Recommended Wayside and Country Inns OF BRITAIN 1997

A Selection of Hostelries of Character
for Food and Drink
and in most cases,
Accommodation

FHG PUBLICATIONS, Paisley

CHESHIRE / CORNWALL   England

Sutton Hall

**Bullocks Lane, Sutton,
Macclesfield, Cheshire SK11 0HE
Tel: 01260 253211
Fax: 01260 252538**

Supplying good ale, good food and good rest Sutton Hall carries on all the best traditions of innkeeping in addition to supplying country house elegance and not a little luxury. Each of the ten guest bedrooms is furnished with an elaborately draped four-poster bed and is appointed to the highest standard with colour television, tea and coffee facilities and bathroom en suite. Cuisine is on a par with accommodation, and a comprehensive range of good bar food is available as well as the more formal fare of the dining room. Hotel membership of adjacent 18 hole golf course enables this facility to be offered to guests free of charge. ♛♛♛ Commended.

Small & Friendly Inns & Hotels

THE OLD CUSTOMS HOUSE *Padstow*

AA★★★   RAC★★   ETB Highly Commended ♛♛♛   JOHANSENS RECOMMENDED

Just one of our Small & Friendly Inn & Hotels throughout Cornwall.
Wherever your destination in Cornwall there is a St.Austell Small & Friendly Inn or Hotel that's right for you. Call now for a FREE colour Brochure:

Tel: 01726 - 627299

ST.AUSTELL EST. BREWERY 1851

END A PERFECT DAY AT ONE OF OUR INNS OR HOTELS

Harbour Lights

**Polkirt Hill, Mevagissey, Cornwall PL26 6UR
Tel: 01726 843249**

This family-run freehouse/hotel is situated in one of the finest clifftop positions in Cornwall, overlooking Mevagissey Harbour and St Austell Bay. All the public rooms and most of the bedrooms enjoy everchanging sea views. En suite rooms available with TV and tea/coffee making facilities. B&B from £19 per person per night. Enjoy a meal in the newly opened restaurant which is only a stone's throw from the water, or watch the fishing boats come in whilst having a drink in the bar. We have our own large car park. **Ring or write for brochure.**

Please mention Recommended Wayside and Country Inns when enquiring

England   CORNWALL / CUMBRIA

The Cornish Arms

16th century coaching inn
Pendogett, Port Isaac,
North Cornwall PL30 3HH

Tel: 01208 880263
Fax: 01208 880335

Situated in the small rural village of Pendogett, just one mile from the coast. Anyone who makes The Cornish Arms a base for exploring the area will not be disappointed by the attractive accommodation or the warmth of welcome extended. Whilst retaining the character of a traditional coaching inn, The Cornish Arms offers all modern amenities in every bedroom; colour and satellite TV, telephone, trouser press, tea and coffee making facilities, etc.

The highly recommended restaurant specialises in locally caught seafood and an extensive range of other dishes. Complement your meal with wine from the extensive cellars of The Cornish Arms. Pendogett Special Bitter is famous for its strength – the locals won't touch it – it's so strong. With Bass straight from the barrel, together with other real ales, you will see why both CAMRA and the Good Pub Guide recommend The Cornish Arms.

ETB ♛♛♛ Commended   RAC ★★   Les Routiers   Good Food Guide

THE BLACKSMITHS ARMS
Talkin Village, Brampton, Cumbria CA8 1LE Tel. 016977 3452

A GETAWAY Place at an affordable price

The Blacksmith's Arms offers all the hospitality and comforts of a traditional country inn, with tasty meals served in the bar lounges, or dinner in the well-appointed restaurant. There are five lovely bedrooms, all en suite. The inn is convenient for the Borders, Hadrian's Wall and the Lake District. There is a good golf course, pony trekking, walking and other country pursuits nearby. Personally managed by the proprietors, Pat and Tom Bagshaw. *FHG Best Bed and Breakfast Diploma Winners 1989.*

THE JOLLY ANGLERS INN
Burneside, Kendal, Cumbria LA9 6QS
Tel. 01539 732552

Situated in the village of Burneside, a mile north of the market town of Kendal and within 6 miles of Lake Windermere. This old traditional Lakeland Inn offers Bed and Breakfast accommodation in Taylors Cottages, (attached to the Inn and once the village Smithy) and Strickland Ketel Guest House situated in a quieter position at the rear. Some rooms have en suite facilities, all have colour T.V. and tea/coffee making facilities. Guests are offered good home cooking in the ground floor rooms of Taylors Cottages. Real Ale is served in the bars, which have low beamed ceilings and log fires. Moderate rates with special bargain breaks. Children and pets welcome. Bed and Breakfast from £14pp. Free Fishing is available, and there is an 18 hole Golf Course close by.   *Cumbria Tourist Board Listed, R.A.C. Listed.*

CUMBRIA / DURHAM / HEREFORD & WORCESTER England

QUEEN'S HEAD HOTEL
ETB ♛♛♛ Commended AA ★★ RAC

Built in the 16th century, the Queen's Head in the heart of traffic-free Hawkshead Village on the edge of Esthwaite Water, has a wonderful atmosphere with low-oak beamed ceilings and panel walls and a warm log fire whenever necessary. The friendly bar and separate dining-room are noted for high-quality food with many locally and organically produced ingredients and a comprehensive wine list. Beer is hand-pulled from the wood.

For overnight stops and holiday breaks, the attractive en suite bedrooms, some with four-poster beds, have colour TV, tea and coffee-making facilities, hair-dryer and phone.

Hawkshead Village was the home of Beatrix Potter and is an excellent centre for fishing, bowling, riding, water ski-ing, cycling and walking.

**QUEEN'S HEAD HOTEL, HAWKSHEAD, CUMBRIA LA22 0NS
TEL: 015394 36271   FAX: 015394 36722**

The Croxdale Inn

The hotel is an ideal place to stay when touring the north-east with its many interesting attractions including Durham City, three miles, with its magnificent Cathedral and Castle; Raby Castle and Bowes Museum are also in close proximity. Other tourist attractions include the famous Beamish Open Air Museum, the Metro Shopping Centre, Hadrian's Wall, Lindisfarne and the lovely east coastline, to name but a few. The Croxdale Inn and Restaurant has recently been refurbished and now boasts a jacuzzi and a sauna. All bedrooms have ensuite amenities with tea/coffee facilities, telephone and remote controlled television. There is also a luxurious four-poster honeymoon suite with whirlpool bath. The restaurant will provide you with a delicious a la carte menu or if you prefer there is an excellent choice of mouthwatering bar meals.

Single room £38; Double room £48; Four poster Suite £58.

**FRONT STREET, CROXDALE, NEAR DURHAM CITY
Tel: 01388 815727 or 01388 420294; Fax: 01388 815368**

YE OLDE SALUTATION INN

This fine, timber-framed black and white building dates back over 500 years, commanding fine views over the medieval village of Weobley and ideally placed for exploring the Welsh Marches, Black Mountains and Brecon Beacons. Accommodation is available in comfortable, centrally heated bedrooms, including a luxury en suite four-poster room. Enjoy a relaxing drink in front of the inglenook fireplace in the lounge bar and contemplate the delights on offer in the Oak Room Restaurant, where great pride is taken in the carefully planned menus and quality of food. AA ★★ 74%, ◎◎

Bed and Breakfast £60 daily per couple. Discounts for stays of 3 or 7 consecutive days.

Market Pitch, Weobley HR4 8SJ Tel: 01544 318443; Fax: 01544 318216 ♛♛♛ Highly Commended

Please mention Recommended Wayside and Country Inns when enquiring

England — HEREFORD & WORCESTER / HERTS / NORFOLK / EAST SUSSEX

Welcome to *The Malvern Hills Hotel*

Set amidst the tranquillity of the Malvern Hills and opposite the Roman Hill Fort and ancient earthworks, this privately owned and run hotel is ideal for walking and enjoying the breathtaking views over 'Elgar's Kingdom'. There are 16 en suite bedrooms with superb views. An oak panelled lounge bar, with open log fire, serves excellent value snacks and real ales, whilst Nightingales Restaurant serves wholesome English cuisine each evening.
Open all year round. Pets welcome.

Commended AA ★★ RAC
Tel: 01684 540237/540690;
Fax: 01684 540327

Malvern Hills Hotel, Wynds Point, by British Camp, Roman Hill Fort, Malvern WR13 6DW

THE SPORTSMAN HOTEL

Dating from the late 19th century, The Sportsman is built on a hillside and is convenient for transport links to London. The 18 comfortable bedrooms are smartly decorated and equipped, all having TV, direct-dial telephone, radio alarm, tea-making facilities and trouser press, as well as ensuite bath/shower rooms. The public areas are light and airy and the attractive *Garden Bar* overlooks the spacious garden. Terrace and children's play area. The hotel has no smoking areas. Children's certificate; baby changing facilities available. Further details and terms on request.

Station Approach, Chorleywood, Herts WD3 5NB Tel: 01923 285155 Fax: 01923 285159

THE LIFEBOAT INN
· An ideal centre for exploring north Norfolk ·

The Lifeboat Inn is a grade II listed building which in its early days was a coaching inn. Everything is within easy walking distance and Wells is an ideal centre for fishing, boating, walking, golf, nature reserves, bird watching, wildlife, train enthusiasts, windsurfing, swimming, sunbathing and historical places of interest. The accommodation offers a comfortable range of full ensuite, half ensuite rooms with showers and single rooms. The inn prides itself in providing an excellent range of real ales, beers, lagers, wines and spirits and in the use of the wonderful local produce which appear on the menu. Fresh sea food, fish, game, poultry and vegetables are available in season together with year round produce all providing scrumptious fayre for all. The Lifeboat Inn also extends the warmest of welcomes and will do its utmost to ensure your stay is memorable and enjoyable. Attractive rates for parties, off-season, long weekends and mid-week breaks are available on request and offer excellent value.

Station Road, Wells-next-the-Sea, Norfolk NR23 1AE   Tel: 01328 710288

HORSE SHOE INN
**Windmill Hill, Herstmonceux, East Sussex BN27 4RU (on A271)
Tel: 01323 833265; Fax: 01323 832001
AA ★★ 60%**

Sympathetically designed in Tudor style, this popular village inn with oak beams throughout has 2 bars – *Squires* being cosier with its wood-burning stove and the *Long Bar*, a locals retreat. In the *Baron of Beef* restaurant excellent food is served and families are welcome. Bedrooms, though a little compact, are furnished with light wood furniture and all have colour TV and private facilities. Children are welcome and pets allowed also, but not in food areas. Large car park. A friendly atmosphere prevails, making this the ideal venue for either a holiday or break, or for a wedding or other function. Facilities available for up to 200 people. Prices per double room – £45 for two persons or £32.50 for one person. Further details on request.

Recommended Wayside and Country Inns 1997

WARWICKSHIRE / WILTS / WEST YORKSHIRE / NORTH YORKSHIRE   England

HALFORD BRIDGE INN
Fosseway, (A429), Halford, Shipston-on-Stour,
Warwickshire CV36 5BN
Tel/Fax: 01789 740382

On the principle that you can't have too much of a good thing Tony and Greta Westwood, proprietors of this charming sixteenth century inn, keep their kitchens open seven days a week to provide sustenance to regulars, residents and hungry passers-by. A wide range of good hot and cold bar food is available, in addition to the excellent fare offered at reasonable prices in the restaurant. Good home cooking is the speciality here, with home-made pickles, sauces, pies etc, as well as fresh vegetables whenever possible. All the comfortably furnished bedrooms have colour television, and tourists who must keep an eye on their budgets as well as the scenery will find them good value for money. Ample parking.

ETB ♛♛, Les Routiers, AA QQ, RAC Recommended, CAMRA, Association of Catering Excellence.

A warm welcome awaits you at
The Queens Head Inn

There are four double rooms, with own bathroom and colour TV, central heating, tea/coffee making facilities and telephone. Self-contained, motel style so that you are free to come and go as you wish. Relax in comfort in the friendly atmosphere of our low-beamed bars with part of the lounge area reserved for non-smokers. Well-behaved children are welcome in the lounge area. Your hosts, Michael and Norma Craggs invite you to enjoy our superb menu available every lunchtime and evening prepared from the finest and freshest food. We also have an excellent selection of real ales (listed CAMRA).

EGON RONAY ♛♛♛ HIGHLY COMMENDED
North Street, Broad Chalke, Salisbury SP5 5EN
TEL/FAX: 01722 780344

The Foresters Arms
Main Street, Grassington, Skipton,
North Yorkshire BD23 5AA Tel: 01756 752349
ETB Listed Approved

The Foresters Arms, Grassington, once an old coaching inn, situated in the heart of the Yorkshire Dales. An ideal centre for walking or touring. A family run business for over 25 years. Serving hand pulled Tetley and Theakstons Beer. Bar meals served lunchtime and evenings. Bedrooms have TVs and tea/coffee making facilities, one en suite. Children and pets welcome. Terms on request. *Proprietor: Rita Richardson*

FALCON INN
Whitby Road, Cloughton, Near Scarborough,
North Yorkshire YO13 0DY   Tel: 01723 870717

Standing in its own 7 acres of pasture and woodland with its southerly aspect towards the sea, this former coaching inn has recently been refurbished. The old coach house has been converted into the Carvery leaving the original stonework and most of the beams exposed. A wide selection of home-cooked English fare is served either here or in the bar lounge. This is a fine touring centre with several coastal resorts within easy reach. To the rear of the inn, a number of delightful bedrooms are furnished to a very high standard with full central heating, colour television and facilities for making hot drinks. *Les Routiers.*

Scotland

ABERDEENSHIRE / DUMFRIESSHIRE

BALLATER

The Green Inn

9 Victoria Road, Ballater, Aberdeenshire AB35 5QQ
Tel/Fax: 01339 755701

Cosy restaurant serving fresh food. Taste of Scotland dishes always available. 3 comfortable bedrooms with private facilities, TV, tea/coffee facilities, hairdryer, etc. Central heating. Pets welcome. Golf, fishing, etc within easy reach. B&B £30 single, £25 double.

♛♛♛ COMMENDED

Kildrummy Inn
Kildrummy
Alford AB33 8QS
Tel. 01975 571227

Small and cosy with only four letting bedrooms, the Kildrummy Inn is ideally situated for fishing, shooting, hillwalking, pony trekking and many other sports including golf. A good base also for 'Castle Trails' and 'Whisky Trails' as well as for touring and visiting many places of interest. All bedrooms have washbasins, tea making facilities and TV and are decorated to a high standard. There is also a residents' dining room, a lounge bar serving bar lunches and suppers, a sun lounge and a public bar. Good parking.

Dinwoodie Lodge
Country House Hotel
Nr. Lockerbie, Dumfriesshire DG11 2SL
Tel: 01576 470289

Grade B Listed Small country house hotel in South-west Scotland Caravan Park and Holiday Cottages adjacent. Fishing, Golf, Shooting available in area. Ideal centre for touring Borders, Galloway; Edinburgh and Glasgow approximately 70 miles. Seven bedrooms, three with private facilities including a room for disabled guests. All rooms have colour TV and tea/coffee facilities. Breakfast, Lunches, Bar Meals, Licensed Bar, Separate Pool Room and Darts Board. Children and Pets welcome.

Terms from £30 for single room, from £49.50 for double room and from £55.00 for a family room (sleeps up to 5 persons – 2 adults, 3 children). Prices include Scottish Breakfast and VAT.

NOTE

All the information in this book is given in good faith in the belief that it is correct. However, the publishers cannot guarantee the facts given in these pages, neither are they responsible for changes in policy, ownership or terms that may take place after the date of going to press. Readers should always satisfy themselves that the facilities they require are available and that the terms, if quoted, still apply.

Recommended Wayside and Country Inns 1997

KIRKCUDBRIGHTSHIRE / WIGTOWNSHIRE   Scotland

Bank O'Fleet Hotel

**47 High Street, Gatehouse of Fleet,
Dumfries & Galloway DG7 2HR Tel/Fax: 01557 814302**

Situated in the heart of this historic and picturesque town, The Bank O'Fleet makes an ideal base for touring Galloway's unspoilt countryside. Fishing, walking and birdwatching can be enjoyed in the area and there are many interesting places to visit. All bedrooms are en suite and have colour TV and tea/coffee facilities. Lounge bar, diningroom, residents' lounge, and function room for ceilidhs, folk nights, Scottish nights, etc. **Bed & Breakfast from £22.50; Dinner, Bed and Breakfast from £32.50. Short Breaks available.**

Ken Bridge Hotel

(Ref.2) New Galloway, Kirkcudbrightshire DG7 3PR

Tel: 01644 420211   Approved   AA & RAC Approved

In the heart of the beautiful Galloway countryside, famed for its associations with Robert the Bruce, this friendly Victorian coach house offers a traditional Scottish welcome and good home cooking. It stands on the banks of the river and residents have free fishing rights. Husband and wife team, Andrew and Ann Ramsay, provide comfortable accommodation in single, double/twin and family rooms. Private parking. **Bed and Breakfast from £17. Open all year.**

Torrs Warren Hotel
By Portpatrick

**Stoneykirk, by Stranraer, Wigtownshire DG9 9DH
Telephone 01776 830204   STB Listed Approved**

The hotel is situated in south west Scotland just 6 miles from Portpatrick and 15 minutes from the ferry to Ireland. All around is tranquil countryside, secluded coves, rugged cliffs, forests and sandy beaches. Ideal for exploring sub-tropical gardens, castles and standing stones. We can arrange most activities for you and we have put together special all-in packages for golf and sea-angling. The comfortable, family-run hotel is set in its own grounds. Ample parking. We offer 8 en-suite bedrooms. B&B from £21. Contact Bernice Camlin.

PHEASANT INN

**Sorbie, Newton Stewart, Wigtownshire
DG8 8EL Telephone: 01988 850223**

Guests can be assured of a warm welcome at the Pheasant Inn which is situated in the peaceful Wigtownshire countryside with its forests, farmlands and coast offering opportunities for golf, fishing, cycling, walking and birdwatching, or just for enjoying the peace and quiet. The well furnished bedrooms have colour TV and tea and coffee facilities. There is a residents' lounge, two comfortable bars, a cosy restaurant serving home cooked meals at reasonable rates, and a large garden. **Full details on request.**

Please mention Recommended Wayside and Country Inns when enquiring

CONTENTS

Recommended Wayside and Country Inns OF BRITAIN

ENGLAND

Bedfordshire	13
Berkshire	14
Buckinghamshire	16
Cambridgeshire	17
Cheshire	19
Cornwall	22
Cumbria	27
Derbyshire	36
Devon	41
Dorset	57
Durham	58
Essex	59
Gloucestershire	61
Hampshire	68
Hereford & Worcester	72
Hertfordshire	77
Isle of Wight	78
Kent	80
Lancashire	82
Lincolnshire	84
Norfolk	85
Northamptonshire	88
Northumberland	90
Oxfordshire	92
Shropshire	95
Somerset	98
Staffordshire	105
Suffolk	105
Surrey	108
East Sussex	110
West Sussex	112
Warwickshire	113
Wiltshire	115
East Yorkshire	119
North Yorkshire	120
West Yorkshire	127

WALES

North Wales	129
Dyfed	132
Powys	133
South Wales	135

SCOTLAND

Aberdeenshire	137
Angus	138
Argyll	139
Caithness	140
Dumfriesshire	141
Inverness-shire	143
Isle of Arran	144
Isle of Skye	144
Kirkcudbrightshire	145
Peeblesshire	146
Perth & Kinross	147
Ross-shire	148
Wigtownshire	149

The Golden Bowl Supplement for Pet-Friendly Pubs 151
Family Friendly Pubs Supplement 174

Other FHG Publications

Recommended Country Hotels of Britain
Recommended Short Break Holidays in Britain
Pets Welcome!
Bed and Breakfast in Britain
The Golf Guide: Where to Play/Where to Stay
Farm Holiday Guide England/Wales, Ireland & Channel Islands
Farm Holiday Guide Scotland
Self-Catering Holidays in Britain
Britain's Best Holidays
Guide to Caravan and Camping Holidays
Children Welcome! Family Holiday and Atttractions Guide
Bed and Breakfast Stops
Scottish Welcome

1997 Edition
ISBN 1 85055 219 3
© FHG Publications Ltd.
No part of this publication may be reproduced by any means or transmitted without the permission of the Publishers.

Cartography by GEO Projects, Reading.
Maps are based on Ordnance Survey Maps with the permission of the Controller of Her Majesty's Stationery Office. Crown Copyright reserved.

Please note: owing to recent boundary changes the following counties no longer exist:

England
Avon — see under Gloucester and Somerset
Cleveland — see under Durham
Humberside — see under Yorkshire(East) and Lincolnshire

Scotland
Banffshire — see under Moray and Aberdeenshire
Kincardineshire — see under Aberdeenshire
Kinross-shire — see under Perth and Kinross

In **Wales** the changes have been more extensive and we have arranged the section as follows:
North Wales — formerly Clwyd and Gwynedd
Dyfed
Powys
South Wales — formerly Glamorgan and Gwent

Typeset by FHG Publications Ltd, Paisley.
Printed and bound in Great Britain by Bemrose Ltd, Derby.

Distribution. **Book Trade**: WLM, Downing Road, West Meadows Ind. Estate, Derby DE21 6HA
(Tel: 01332 343332 Fax: 01332 340464).
News Trade: USM Distribution Ltd, 86 Newman Street, London W1P 3LD
(Tel: 0171-396 8000. Fax: 0171-396 8002). E-mail:usm.co.uk

Published by FHG Publications Ltd,
Abbey Mill Business Centre, Seedhill, Paisley PA1 1TJ (0141-887 0428; Fax: 0141-889 7204).

Cover design: Cyan Creative Consultants, Glasgow.
Cover picture: The Old Custom House, Padstow, courtesy of St. Austell Brewery, Cornwall.
Inset: The Queen's Head Hotel, Hawkshead, Cumbria.

US ISBN 1-55650-765-8
Distributed in the United States by
Hunter Publishing Inc.,300 Raritan Center, Parkway, CN94, Edison, N.J., 08818, USA.

Recommended
WAYSIDE & COUNTRY INNS OF BRITAIN 1997

PUBS, INNS AND SMALL HOTELS in Britain have changed enormously since the first edition of RECOMMENDED WAYSIDE & COUNTRY INNS appeared in 1963. There is a steady trend towards a more sociable 'family' atmosphere, towards serving a broader range of interesting food as well as beer, wine and spirits, and towards creating an 'entertainment' centre, often with a theme. In recent years we have even seen the appearance of highly successful 'Inns' which don't have a bar! Best of all is any move which tries to retain the character of old British inns alongside the best of modern practice in accommodation, facilities, amenities, hospitality and service.

Our selection of pubs, inns and small hotels is 'recommended' on the basis of reputation, written descriptions, facilities and long association rather than through personal inspection. We cannot accept responsibility for errors, misrepresentations or the quality of hospitality but we are always interested to hear from readers about their own experiences. Fortunately complaints are few, and rarely serious, but if you do have a problem which cannot be settled on the spot (the best solution, by the way), please let us know. We cannot act as intermediaries or arbiters but we will record your complaint and follow it up with the establishment.

As far as we can establish, the details of all our entries are accurate as we go to press. We suggest, however, that you confirm prices and other specific points at the same time as you make an enquiry or booking – and please also mention *Recommended Wayside and Country Inns of Britain*.

Amongst the hundreds of entries in this most recent edition are examples of both old and new. We hope that readers will continue to enjoy the old and that they will give a hearty welcome to the new. What is old is not in itself necessarily a recommendation. The venerable Doctor Johnson found conditions in a tavern in 18th-century Bristol such that he said. "Why, it was so bad that Boswell wished to be in Scotland!". And well he might – there are some very fine 'wayside and country inns' in Scotland!

Peter Stanley Williams
Editorial Consultant

Peter Clark
Publishing Director

ENGLAND

Bedfordshire

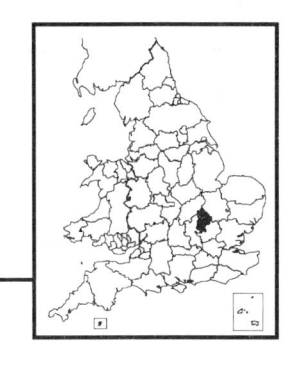

THE KNIFE & CLEAVER,
The Grove, Houghton Conquest,
Bedfordshire MK45 3LA

Tel: 01234 740387
Fax: 01234 740900

9 bedrooms, all with private bathroom; Free House with real ale; Historic interest; Children welcome, pets by arrangement; Bar and restaurant meals; Car park (36); Ampthill 2 miles; ££££.

Deep in the heart of rural Bedfordshire, this friendly country inn offers a warm welcome to locals and visitors alike, and proves equally popular with both. One of the main reasons for its enviable reputation is the quite exceptional Victorian-style conservatory restaurant, where the finest of fresh ingredients are prepared with care and imagination by first-class chefs and where the accompanying wine list has been selected with quality and value as the highest priorities. Nine well-appointed bedrooms, all with bathroom and power shower, provide comfortable overnight accommodation for those wishing to explore this lovely area. *RAC*** and Restaurant Merit Award, Les Routiers, Logis.*

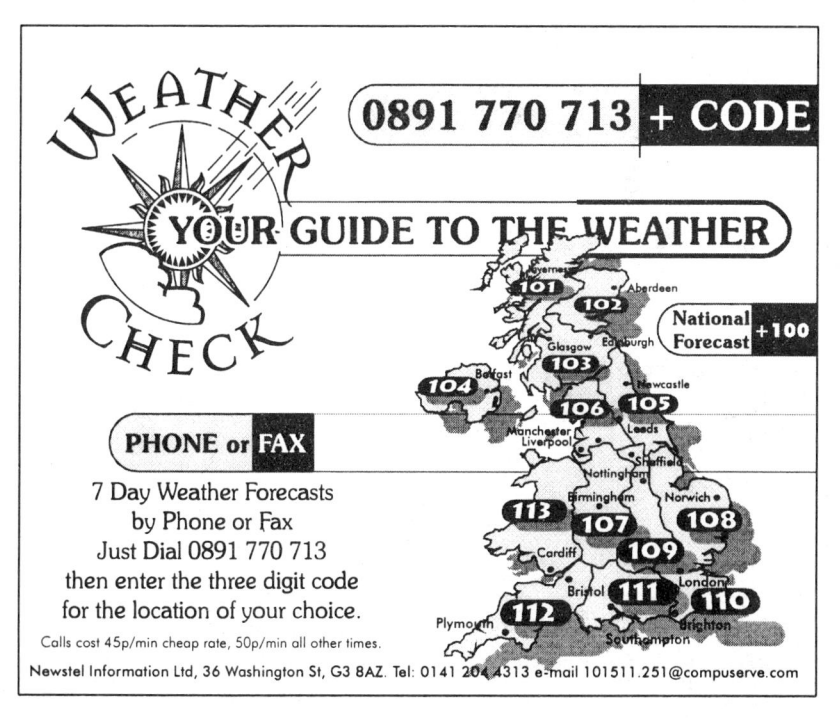

WEATHER CHECK

0891 770 713 + CODE

YOUR GUIDE TO THE WEATHER

National Forecast +100

PHONE or FAX

7 Day Weather Forecasts
by Phone or Fax
Just Dial 0891 770 713
then enter the three digit code
for the location of your choice.

Calls cost 45p/min cheap rate, 50p/min all other times.
Newstel Information Ltd, 36 Washington St, G3 8AZ. Tel: 0141 204 4313 e-mail 101511.251@compuserve.com

Berkshire

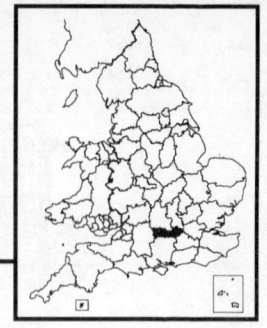

THE INN ON THE GREEN,
The Old Cricket Common, Cookham Dean,
Berkshire SL6 9NZ

Tel: 01628 482638
Fax: 01628 487474

6 bedrooms, all with private bathroom; Free House; Historic interest; Bar lunches and restaurant meals; Children welcome; Car park (50); Maidenhead 3 miles; ££££.

Fashionable without being pretentious, this happy place is truly a resort of knowledgeable gourmets for the fame of Head Chef, Adrian Hutchinson is spreading forever wider. The exceptional cuisine is a blend of traditional English and classical European fare. A la carte and table d'hôte dishes are offered seven days a week with Sunday lunchtime roasts a popular feature. Relaxation comes easily in the oak-beamed bar where a log fire blazes in winter months with a variety of real ales no doubt contributing to the mood. For a few days' break by the Thames, this is a well recommended venue; the en suite guest rooms an attractive amalgam of old-fashioned charm and modern conveniences. Excellent corporate facilities also exist.

THE SWAN,
East Ilsley, Near Newbury,
Berkshire RG20 7LF

Tel: 01635 281238
Fax: 01635 281791

10 bedrooms, all with private bathroom; Morlands House with real ale; Historic interest; Children and pets welcome; Bar and restaurant meals; Car park (26); Newbury 9 miles; ££/£££.

A thoroughly delightful inn with its roots in the 16th century, the Swan's recent refurbishment has added much in the way of comfort, while retaining the atmosphere which enchants visitors old and new. Good food is served in the open-plan bar, where blackboard specialities supplement the usual menu which includes individual steak and kidney pie, spicy chilli con carne, and wonderfully fragrant steak and onions braised in ale. On the subject of ale, a good range is kept and served with friendly good cheer. Guest rooms have en suite facilities, colour television and hospitality trays. Situated just off the A34 and close to the M4 for Heathrow Airport, the Swan is also within easy reach of Newbury, the racecourse, the Ridgeway Walk and the beautiful city of Oxford.

THE BELL AT BOXFORD,
Lambourn Road, Newbury,　　　　　　　Tel: 01488 608721/2
Berkshire RG20 8DD　　　　　　　　　　Fax: 01488 608749

11 bedrooms, all with private bathroom; Free House with real ale; Children and pets welcome; Bar and restaurant meals; Car park; Reading 16 miles; ££££.

The smart exterior of this traditional country inn between Newbury and Lambourn will attract the attention of passers by, maybe and possibly disciples of the turf. To venture within is to discover homely comforts in the form of log fires and real ales as well as bags of character. Widely recommended, the international fare on offer in the candlelit restaurant is a lure in itself, there being a mouth-watering choice of reasonably-priced dishes on the à la carte menu, not forgetting the daily 'blackboard specials'. Excellent accommodation is available at this hostelry run in distinguished style by Paul and Helen Lavis, bedrooms having en suite facilities, direct-dial telephone and modern appointments. *Egon Ronay Recommended.*

THE GEORGE,
479 Wokingham Road, Earley, Reading,　　Tel: 01734 261844
Berkshire RG6 1EN　　　　　　　　　　　　Fax: 01734 351389

No accommodation; Chef & Brewer House with real ale; Historic interest; Bar meals; Reading 2 miles.

Loddon Bridge, built over the river of that name near Reading, is the setting for this picturesque English pub. Dating back to the 18th century, with exposed beams, grandfather clock and log fires, the pub still retains a wealth of character as well as plenty of old fashioned hospitality. The beer garden alongside the river is ideal for leisurely summer days. As well as a wide choice of cask conditioned ales, lagers and soft drinks, there is an extensive blackboard menu which features imaginative pub food, all beautifully presented at reasonable prices. A wide range of quality wines has been chosen to accompany the food and all are available by the bottle and by the glass. There are over 40 main courses to choose from and an interesting selection of hot and cold snacks is also served. The choice of desserts is equally tempting and delicious. The George is open all day every day for food and drink. Local attractions include Mapledurham House and Watermill, Wellington Country House in Riseley, Beale Wildlife Gardens and Reading Abbey.

Buckinghamshire

THE CARRINGTON ARMS,
Cranfield Road, Moulsoe,
Buckinghamshire MK16 0HB

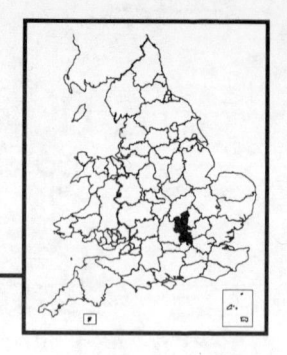

Tel: 01908 218050
Fax: 01908 217850

8 bedrooms, all with private bathroom; Free House with real ale; Historic interest; Children welcome; Bar and restaurant meals; Car park (100); Newport Pagnell 3 miles; £££.

Heard described, somewhat ungraciously, as a rather forbidding cross between a 1930's public library and an ecclesiastical 'grace and favour' house, the intriguing Carrington Arms is actually a Grade II listed building and a veritable 'Mecca' for those who know a thing or two about the culinary arts. The open cooking area is a revelation, literally. 'You see what you get' is the house motto — and what you see will certainly activate the taste buds. Quality steaks, fresh fish and other palate tempters are there on view to be selected for one's gastronomic delight. Watch your meal being cooked and preface the joys to come with, maybe, a visit to the oyster bar and a glass of chilled champagne. Splendiferous stuff!

ROSE AND CROWN HOTEL,
Saunderton, Near Princes Risborough,
Buckinghamshire HP27 9NP

Tel: 01844 345299
Fax: 01844 343140

17 bedrooms, 14 with private bathroom; Free House with real ale; Bar and restaurant meals; Car park (60); London 39 miles, Oxford 20, Aylesbury 9; ££££.

On the main road (A4010) between Aylesbury and High Wycombe, this attractive Georgian-style free house has facilities that would put many multi-starred hotels in the shade, at the same time retaining its appealing wayside inn atmosphere. A recommended base from which to explore the Chilterns and a lush and gentle countryside, the inn has welcoming bars where traditional ales are sure to be appreciated, and the excellent restaurant operates an interesting menu throughout the week. The accommodation is of the highest order, guest rooms all having colour television, direct-dial telephone and tea and coffee makers.

The **£** symbol when appearing at the end of the italic section of an entry shows the anticipated price, during 1997, for single full Bed and Breakfast.

Under £25	£	Over £36 but under £45	£££
Over £25 but under £36	££	Over £45	££££

This is meant as an indication only and does not show prices for Special Breaks, Weekends, etc. Guests are therefore advised to verify all prices on enquiring or booking.

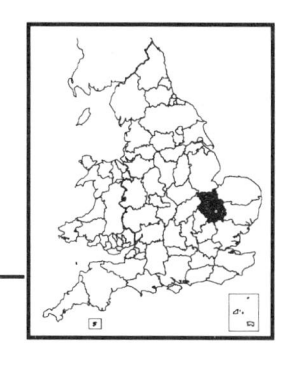

Cambridgeshire

THE CROSS KEYS,
12-16 Market Hill, Chatteris,
Cambridgeshire PE16 6BA
Tel and Fax: 01354 693036

7 bedrooms, 5 with private bathroom; Free House with real ale; Historic interest; Children welcome; Bar and restaurant meals; Car park (10); March 7 miles; ££

No lesser personages than Dick Turpin, Samuel Pepys and Oliver Cromwell are reputed to have passed through the pleasant little Fenland town of Chatteris, and although it is not recorded whether or not they chose to rest awhile at this fine establishment, if they did in fact do so, those noble gentlemen would no doubt have experienced the same warm hospitality and excellent standards of service that are available to today's traveller. Particular attention is paid to providing for the needs of the inner man, with daily deliveries of fresh fish ensuring its prominent position on the extensive bar and restaurant menus. An ideal base for an active or more leisurely break, The Cross Keys provides delightful, individually decorated and colour co-ordinated bedrooms, which are available at most reasonable rates. ☙☙☙ *Commended, RAC and AA *.*

LEEDS ARMS,
The Green, Eltisley,
Cambridgeshire PE19 4TG
Tel: 01480 880283
Fax: 01480 880379

9 motel rooms, all with private bathroom; Free House with real ale; Bar food; Car park (40); Cambridge 10 miles, St. Neots 6; ££.

Long before community centres were thought of, the village hostelry was the place to hear all the news, and a lovely old inn like the Leeds Arms is still the hub of local social life, and well deserves to be. Attractively decorated yet still retaining the old oak beams and an inglenook fireplace with copper hood over a blazing log fire to bring a touch of the old days to modern times, the Leeds Arms offers a range of meals to suit all tastes. There is an extensive bar menu with appetisers, succulent steaks and delicious desserts available all week; also Sunday lunch. Accommodation is of an equally high standard, and rooms are well equipped with colour television, telephone and drinks making facilities. *ETB Listed.*

BRIDGE HOTEL,
Clayhithe, Near Waterbeach, Cambridgeshire CB5 9NZ

Tel: 01223 860252
Fax: 01223 440448

26 bedrooms, all with private bathroom; Free House with real ale; Historic interest; Children welcome; Restaurant meals; Car park (100); Cambridge 4 miles; £££.

The historic Bridge Hotel is not only one of the most popular luncheon and dinner rendezvous in the area but is also internationally famous as a riverside hotel. Situated beside the River Cam just four miles north of Cambridge, the hotel can easily be reached by road or rail. Our riverside restaurant offers you service and individual attention, and a full à la carte menu is always available. The Bridge Hotel is fully licensed and can cater for all kinds of business and private functions.

THE CROWN AND PUNCHBOWL INN,
Horningsea, Cambridgeshire CB5 9JG

Tel: 01223 860643
Fax: 01223 441814

5 bedrooms, all with private bathroom; Free House with real ale; Historic interest; Bar meals, restaurant evenings only; Car park; Cambridge 4 miles; ££.

This charming, recently restored 17th century inn, situated in the centre of the unspoilt riverside village of Horningsea which lies four miles north-east of Cambridge, is an ideal stopover, not only for visitors to the city, but also for those touring East Anglia. In the old bars, with their exposed timbers and inglenook fireplace, open fires throughout the winter months add to the warm welcome provided by the proprietors. The inn has an enviable reputation for its food, which, while quintessentially English, provides many original dishes with a menu changing weekly. A speciality of the house is a five-course dinner included in the daily and weekend rates. The bedrooms all offer the highest standards of comfort with private bathrooms, tea and coffee making facilities, telephones and colour television.

OLD RED LION,
Linton Road, Horseheath, Cambridgeshire CB1 6QF

Tel: 01223 892909
Fax: 01223 894217

12 bedrooms, all with private bathroom; Free House with real ale; Historic interest; Children welcome; Bar lunches, restaurant evenings only; Car park (54); Haverhill 4 miles; ££££.

With Cambridge less than half-an-hour's drive away along the A604, this beautiful, 17th century pub is open all day every day dispensing a fine selection of real ales, lunchtime snacks, cream teas and appetising dinners. Whatever one's needs, there can be no more pleasing a setting, the ambience being created by flagstone floors, open fires and a wealth of timber beams. That being said, the old inn has been subjected to total refurbishment which provides a number of en suite bedrooms, equipped with television and tea and coffee-making facilities. For business in Cambridge and set in delightful, unspoiled countryside, we found this recommended hostelry to satisfy requirements both practical and aesthetic. *Les Routiers.*

THE EATON OAK,
Cross Hall Road, Eaton Ford, St. Neots, Cambridgeshire PE19 4AH

Tel: 01480 219555
Fax: 01480 407520

9 bedrooms, all with private bathroom; Charles Wells House with real ale; Children welcome; Bar and restaurant meals; Car park (50); Bedford 11 miles, Huntingdon 9; £££.

Just a moment from the A1, this Georgian-style inn is the ideal place for the family to stop for excellent and reasonably-priced meals in the Charterhouse Restaurant which is open seven days a week. Children are most welcome to dine with their parents and they have their own menu. As an alternative, hot and cold bar snacks are served in the lounge and Charles Wells' real ale is a recommended tipple. Grenville and Pauline are your friendly hosts and visitors lured by the conviviality of the house may be tempted to stay overnight; a wise decision, for the accommodation is first-class, all guest rooms having en suite facilities, with colour television, telephone and tea and coffee makers.

RED LION HOTEL,
Station Road East, Whittlesford, Cambridgeshire CB2 4NL

Tel: 01223 832047/832115
Fax: 01223 837576

17 bedrooms, all with private bathroom; Free House with real ale; Historic interest; Children welcome; Bar meals, restaurant evenings only; Car park (40); Cambridge 7 miles; £££.

Visiting Cambridge? Look no further for somewhere to stay or somewhere to meet friends or relations than this lovely, historic inn which fairly exudes character. Founded as a Carmelite Priory in the 13th century, it has a proud record of providing rest and refreshment over the years to both high and lowly. Service is certainly courtly and the cuisine is of like standard. In introducing modern refinements, much care has been taken in retaining the time-hallowed ambience. Thus impressive beams, hand-carved by monks, share attention with beautifully furnished en suite rooms with colour television, telephone and beverage makers. Romance in the air? There is a superb Honeymoon Suite and some four-poster beds are available.

Cheshire

TURNERS ARMS,
Ingersley Road, Bollington, Macclesfield, Cheshire SK10 5RE

Tel: 01625 573864

8 bedrooms, 5 with private bathroom; Free House with real ale; Historic interest; Children welcome; Bar food; Macclesfield 3 miles; ££.

Offering all the homely comforts of a traditional northern, family-run inn, the Turners Arms has just eight nicely appointed letting bedrooms, all with colour television, beverage-making facilities and washbasin. A good range of excellent and reasonably priced bar snacks is served, and even the splendid à la carte menu available Tuesday to Sunday will not stretch the budget too far. Two of Bollington's old cotton mills still stand, a testament to the town's peak of prosperity in the last century, and there is much of historic and natural interest in the surrounding area.

CHOLMONDELEY ARMS,
Malpas,
Cheshire SY14 8BT

Tel: 01829 720300
Fax: 01829 720123

6 bedrooms, all with en suite showers; Free House with real ale; Historic interest; Children welcome; Bar and restaurant meals; Car park (80); Wrexham 8 miles.

Perfect for those seeking somewhere a little bit different, this appealing pub was until 1982 the village school. People come from far beyond the area to sample the Cholmondeley cuisine, with a fine range of starters, main courses such as home-made pies, curries and filled savoury pancakes, and a mouth-watering selection of speciality puddings. Overnight guests are accommodated in the school house, just a step across the playground, where individually styled bedrooms offer tea and coffee facilities, colour television, radio alarm, hairdryer and direct-dial telephone as well as smart decor and furnishings and supreme comfort. This unique establishment is to be found on the A49, next to the park and gardens of Cholmondeley Castle. *Good Pub Guide "Dining Pub of the Year" 1996.*

SYCAMORE INN,
Sycamore Road, Birch Vale, Stockport,
Cheshire SK12 5AB

Tel: 01663 742715
Fax: 01663 747382

6 bedrooms, all with private bathroom; Free House with real ale; Historic interest; Children welcome; Bar and restaurant meals; Car park; Manchester 6 miles; ££.

Picturesquely set in open countryside on the Cheshire/Derbyshire border, this friendly free house on the banks of the River Sett is ideally placed for excursions to the Peak District as well as the urban pleasures of Manchester. Parents love this well-run hostelry and not just for the excellent food, drink and accommodation it provides but for the attention it pays to children's needs. Prime amongst such amenities is the superb Adventure Trail Playground where youngsters may disport themselves happily for ages whilst parents can relax with a drink and smile indulgently at the periodic return of the prodigal requesting another Coke and packet of crisps. However, more formal dining of high calibre is recommended with two sizeable restaurants presenting a delicious selection of home-cooked dishes and choice wines; children have their own special menu. Such is the inn's popularity that bookings are advised if possible. The convivial and comfortable bars engender conversation and bonhomie with cask-conditioned real ales playing a prominent role. Parting is such sweet sorrow — so why not make this the family holiday base? Guest rooms are delightfully appointed with en suite facilities, satellite television and tea and coffee-makers. And, for good measure, the young (in heart as well!) can strut their stuff in the evening in the music and cocktail bar under the inspiration of a resident DJ. Family fun in idyllic surroundings. *Egon Ronay Recommended.*

SUTTON HALL,
Bullocks Lane, Sutton, Macclesfield,
Cheshire SK11 0HE

Tel: 01260 253211
Fax: 01260 252538

10 bedrooms, all with private bathroom; Free House; Historic interest; Bar and restaurant meals; Car park; Manchester 18 miles, Airport 10, Stockport 10; ££££.

One hesitates to describe this one-time baronial residence and former convent standing in extensive grounds and farmland as an inn — and yet in its virtues of good ale, good food and good rest it ably carries on all the best traditions of innkeeping in addition to supplying country house elegance and not a little luxury. Each of the ten guest bedrooms is furnished with an elaborately draped four-poster bed and is appointed to the highest standard with colour television, tea and coffee facilities and bathroom en suite. Cuisine is on a par with accommodation, and a comprehensive range of good bar food is available as well as the more formal fare of the dining room. Hotel membership of adjacent 18 hole golf course enables this facility to be offered to guests free of charge. ❦❦❦ *Commended*. **See also Colour Advertisement on page 2.**

SWAN HOTEL,
50 High Street, Tarporley,
Cheshire CW6 0AG

Tel: 01829 733838
Fax: 01829 732932

20 bedrooms, all with private bathroom; Free House with real ale; Historic interest; Children and small dogs welcome; Bar and restaurant meals evenings only; Car park (25); Nantwich 9 miles; ££££.

Full of character, this welcoming hostelry retains all the charm of its Georgian origins to which modern refinements have been skilfully added. The Tarporley Hunt has met here for over two centuries and the historic Hunt Room with its impressive art collection is worth a visit in its own right. Good ales are served in the snug, flagstoned bar with its open fire and gleaming copperware, and the elegant brasserie presents an appetising selection of freshly prepared dishes. The stylish guest accommodation comprises family, double and single rooms, all tastefully decorated and appointed to a high standard. ✿✿✿ *Commended.*

THE PHEASANT INN,
Higher Burwardsley, Tattenhall,
Cheshire CH3 9PF

Tel: 01829 770434
Fax: 01829 771097

10 bedrooms, all with private bathroom; Free House with real ale; Historic interest; Children welcome; Bar and restaurant meals; Car park (60); Chester 9 miles; £££.

For 300 years the lovely half timbered and sandstone Pheasant Inn has stood atop the Peckforton Hills, gazing out over the Cheshire Plain to distant Wales. Panoramic views are to be enjoyed from most of the nicely decorated bedrooms, which are complete with en suite bathroom, colour television, radio alarm, hairdryer and beverage making facilities. Accommodation is in the beautifully converted barn, tucked quietly away from the convivial bar with its huge log fire, and the Bistro Restaurant which enjoys a well-deserved reputation for fine fare, well presented and served with cheerful efficiency. Weekend mini-breaks are a popular feature of this commendable establishment. ✿✿✿ *Commended, AA and RAC**.*

PLEASE MENTION THIS GUIDE WHEN YOU WRITE

OR PHONE TO ENQUIRE ABOUT

ACCOMMODATION.

IF YOU ARE WRITING, A STAMPED,

ADDRESSED ENVELOPE IS ALWAYS APPRECIATED.

Cornwall

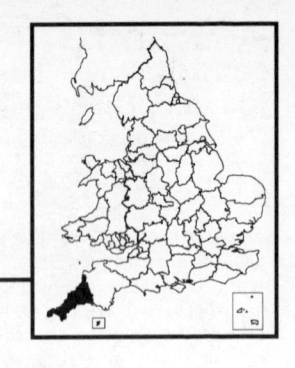

THE WELLINGTON HOTEL,
**The Harbour, Boscastle,
Cornwall PL35 0AQ**

Tel: 01840 250202
Fax: 01840 250621

19 bedrooms, 16 with private bathroom; Free House with real ale; Historic interest; Children and pets welcome; Bar meals, restaurant evenings only; Car park (20); Camelford 5 miles; £/££.

This historic 16th century coaching inn is situated by the Elizabethan harbour and is surrounded by National Trust countryside. It is ideally situated for walking, touring and golfing holidays and close to glorious sandy beaches, beautiful wooded valleys and dramatic moorland. The Wellington Hotel is a free house, and offers real ales, pub grub, open fires and beams; the fine Anglo-French restaurant specialises in regional cuisine and seafood. There are 10 acres of private woodland walks and pets are very welcome. ♛♛♛ *Commended, AA and RAC **.*

JUBILEE INN,
**Pelynt, Near Looe,
Cornwall PL13 2JZ**

Tel: 01503 220312
Fax: 01503 220920

9 bedrooms, all with private bathroom; Free House with real ale; Historic interest; Children welcome; Bar and restaurant meals; Car park; Fowey (ferry) 5, Looe 4; ££.

The old world is preserved to a very high standard in this comfortable and spacious Wayside Inn. This 16th century country inn, situated on the Looe-Lostwithiel road is attractively furnished throughout, has en suite rooms with colour television, central heating, and log fires in winter. The village of Pelynt is situated only two miles from the sea, excellent for sailing, boating, bathing and fishing. The inn has attractive gardens and lawns with a safe children's play area. An evening barbecue is a weekly feature in high season (weather permitting). Special Christmas and New Year Breaks. *ETB* ♛♛♛ *Commended, AA and RAC **.*

SHIP INN,
Lerryn, Lostwithiel,
Cornwall PL22 0PT

Tel: 01208 872374

4 bedrooms, all with private bathroom; Free House with real ale; Children and pets welcome; Restaurant meals; Lostwithiel 3 miles; £.

This charming and traditional Cornish country inn can be found in what surely must be the prettiest riverside village in Cornwall. The wooded river banks were the inspiration for Kenneth Grahame's *The Wind in the Willows*. Popular with walkers and sailors alike, it offers a warm welcome to all. A log fire and central heating ensure year round comfort and make this a cosy choice for an out of season break. The attractive guest rooms all have en suite bathrooms, beverage-making facilities, colour television and radio. One bedroom is on the ground floor, making it ideal for elderly or disabled visitors. Excellent home-cooked fare is available in the restaurant lunchtimes and evenings, where you can choose from our extensive menu which also includes a good choice for vegetarians; an extensive wine list will complement any meal. The bar offers a choice of real ales and a large selection of malt whiskies. Conveniently situated for the coast, valleys and moors of central and east Cornwall. *Good Pub Guide.*

ROYAL OAK INN,
Duke Street, Lostwithiel,
Cornwall PL22 0AH

Tel and Fax: 01208 872552

6 bedrooms, all with private bathroom; Free House with real ale; Historic interest; Children and pets welcome; Bar and restaurant meals; Car park; Bodmin 5 miles; ££.

Full of character and with two beautifully kept bars, one of which does duty as a restaurant where splendid and reasonably priced meals are served nightly, the 13th century Royal Oak is tucked away just off the main road. An underground tunnel is said to connect its cellar to the dungeons of nearby 12th and 13th century Restormel Castle, providing a smuggling and, possibly, an escape route. No-one will surely wish to escape from this warmly welcoming hostelry with its log fire and the kind attention of hosts, Malcolm and Eileen Hine. Overnight guests are accommodated in attractively decorated bedrooms, all appointed with en suite facilities, television, radio and tea-makers. *RAC**.*

GLOBE INN,
3 North Street, Lostwithiel,
Cornwall PL22 OEG
Tel: 01208 872501

3 bedrooms, all with private bathroom; Free House with real ale; Historic interest; Children welcome; bar and restaurant meals; Bodmin 5 miles; £/££.

Excellent home-cooked food is just one of the attractions of this delightful 13th century inn beside the River Fowey. There is plenty of choice and prices are extremely reasonable. A fine centre for touring the county, the inn is homely and warmly welcoming; excellent en suite accommodation is available — but limited, so book early! All rooms have television, radio and tea and coffee-making facilities. Evening meals are served in a pleasant restaurant and summer days will find the beer garden well patronised. Lostwithiel, the ancient capital of Cornwall, is a lovely old town with several historic sites, including Restormel Castle, home of the Black Prince. Good opportunities exist nearby for golf, sailing and salmon and trout fishing.

HARBOUR LIGHTS,
Polkirt Hill, Mevagissey,
Cornwall PL26 6UR
Tel: 01726 843249

7 bedrooms, 5 with private bathroom; Free House with real ale; Children welcome; Bar meals, restaurant Thu/Fri/Sat evenings only; Car park; St Austell 5 miles; £.

This family-run freehouse is situated in one of the finest cliff top positions in Cornwall, overlooking Mevagissey Harbour and St Austell Bay. All the public rooms and most of the bedrooms enjoy ever-changing sea views. En suite rooms are available with television and tea/coffee making facilities. Enjoy a meal in the newly opened restaurant which is only a stone's throw from the water, or watch the fishing boats come in while having a drink in the bar. We have our own large car park. Ring or write for brochure. **See also Colour Advertisement on page 2.**

THE CORNISH ARMS,
Pendoggett, Port Isaac,
Cornwall PL30 3HH
Tel: 01208 880263
Fax: 01208 880335

7 bedrooms, 5 with private bathroom; Free House with real ales; Historic interest; Children welcome; Bar and restaurant meals; Wadebridge 8 miles, Polzeath 6, Port Isaac 1; £.

A delightful 16th century Coaching Inn in the small rural village of Pendoggett, just one mile from the coast. Anyone who makes The Cornish Arms a base for exploring the area will not be disappointed by the attractive accommodation or the warmth of welcome extended. Whilst retaining the character of a traditional coaching inn, The Cornish Arms offers all modern amenities in every bedroom; colour and satellite TV, telephone, trouser press, tea and coffee making facilities, etc. The highly recommended restaurant specialises in locally caught seafood and an extensive range of other dishes. Complement your meal with wine from the extensive cellars of The Cornish Arms. Pendoggett Special Bitter is famous for its strength — the locals won't touch it, it's so strong. With Bass straight from the barrel, together with other real ales, you will see why both CAMRA and The Good Pub Guide recommend The Cornish Arms. ETB ❀❀❀ Commended, RAC **, Les Routiers, Good Food Guide. **See also Colour Advertisement on page 3.**

GOLDEN LION,
Fore Street, Port Isaac,
Cornwall PL29 3RB

Tel: 01208 880336

No accommodation; St Austell House with real ale; Historic interest; Children and pets welcome; Bar and restaurant meals; Wadebridge 5 miles.

No Cornish holiday would be complete without a visit to this quaint old fishing village, where steep, narrow streets with their fishermen's cottages slope down to an attractive, still-working harbour. Likewise, no visit to Port Isaac would be complete without taking some refreshment in this well-cared for 18th century hostelry overlooking the rocky harbour far below. Lunchtime snacks are particularly good value — try the fresh crab sandwiches or one of the tasty seafood specials. Accompanied by a glass of well-kept ale they are guaranteed to revive the most leg-weary tourist!

DRIFTWOOD SPARS HOTEL,
Trevaunance Cove, St Agnes,
Cornwall TR5 0RT

Tel: 0187-255 2428/3323

10 rooms, all with private facilities; Free House with real ale; Historic interest; Children welcome; Bar and restaurant meals; Large car park; Newquay 12 miles, Truro 8, Redruth 7; ££.

Situated only a hundred yards from the beach, the building which is now the popular Driftwood Spars Hotel is over 300 years old and has seen active service as a tin miners' store, a chandlery, a sailmaker's workshop and a fish cellar. But nowadays the emphasis is strictly on providing guests with good food, ale and atmosphere. There are three bars — one has a children's room — serving a selection of real ales, including a weekly guest beer, and appetising home-cooked food. Delicious candlelit dinners, featuring fresh local seafood, game and steaks, can be enjoyed in the restaurant. Driftwood Spars offers ten bedrooms, all with private facilities, colour television, telephone, tea-making equipment and sea views. Arts and Crafts Breaks available. Please telephone or write for brochure.

RASHLEIGH ARMS,
Charlestown, St Austell,
Cornwall PL25 3NJ

Tel: 01726 73635
Fax: 01726 69246

5 bedrooms, all with private bathroom; Free House with real ale; Historic interest; Children welcome; Bar and restaurant meals; Car park (100); Truro 13 miles; £.

The little working port of Charlestown is an idyllic relic from another age, hence its popularity with film and television producers. Today, it primarily serves the clay industry. It was originally constructed under the orders of Charles Rashleigh who gave his name to the village and this homely inn. With a large and attractive main bar which boasts a choice of eight real ales, the hostelry has a popular restaurant with a fine salad bar and carvery. There is a wide selection of dishes and children have their own special menu. Accommodation of a very high standard is now available, all bedrooms having en suite facilities, colour television and tea and coffee-makers. *ETB Listed Highly Commended, AA, Egon Ronay.*

THE OLD CUSTOM HOUSE,
South Quay, Padstow,
Cornwall PL28 8ED

Tel: 01841 532359
Fax: 01841 533372

26 bedrooms, all with private bathroom; St Austell Brewery House; Children and pets welcome; Bar and restaurant meals; Wadebridge 5 miles; £££.

This delightfully situated hotel has 26 bedrooms, including a honeymoon suite, all with private bathrooms, colour television, tea and coffee making facilities and central heating. Excellent bar meals are served daily and the restaurant offers a wide range of dishes, including locally caught fish, on both table d'hôte and à la carte menus. Padstow is ideal for holidays, with swimming, fishing, golf, tennis, horse riding and walking — something for everyone. Special Short Break terms available, details on request. ♕♕♕ *Commended.* **See also Colour Advertisement on page 2.**

MOLESWORTH ARMS HOTEL,
Wadebridge,
Cornwall PL27 7DP

Tel: 01208 812055
Fax: 01208 814254

16 bedrooms, 14 with private bathroom; Free House with real ale; Children welcome; Bar food, restaurant evenings only; Car park (20); Bodmin 6 miles; ££.

Cars have now replaced the coaches and carriages that once clattered across the cobbled courtyard of this 16th century coaching inn. Rich panelling, beamed ceilings, cheerful log fires and traditional Cornish hospitality are reminders of those days, although the splendid facilities now to be found at this welcoming hostelry would be well beyond the ken of guests of former years. Under the kind supervision of hosts, Nigel and Shelley Cassidy, the inn is elegantly furnished; two bars invariably buzz with amiable conversation, some guests no doubt studying the comprehensive selection of bar meals. For formal dining, the Coach House Restaurant is justly popular, especially for its fresh local seafood. Excellently appointed overnight accommodation is available. *AA**, Les Routiers.*

Key to Tourist Board Ratings

The Crown Scheme
(England, Scotland & Wales)

Covering hotels, motels, private hotels, guesthouses, inns, bed & breakfast, farmhouses. Every Crown classified place to stay is inspected annually. *The classification*: Listed then 1-5 Crown indicates the range of facilities and services. Higher quality standards are indicated by the terms APPROVED, COMMENDED, HIGHLY COMMENDED and DELUXE.

The Key Scheme
(also operates in Scotland using a Crown System)

Covering self-catering in cottages, bungalows, flats, houseboats, houses, chalets, etc. Every Key classified holiday home is inspected annually. *The classification*: 1-5 Key indicates the range of facilities and equipment. Higher quality standards are indicated by the terms APPROVED, COMMENDED, HIGHLY COMMENDED and DELUXE.

The Q Scheme
(England, Scotland & Wales)

Covering holiday, caravan, chalet and camping parks. Every Q rated park is inspected annually for its quality standards. The more ✔ in the Q – up to 5 – the higher the standard of what is provided.

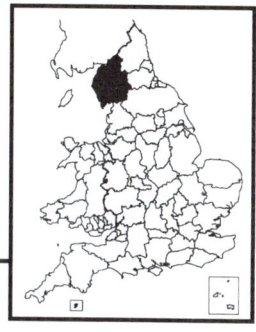

GLEN ROTHAY HOTEL,
Rydal, Ambleside,
Cumbria LA22 9LR

Tel: 015394 32524
Fax: 015394 31079

11 bedrooms, all with private bathroom; Free House with real ale; Historic interest; Children and pets welcome; Bar meals, restaurant evenings only; Car park (40); Windermere 4 miles; ££.

Close to the shores of peaceful Rydal Water, this is an outstanding example of a traditional country hotel. Standing in its own grounds, the lovely house was built in the early 17th century and its beamed ceilings, oak-panelled lounge and open log fires remain to captivate modern-day guests. Tastefully decorated bedrooms are blessed with such contemporary facilities as bath or shower en suite, w.c., colour television, telephone, tea and coffee makers and central heating. The cuisine here represents English cooking at its very best, with a good choice of delicious five-course table d'hôte dinners. Coffee and liqueurs are served in the relaxing comfort of the Oak Lounge whilst the attractive Badger Bar dispenses local real ale and a selection of malt whiskies. ☕☕☕, *AA and RAC ***.

SAWREY HOTEL,
Far Sawrey, Near Ambleside,
Cumbria LA22 0LQ

Tel: 015394 43425

20 bedrooms, 18 with private bathroom; Free House with real ale; Historic interest; Children and pets welcome; Bar lunches, restaurant meals; Car park (30);

This recommended port of call we find interesting for a variety of reasons. It was originally three separate buildings, the central part dating from about 1700. The bar was created out of the old stables and is named after the ghost of a monk who spent his time rescuing fallen women — with disastrous results! The old beams are believed to be from ships wrecked nearby, some possibly from the scattered Armada. One mile from Windermere car ferry and with a vast number of country pursuits to be enjoyed, Sawrey Hotel backs up its inn traditions with excellent cuisine in restaurant and bar and first-class accommodation. ☕☕☕ *Commended, RAC**, Relais Routiers.*

RED LION INN,
Hawkshead, Ambleside, Cumbria

Tel: 015394 36213
Fax: 015394 36747

*All bedrooms with private bathroom; Free House; Pets welcome;
Bar meals; Ambleside 5 miles; ££.*

The Red Lion is a former coaching inn situated in the delightful village of Hawkshead in the beautiful Vale of Esthwaite, an area which has inspired artists and poets over the years. Complete with old beams and open fire, the inn provides an atmosphere of bonhomie where guests can relax and enjoy the excellent service, memorable meals and all the comforts of home. Everything is provided to make your stay enjoyable, and all bedrooms are en suite with televison and tea/coffee making facilities. Hawkshead village has much to interest the visitor — it is home to the Beatrix Potter Gallery, a museum and William Wordsworth's Grammar School, as well as many interesting shops — and makes an ideal base for exploring the many attractions of this scenic area.

BARBON INN,
Barbon, Near Kirkby Lonsdale, Via Carnforth, Lancashire LA6 2LJ

Tel and Fax: 015242 76233

10 bedrooms, 4 with private bathroom; Free House with real ale; Historic interest; Children and pets welcome; Bar meals, restaurant evenings only; Car park (6); Kirkby Lonsdale 3 miles; ££.

If you are torn between the scenic delights of the Lake District and the Yorkshire Dales, then you can have the best of both worlds by making your base this friendly 17th coaching inn nestling in the pretty village of Barbon. Individually furnished bedrooms provide cosy accommodation, and for that extra touch of luxury enquire about the elegant mini-suite with its oak four-poster bed. Fresh local produce is featured on the good value menus presented in the bar and restaurant, and the Sunday roast lunch with all the trimmings attracts patrons from near and far. A wide range of country pursuits can be enjoyed in the immediate area, and the helpful staff will be happy to give information and advice.

DRUNKEN DUCK INN,
Barngates, Ambleside,
Cumbria LA22 ONG

Tel: 015394 36347
Fax: 015394 36781

9 bedrooms, all with private bathroom; Free House with real ale; Historic interest; Children and pets welcome; Bar meals; Car park (40); Windermere 4 miles; ££.

Dating from the 16th century, this unique establishment was known originally as the 'Barngates Inn'. Its present name appears to have been acquired less than a century ago when a barrel on stillage in the cellar slipped its hoops and the contents seeped into the ducks' feeding ditch. The result can be imagined — "Qua-hic"! Thus was born a name which is as memorable and unusual as the inn itself. Veritably, this is a mellow place with the bars offering a variety of real ales and over 60 whiskies. Food is plentiful, varied and beautifully cooked with old favourites like Cumberland sausage casserole, game pie and beefsteak and kidney pie vying with smoked trout from the home tarns and other imaginative dishes to tempt the palate. Hearty old-fashioned puddings such as spotted dick and syrup roly poly are specialities, too — though how diners can cope with them on a day which has begun with the Duck's 'Compleat Breakfast' is a mystery indeed! Set in 60 acres of enchanting Cumbrian scenery and with all the pleasures of Lakeland within easy reach, the Drunken Duck offers splendid accommodation, guest rooms being furnished in traditional style with antiques, tester beds and patchwork quilts but with such modern conveniences as en suite facilities, colour television, hair dryer and tea and coffee-makers. Definitely, delightfully different! ♛♛♛ Commended, AA QQQQ, Good Pub Guide Vegetarian Food Pub of the Year 1996, Egon Ronay, Which? Hotel Guide.

THE BURNMOOR INN,
Boot, Eskdale,
Cumbria CA19 1TG
Tel and Fax: 019467 23224

8 bedrooms, 6 with private bathroom; Free House with real ale; Historic interest; Children welcome; Bar food, restaurant evenings only; Car park (30); Ravenglass 6 miles; ££.

Those searching out the unspoiled charm of the Lakes will not be disappointed in this fine old inn in the ancient village of Boot, nestling amid the hills at the foot of Scafell. Lakeland hospitality is legendary, and hosts Tony and Heidi Foster are proud upholders of this tradition, offering excellent food (both in the restaurant and the bar), fine wines and a selection of good ales. Comfortable, cosy en suite twin and double bedrooms make this a perfect base for walkers, climbers and ramblers all year round. Very competitive room rates make an "Escape to Eskdale" a most appealing prospect.

THE BLACKSMITH'S ARMS,
Talkin Village, Brampton,
Cumbria CA8 1LE
Tel: 016977 3452

5 bedrooms, all with private bathroom; Free House; Historic interest; Bar and restaurant meals; Car park (30); Carlisle 9 miles, Brampton 1; ££.

"A getaway place at an affordable price". The Blacksmith's Arms offers all the hospitality and comforts of a traditional country inn. Enjoy tasty meals served in the bar lounges, or linger over dinner in the well-appointed restaurant. The inn is personally managed by the proprietors, Pat and Tom Bagshaw, who guarantee the hospitality one would expect from a family concern. Guests are assured of a pleasant and comfortable stay. There are five lovely bedrooms, all en suite and offering every comfort. Peacefully situated in the beautiful village of Talkin, the inn is convenient for the Borders, Hadrian's Wall and the Lake District. There is a good golf course, pony trekking, walking and other country pursuits nearby. *FHG Diploma Winners 1989.* **See also Colour Advertisement on page 3.**

JOLLY ANGLERS INN,
Burneside, Kendal,
Cumbria LA9 6QS
Tel: 01539 732552

8 bedrooms, 1 with private bathroom; Real ale; Children and pets welcome; Bar meals, restaurant evenings only; Windermere 6 miles, Kendal 2; £.

The Jolly Anglers is situated in the village of Burneside, two miles north of the market town of Kendal and within six miles of Lake Windermere. This old tradtional Lakeland inn offers bed and breakfast accommodation in Taylors Cottages (attached to the inn and once the village smithy) and Strickland Ketel Guest House, situated in a quieter position at the rear. Some rooms have en suite facilities, all have colour television and tea/coffee making facilities. Guests are offered good home cooking in Taylors Cottages. Real ale is served in the bars, which have low beamed ceilings and log fires. Rates are moderate, with special bargain breaks. Free fishing is available, and there is an 18-hole golf course nearby. *Cumbria Tourist Board Listed, RAC.* **See also Colour Advertisement on page 3.**

NOTE

All the information in this book is given in good faith in the belief that it is correct. However, the publishers cannot guarantee the facts given in these pages, neither are they responsible for changes in policy, ownership or terms that may take place after the date of going to press. Readers should always satisfy themselves that the facilities they require are available and that the terms, if quoted, still apply.

DUKE'S HEAD HOTEL,
Armathwaite, Near Carlisle,
Cumbria CA4 9PB
Tel: 016974 72226

5 bedrooms, all with private bathroom; Pubmaster House with real ale; Children and pets welcome; Bar and restaurant meals; Car park (30); Carlisle 9 miles; ££.

Serene and secure in the unspoilt Eden Valley, the Duke's Head claims to be the house of "probably the best roast duckling in Cumbria" and we are not disposed to argue or insist on the "probably". Excellent and moderately-priced meals are served in the bar and restaurant daily. Peacefully situated between the Border Country and the Lake District, yet easily accessible from the M6, A1, A6 and A69, this hospitable inn is also in demand for its comfortable accommodation and bookings are advisable. There are numerous country pursuits to be enjoyed in the immediate vicinity, including walking, fishing, shooting, canoeing and rock climbing. The scenic Settle to Carlisle railway provides a delightful way to view the enchanting countryside.

PHEASANT INN,
Casterton, Kirkby Lonsdale,
Cumbria LA6 2RX
Tel and Fax: 015242 71230

10 bedrooms, all with private bathroom; Free House with real ale; Historic interest; Bar meals, restaurant evenings only (not Mon.); Children and pets welcome; Car park (40); Kirkby Lonsdale 1 mile; £££.

Perfectly located between the Lake District and Yorkshire Dales, this lovely old country inn has a peerless reputation for its outstanding cuisine, from the hearty Cumbrian breakfast to start the day to the superbly-presented dishes served in the beautiful panelled restaurant. May and Melvin Mackie are convivial hosts and are to be congratulated on the high standards of decor and appointments. Hand-pulled beers and appetising meals are on offer in the welcoming bar or the non-smoking Fox Room, which is also suitable for small private parties. A fine touring base, the inn has delightfully furnished guest rooms, all with en suite bath or shower, colour television, direct-dial telephone and tea and coffee making facilities. ♛♛♛ Commended.

Taking a pet on holiday? Then buy
"PETS WELCOME"
THE ANIMAL LOVERS' HOLIDAY GUIDE
Details of Hotels, Guest Houses, Furnished Accommodation, Caravans, etc, where holiday makers and their pets are made welcome.
Available from most newsagents and bookshops price £4.60
or from Publishers (£5.50 including postage, UK only).
FHG PUBLICATIONS LTD
Abbey Mill Business Centre, Seedhill, Paisley, Renfrewshire PA1 1TJ

SUN HOTEL AND COACHING INN,
Coniston,
Cumbria LA21 8HQ
Tel: 015394 41248

11 bedrooms, all with private bathroom; Free House with real ale; Children and pets welcome; Bar food, restaurant evenings only; Car park (15); Ambleside 6 miles; ££.

Hand in hand, this fine country hotel and its adjacent 16th century coaching inn stand in the shadow of Coniston's spectacular 'Old Man', ready to serve Lakeland visitors in traditional style. With inspiring views on all sides, here is a rewarding blend of warm, wayside inn hospitality and sophisticated modern conveniences. Delicious home-made bar food is served daily, whilst the hotel menu offers a broad range of interesting dishes in plush and tasteful surroundings. Special diets are willingly catered for. The accommodation is of a high standard, the majority of the charming rooms having en suite facilities, colour television, telephone and beverage-makers; two rooms have four-poster beds and all are centrally heated. *ETB* ♛♛♛ *Commended, AA/RAC**.*

SUN INN,
Main Street, Dent, Sedbergh,
Cumbria LA10 5QL
Tel: 01539 625208

3 bedroom;, Free House with real ale; Historic interest; Children welcome, pets in bar area only; Bar meals; Sedbergh 4 miles; £.

A typical Dales village inn, the Sun's beamed bar is a convivial retreat that will soon cast its spell on the first-time visitor, a happy mood no doubt influenced by its traditional ales and tempting variety of bar meals. Dent, with its quaint narrow cobbled street lined with stone cottages, some dating from the 15th and 16th centuries, is within the Yorkshire Dales National Park and, completely unspoiled, is a most relaxing holiday venue. And where better to stay than this friendly inn where each bedroom has colour television, washbasin, shaver socket and tea and coffee making facilities. What is more, the bed and breakfast charges are extremely reasonable. *Cumbria Tourist Board Listed.*

BOWER HOUSE INN,
Eskdale, Holmrook, Cumbria CA19 1TD

Tel: 019467 23244
Fax: 019467 23308

24 bedrooms, all with private bathroom; Free House with real ale; Historic interest; Children welcome; Bar meals, restaurant evenings only; Car park (60); Gosforth 6 miles; £££.

A 17th century inn of considerable character, the Bower House is as popular with the locals as it is with tourists, always a good recommendation for any establishment. Decor and furnishings throughout are tasteful and designed with an eye to comfort as well as style, and all guest rooms have private facilities, colour television and telephone. Cuisine is of a consistently good standard, with fresh produce from nearby farms featuring extensively in skilfully prepared and well presented dishes, and the wine cellar should satisfy the most demanding palate. Mature gardens make a fine setting for this gem of an inn. ❀❀❀❀ Commended, AA ** and Red Rosette.

HARE AND HOUNDS INN,
Bowland Bridge, Grange-over-Sands, Cumbria

Tel: 015395 68333

16 bedroooms, most with private bathroom; Free House with real ale; Historic interest; Bar food; Car park (80); Grange-over-Sands 9 miles, Kendal 6, Windermere 6; £.

Situated in the Beautiful Winster Valley yet only six miles from Windermere. The Hare and Hounds is a delightful inn, run by ex-England and Liverpool football player, Peter Thompson, and his wife Debbie. All bedrooms have a telephone, colour television and tea/coffee making facilities, and there is a beer garden and comfortable resident's lounge. The lounge bar, which dates from 1600 with oak beams, stone walls and log fires, has a typical Lakeland atmosphere, and meals are served at midday and in the evening. Terms for overnight accommodation represent good value and special bargain breaks are available. Access and Visa welcome. ETB ❀❀❀, Egon Ronay Recommended.

QUEEN'S HEAD HOTEL,
Main Street, Hawkshead, Cumbria LA22 0NS

Tel: 015394 36271
Fax: 015394 36722

13 bedrooms, all with private bathroom; Hartleys House with real ale; Historic interest; Children and pets welcome; Bar and restaurant meals; Ambleside 4 miles; ££.

The 16th century Queen's Head, set in the traffic-free village of Hawkshead on the edge of Esthwaite Water, has a wonderful atmosphere, with low oak-beamed ceilings, panelled walls and a warm log fire whenever necessary. The friendly bar and separate dining room are noted for high quality food, with many locally and organically produced ingredients and a comprehensive wine list. Beer is hand-pulled from the wood. The attractive en suite bedrooms, some with four-poster beds, have colour television, tea and coffee making facilities, hairdryer and telephone. The village was the home of Beatrix Potter and is an excellent centre for fishing, bowling, riding, water ski-ing, cycling and walking. ❀❀❀ Commended, AA and RAC **. See also Colour Advertisement on page 4.

Cumbria 33

COLEDALE INN,
Braithwaite, Near Keswick, Cumbria CA12 5TN

Tel: 017687 78272

12 bedrooms, all with private shower/WC; Free House with real ale; Children and pets welcome; Bar and restaurant meals; Car park (14); Carlisle 30 miles, Cockermouth 10, Keswick 2; ££.

A friendly, family-run Victorian Inn in a peaceful hillside position above Braithwaite, and ideally situated for touring and walking, with paths to the mountains immediately outside our gardens. All bedrooms are warm and spacious, with en suite shower room and colour television. Children are welcome, as are pets. Home-cooked meals are served every lunchtime and evening, with a fine selection of inexpensive wines, beers and Coledale XXPS and Yates real cask ale. Open all year except midweek lunches in winter. Tariff and menu sent on request.

SNOOTY FOX TAVERN,
Main Street, Kirkby Lonsdale, Cumbria LA6 2AH

Tel: 015242 71308
Fax: 015242 72642

5 bedrooms, all with private bathroom; Free House with real ale; Historic interest; Bar and restaurant meals; Car park (8); Lancaster 14 miles; ££.

For years now Proprietor, Jack Shone, and his seventeenth century coaching inn have consistently tended to the needs of weary travellers. Well-kept beers: Timothy Taylors, Theakstons Best and Hartleys XB seduce all explorers into the timeless ambience of the bar. Bed and breakfast presented in five homely bedrooms ensure that the Fox is more soporific than Snooty! The ambitious menu, prepared by nationally acclaimed chefs, is served all day throughout the inn and has something for everyone, confirming that food is definitely the speciality. Explore both the Lakes and the Dales through the heart of the Snooty Fox.

BAY HORSE INN,
Winton, Near Kirkby Stephen,
Cumbria CA17 4HS
Tel: 017683 71451

3 bedrooms, all with private bathroom; Free House with real ale; Historic interest; Bar food; Car park (6); M6 (Junction 38) 11 miles, Appleby 10, Brough 3, Kirkby Stephen 1; £.

A warm and welcoming little inn situated on the western side of the scenic Cumbrian Pennines, and ideally placed as a stopping-off point on your journey north or south on the nearby M6. Resident proprietors Sheila and Derek Parvin offer the warmest of welcomes to all guests, with the finest of traditional ales, good food and comfortable accommodation. Lying as it does in the picturesque Eden Valley, the Bay Horse is also ideal as a touring base for those wishing to stay longer in this lovely part of the country. Open all year.

THE BLACK SWAN,
Ravenstonedale, Kirkby Stephen,
Cumbria CA17 4NG
Tel: 015396 23204
Fax: 015396 23604

15 bedrooms, all with private bathroom; Free House with real ale; Historic interest; Children and pets welcome; Bar and restaurant meals; Car park (30); Kirkby Stephen 4 miles; £££.

Built of Lakeland stone at the turn of the century, this homely hostelry is tucked away in the tranquil Eden Valley — just the place to get away from it all, commune with nature and revivify body and spirit. Under the care of resident owners, Gordon and Norma Stuart, the hotel has a jealously guarded reputation for good food from the big breakfast to the set five-course dinner with a modest à la carte menu also available. The views from the nearby Howgill Fells are spectacular and this is a wonderful centre for walking. Sport on the Eden and Lune is first-rate with the hotel holding private fishing rights. Guest rooms are tastefully furnished and superbly appointed. ♚♚♚♚ *Commended, AA** and Rosette, RAC** and Hospitality Award.*

MANOR HOUSE INN,
Oxen Park, Near Ulverston,
Cumbria LA12 8HG
Tel: 01229 861345

5 bedrooms, 4 with private bathroom; Robinsons & Hartleys House with real ale; Historic interest; Children and well behaved pets welcome; Bar and restaurant meals; Car park (30); Greenodd 3 miles; ££.

Nestling 'twixt lakes, mountains and coast, Oxen Park is one of the few undiscovered, unspoilt beauty spots in South Lakeland. Set in this hamlet frozen in time, is Manor House, an inn of distinction. Here a warm welcome awaits as soon as you enter the large bar, with beamed ceiling and log fire. The guest bedrooms offer spacious, comfortable accommodation with tea/coffee facilities and colour television. Breakfast is hearty and traditional, as are all the meals on the extensive menu which offers freshly prepared dishes, many to order, catering for most tastes including vegetarian, special diets and smaller appetites. Hosts, John and Jean Mitchell, strive to maintain a high standard of service and presentation in an informal and friendly atmosphere. Forget the crowds, rub shoulders with the locals, and enjoy our relaxed pace. ♚♚♚ *Commended, Egon Ronay.*

Derbyshire

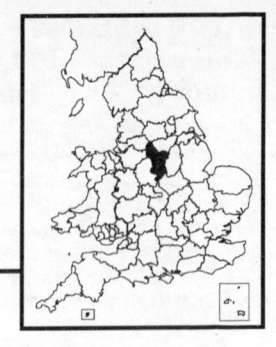

THE DOG AND PARTRIDGE COUNTRY INN,
Swinscoe, Ashbourne,
Derbyshire DE6 2HS

Tel: 01335 343183
Fax: 01335 342742

29 bedrooms, all with private bathroom; ; Free House; Historic interest; Children welcome; Bar and restaurant meals; Car park (100); Ashbourne 3 miles; £.

Mary and Martin Stelfox welcome you to a family-run seventeenth century inn and motel set in five acres, five miles from Alton Towers and close to Dovedale and Ashbourne. We specialise in family breaks, and special diets and vegetarians are catered for. All rooms have private bathrooms, colour television, direct-dial telephone, tea-making facilities and baby listening service. It is ideally situated for touring Stoke Potteries, Derbyshire Dales and Staffordshire moorlands. The restaurant is open all day, and non-residents are welcome. Open Christmas and New Year.

BERESFORD ARMS HOTEL,
Station Road, Ashbourne,
Derbyshire DE6 1AA

Tel: 01335 300035
Fax: 01335 300065

12 bedrooms, all with private bathroom; Free House with real ale; Historic interest; Children welcome; Restaurant meals; Car park (30); Derby 13 miles; £.

Situated at the gateway to the Peak District, this family-run hotel is ideal for visiting such places as Alton Towers, Carsington Water and Dovedale, as well as many historic buildings. Built at the turn of the century, it offers a warm welcome in a pleasant environment of olde worlde charm. The comfortable en-suite bedrooms have colour television, direct-dial telephone and tea/coffee making facilities. The hotel has a restaurant and two bars, and there is parking for guests' use. Open Christmas and New Year.

THE WALTZING WEASEL,
New Mills Road, Birch Vale, Stockport,
Derbyshire SK12 5BT

Tel and Fax: 01663 743402

8 bedrooms, all with private bathroom; Free House with real ale; Historic interest; Children and pets welcome; Bar meals, restaurant evenings only; Car park (40); Stockport 10 miles; ££££.

There are pub names of infinite variety but this one must take the biscuit for originality (or eccentricity!). This is, in fact, a dyed-in-the-wool traditional country inn that is without the need of gimmicks to attract lovers of good food and drink. Bang in the heart of the Peak District, the inn may be architecturally unremarkable from the exterior but, within, it possesses an ambience induced by subdued lighting, antiques and mullioned windows through which there are fine views of Kinder Scout. Wholesome fare is served in a cosy restaurant and those seeking first rate accommodation in this lovely area have handsome en suite bedrooms at their disposal, all with colour television, direct-dial telephone and tea and coffee making facilities.

JINGLERS INN/THE FOX & HOUNDS,
Belper Road, Bradley, Ashbourne, Derbyshire DE6 3EN
Tel: 01335 370855

6 bedrooms, most en suite; Free House with real ale; Children and pets welcome; Bar food; Car park; Ashbourne 4 miles; £.

Character country inn, famous for having two names, set adjacent to 18 acres (A517). Pub food is served along with real ale; the menu ranges from filled cobs to steaks. There are six bedrooms available for bed and breakfast; some are en suite and all have separate entrances, television and tea/coffee making facilities. Children and pets are most welcome. There is a pool/family room, public/lounge bar, pool, dominoes and darts. Conveniently placed for Derbyshire Dales, Alton Towers, Chatsworth House, Dovedale, American Adventure and several golf courses. Carsington Water is only two miles away, where sailing, windsurfing, cycle hire and fishing are available. Clay pigeon shooting. Everyone welcome. Licensed site for 34 caravans with hook-ups and hard standings. *ETB Listed.*

THE CHARLES COTTON HOTEL,
Hartington, Near Buxton, Derbyshire SK17 0AL
Tel: 01298 84229
Fax: 01335 42742

13 bedrooms; Free House with real ale; Historic interest; Children welcome; Bar and restaurant meals; Car park (16); Ashbourne 9 miles; £.

The Charles Cotton is a small comfortable hotel with a starred rating for the RAC and AA. The hotel lies in the heart of the Derbyshire Dales, pleasantly situated in the village square of Hartington, with nearby shops catering for all needs. It is renowned throughout the area for its hospitality and good home cooking. Pets and children are welcome; special diets are catered for. The Charles Cotton makes the perfect centre to relax and enjoy the area, whether walking, cycling, pony trekking, brass rubbing or even hang gliding. Open Christmas and New Year.

PUBLISHER'S NOTE

While every effort is made to ensure accuracy, we regret that FHG Publications cannot accept responsibility for errors, omissions or misrepresentations in our entries or any consequences thereof. Prices in particular should be checked because we go to press early. We will follow up complaints but cannot act as arbiters or agents for either party.

YE OLDE NAGS HEAD,
Cross Street, Castleton,
Derbyshire S30 2WH

Tel: 01433 620248
Fax: 01433 621604

8 bedrooms, all with private bathroom; Free House with real ale; Historic interest; Children welcome; Bar and restaurant meals; Car park (10); Hathersage 5 miles; ££££.

In the shadow of Scott's Peveril Castle, the picturesque village of Castleton is a perfect setting from which to plan excursions into the Peak District National Park. And what finer base for a stay in such a tranquil spot than this 17th century coaching house, where comfort and congeniality blend seamlessly with the finest modern amenities. The friendly bars warm the spirit with a good selection of real ales and other refreshments, with tasty bar meals to provide sustenance. For more serious dining, traditional English and Continental fare of the highest quality is served in the elegant restaurant. Charmingly decorated throughout, Ye Olde Nags Head has exemplary accommodation, all rooms having private bathrooms or showers, direct-dial telephone, hairdryers and tea/coffee making facilities. ♛♛♛♛ *Highly Commended.*

BULL'S HEAD INN,
Foolow, Near Eyam,
Derbyshire S30 1QR

Tel: 01433 630873
Fax: 01433 631738

3 bedrooms, all with private bathroom; Free House with real ale; Historic interest; Children welcome; Bar and restaurant meals; Car park (15); Tideswell 3 miles; ££.

One of the prettiest pubs in the Peak District, the Bull's Head is situated in an old-world village complete with pond and resident ducks. Open log fires, oak beams and a copper-decked inglenook fireplace enhance the traditional bar where cask-conditioned ales and numerous malt whiskies are on offer. Bar meals are served and there is a cosy oak-panelled restaurant presenting fish and game dishes and home-cooked pies, all garnished with fresh vegetables. This is a lovely place in which to stay, the en suite accommodation including one room with a four-poster bed. For the (resident) fisherman, two rods are available on the Derbyshire Wye with $4^{3}/_{4}$ miles of double bank fishing, brown and rainbow trout providing good sport.

THE MANIFOLD INN,
Hulme End, Hartington,
Derbyshire SK17 0EX

Tel: 01298 84537

5 bedrooms, all private shower/toilet; Free House with real ale; Bar meals and dining room; Car park (35); Buxton 10 miles, Ashbourne 10, Bakewell 10, Leek 8; £/££.

The Manifold Inn is a 200-year-old coaching inn now owned by Frank and Bridgette Lipp. It offers warm hospitality and good pub food at sensible prices. This lovely mellow stone inn nestles on the banks of the River Manifold opposite the old toll house that used to serve the turnpike and river ford. All guest accommodation is in the old stone blacksmith's shop in the secluded rear courtyard of the inn. The bedrooms have en suite showers, colour television, tea/coffee making facilities and telephone. ♛♛♛

MAYNARD ARMS HOTEL,
Main Road, Grindleford,
Derbyshire S30 1HP

Tel: 01433 630321
Fax: 01433 630445

10 bedrooms, all with private bathroom; Free House with real ale; Bar and restaurant meals; Children welcome, pets by arrangement; Car park (60); Hathersage 3 miles; ££.

With the tranquillity and scenic grandeur of the Peak District National Park surrounding it, it is hard to believe that the urban centres of Sheffield and Manchester are only minutes away from this splendid hotel which stands in a beautiful garden. A reasonably-priced and interesting range of bar meals is served daily in the informal Longshaw Bar, where traditional ales are on offer; alternatively, diners may opt for the more formal setting of the Padley Restaurant where the dishes are of international flavour as well as classic British fare. Over-indulgence may be countered by following one of the delightful walks in which the area abounds. Accommodation is appointed to a very high standard with some rooms with four-posters available. ❦❦❦❦ Highly Commended, AA, RAC, Johansens.

THE SPORTSMAN,
Kinder Road, Hayfield,
Derbyshire SK22 5LE

Tel: 01663 741565

7 bedrooms, all with private bathroom; Thwaites House with real ale; Children and pets welcome; Bar and restaurant meals; Glossop 4 miles; ££.

Between the pretty village of Hayfield and lofty Kinder Scout (2088ft), highest point in the Peak District National Park, this homely inn is a recommended port of call, especially for those following the picturesque Kinder Trail. Family-run and with a traditional bar with a log fire providing an unselfconscious welcome to all, the hostelry dispenses wholesome, freshly home-cooked fare using the best local produce in company with hand-pulled Thwaites real ale. There is a first-rate choice of casseroles, fish and grills with vegetarian alternatives. This is a fine base for a walking or sightseeing holiday amidst glorious countryside and the inn offers extremely comfortable accommodation in rooms with en suite facilities.

POACHERS ARMS HOTEL,
Castleton Road, Hope, Via Sheffield,
Derbyshire S30 2RD

Tel: 01433 620380

6 bedrooms, all with private bathroom; Free House with real ale; Children and pets welcome; Bar and restaurant meals; Car park (30); Hathersage 4 miles; £££.

The first thing that impressed us about this homely Peak District retreat was its intriguing (and almost bewildering!) selection of starters, light snacks, vegetarian dishes, main bar meals and even children's specials on offer and at extremely realistic prices, too! Conveniently placed for all types of countryside recreation, this little inn-cum-hotel is well worth a visit for sustenance alone, although discerning holidaymakers have already discovered the full worth of the accommodation offered. Under the personal supervision of Gladys Bushell and family, comforts abound, guest rooms having private bath/shower, colour television, radio and tea and coffee-making facilities amongst their excellent appointments. ❦❦❦, Egon Ronay.

Please mention
Recommended WAYSIDE & COUNTRY INNS
when seeking refreshment or
accommodation at a Hotel
mentioned in these pages.

BOATHOUSE INN,
Dale Road, Matlock,
Derbyshire DE4 3PP
Tel: 01629 583776

4 bedrooms; Real ale; Historic interest; Bar food; Car park; Nottingham 24 miles, Buxton 20, Derby 18, Ashbourne 13, Chesterfield 10; £.

With comfortable bedrooms overlooking the River Derwent this is, indeed, a pleasant place in which to stay. It is an ideal base from which to explore an area of great beauty yet shops are near at hand. Fine meals are served in the quaint bars with the enjoyment heightened, perhaps, with a jar of real ale.

GEORGE HOTEL,
Tideswell,
Derbyshire
Tel: 01298 871382
Fax: 01298 872408

4 bedrooms; Historic interest; Bar and restaurant meals; Car park (30); Chatsworth 10 miles, Buxton 9, Bakewell 8; £.

The church of this ancient market town is known as the "Cathedral of the Peak" and visitors come from far and wide to see it. Next door, the George offers tourists to the Peak District hospitality in keeping with its history as an old coaching inn dating from 1730. A four-poster suite is available for honeymoons or other special occasions. All meals are served every day of the week and a wide range of appetising snacks is also obtainable over the bar. Live 60s music every Friday evening. Used in the TV series "Yesterday's Dreams" set in this "best kept" Derbyshire village.

Devon

CHURCH HOUSE INN,
Holne, Near Ashburton,
Devon TQ13 7SJ
Tel: 01364 3208

6 bedrooms, 4 with private facilities; Free House with real ale; Historic interest; Children welcome; Bar and restaurant meals; Car park (6); Ashburton 3 miles; £/££.

Very much the heart of the village in both location and spirit, this family-run inn dates from 1329 and is a Grade II Listed building. Up to twelve guests can be accommodated, and four of the pleasantly furnished, comfortable bedrooms have their own private facilities. All are provided with tea and coffee facilities and colour television, and residents have use of an attractive private sitting room where books, magazines and writing materials are available. Wherever possible local produce is used in the freshly prepared dishes served in the bar and in the restaurant, and a nice range of wines, real ale and cider meets all tastes in refreshment. ☙☙☙ Commended, Egon Ronay, Good Pub Guide, Which? Guide to Country Inns, CAMRA.

THE SHIP INN,
Church Street, Axmouth,
Devon EX12 4AF
Tel: 01297 21838

No accommodation; Real ale; Bar food; Car park; Seaton 1 mile.

Especially pretty on summer evenings when fairy lights twinkle in the garden trees, this fine, creeper-clad inn extends a warm welcome at any time of year and guaranteed Devonshire hospitality. Excellent lunchtime bar food includes sandwiches, various hot dishes and daily specials, including local fish and game, and there is a more extensive evening menu. Licensee Jane Chapman and her husband Christopher are devoted supporters of The Barn Owl Trust and often take in injured birds (including owls) to convalesce in the back garden (enquire about visiting hours!).

RIVERSIDE INN,
Bovey Tracey,
Devon TQ13 9AF

Tel: 01626 832293
Fax: 01626 833880

10 bedrooms, all with private bathroom; Free House with real ale; Historic interest; Bar and restaurant meals; Car park (100); Newton Abbot 5 miles; £/££.

Beautifully placed only three miles from Dartmoor's rugged slopes and 20 minutes from the South Devon coast, this pleasant inn is the ideal venue for a combined sea and country holiday. New friends will soon be made in the old-world atmosphere of the well-stocked Tracey Bar and relaxing moments may be spent strolling along the leafy banks of the River Bovey on which the inn enjoys fishing rights, whilst Bovey itself is a charming and historic little town. The accommodation is excellent, each one of the en suite bedrooms being appointed with colour television, radio, direct-dial telephone, tea and coffee-making facilities and hair dryer. Diners have the choice of à la carte and table d'hôte menus, plus bar snacks and daily specials. *AA/RAC***

THE MASONS ARMS,
Branscombe,
Devon EX12 3DJ

Tel: 01297 680300
Fax: 01297 680500

21 bedrooms, 19 with private bathroom; Free House with real ale; Historic interest; Children and pets welcome; Bar and restaurant meals; Car park (45); Sidmouth 5 miles; ££/£££.

Once the haunt of smugglers bringing ashore brandy from the coast half a mile away, this creeper-clad hostelry is very much part of the area of outstanding natural beauty in which it stands. Original antique furnishings contribute markedly to the atmosphere and character of a seasoned village inn. The oldest part of the building contains the bar built round a central fireplace which radiates living warmth on chilly days whilst further pleasures await in an oak-beamed restaurant renowned for its splendid à la carte cuisine backed by carefully chosen wines. Thatched cottages, sensitively converted, supplement the guest accommodation in the hostelry itself, all rooms having en suite facilities and fine modern appointments. *AA** and Rosette.*

COACH AND HORSES INN,
Buckland Brewer, Near Bideford,
Devon EX39 5LU

Tel: 01237 451395

2 bedrooms, both with private bathroom; Free House with real ale; Historic interest; Children welcome; Bar and restaurant meals; Car park (15); Bideford 4 miles; £.

Parts of this family-run thatched inn have been dated as 16th and 17th century, but the original building is believed to go back as far as the 13th century. Good bar meals and snacks are available lunchtimes and evenings, and more substantial fare is on offer in the attractive dining room, where a full traditional English roast lunch is served on Sundays. Two cosy bedrooms, each with private bathroom, provide comfortable overnight accommodation.

Available from most bookshops, the 1997 edition of THE GOLF GUIDE covers details of every UK golf course – well over 2000 entries – for holiday or business golf. Hundreds of hotel entries offer convenient accommodation, accompanying details of the courses – the 'pro', par score, length etc.

Endorsed by The Professional Golfers' Association (PGA) and including Holiday Golf in Ireland, France, Portugal, Spain and the USA.

**£8.99 from bookshops or £9.80 including postage (UK only) from FHG Publications,
Abbey Mill Business Centre, Paisley PA1 1JT**

THE POACHER'S POCKET,
Burlescombe, Near Tiverton,
Devon EX16 7JY
Tel: 01823 672286

9 bedrooms; Free House with real ale; Historic interest; Children and pets welcome; Bar and restaurant meals; Car park (50); Wellington 5 miles; £.

Retaining all the character of yesteryear, this tidy little hostelry dates from the 17th century. We have known of its merits for some years and its amenities have remained consistently well above average. Whether your visit be long and lingering or short and sweet, you may be sure of a warm welcome from present hosts, John and Pat Whitlock, aided in practical terms by central heating and a real log fire in the bar. A full à la carte menu is available until 10 pm and there is also a wide range of bar meals. Direct on the A38 between Junctions 26 and 27 of the M5 and within easy reach of Exmoor and several areas of outstanding beauty, this former coaching inn provides excellent accommodation at very reasonable rates.

MANOR HOTEL,
2-4 Fore Street, Cullompton,
Devon EX15 IJL
Tel: 01884 32281
Fax: 01884 38344

10 bedrooms, all with private bathroom; Free House with real ale; Historic interest; Children and pets welcome; Bar lunches, restaurant evenings only; Car park (40); Tiverton 5 miles; £££.

Built in 1603 and formerly the grand town house of a local wool merchant, the Manor has been refurbished to a high standard to fulfil its present-day function as a hostelry of some distinction. Its elegant timbered facade graces the heart of this pleasant Devon town. Within, the ambience of former days remains in company with services that previous occupants would marvel at. A mouth-watering à la carte menu is served in a delightfully intimate restaurant; alternatively, one may try the splendid Veryards Bar. Catering for holidaymaker and businessman alike, the accommodation consists of beautifully-appointed period bedrooms now blessed with en suite bathrooms, colour television, direct-dial telephone, tea and coffee-making facilities, trouser press and hairdryer. ♛♛♛ *Commended.*

RECOMMENDED SHORT BREAK HOLIDAYS IN BRITAIN
Introduced by John Carter, TV Holiday Expert and Journalist.

Specifically designed to cater for the most rapidly growing sector of the holiday market in the UK. Illustrated details of hotels offering special "Bargain Breaks" throughout the year. Available from newsagents and bookshops for £4.25 or direct from the publishers for £4.80 including postage (UK only).

FHG PUBLICATIONS LTD
Abbey Mill Business Centre, Seedhill, Paisley, Renfrewshire PAl ITJ

THE COTT INN,
**Dartington, Totnes,
Devon TQ9 6HE**

Tel: 01803 863777
Fax: 01803 866629

6 bedrooms, all with private bathroom; Free House with real ale; Historic interest; Children and pets welcome; Bar meals, restaurant evenings only; Car park (30); Totnes 2 miles; £££.

This rambling thatched inn is one of the oldest in the country (AD 1320), and is certainly one of the most beautiful. A free house, the inn is on the Buckfastleigh to Totnes road and travellers will find ample room to park their cars and relax for a while in an atmosphere of timeless charm. The cottage-style bedrooms are spotless, and in addition to bed and breakfast, special terms are offered for short breaks. A superb hot and cold buffet table offers excellent refreshment at lunchtime, and during the evening there is an à la carte menu presenting home-cooked dishes using local produce. *Wine Pub of the Year 1996, Good Food Guide; Good Pub Guide Licensees of the Year 1995.*

THE RED LION INN,
**Dittisham, Near Dartmouth,
Devon TQ6 0ES**

Tel: 01803 722235

6 bedrooms, all with private facilities; Free House with real ale; Children over 12 years welcome; Bar and restaurant meals; Car park (12); Dartmouth 6 miles; ££.

The Red Lion has been offering generous hospitality since 1750 when it was a Coaching House. Log fires and gleaming brass in a friendly old bar, hearty English breakfasts, terraced gardens overlooking the River Dart, and an exceptionally warm welcome all await you. Bedrooms are individually furnished, with comfortable beds, central heating, colour television, tea-making facilities and telephones. An extensive menu includes daily specials and features fresh produce, prime local meats, fresh fish and locally grown vegetables. Picturesque countryside and a mild climate make this a perfect holiday retreat.

THE ROYAL OAK INN,
**Dunsford, Near Exeter,
Devon EX6 7DA**

Tel: 01647 252256

8 bedrooms, 5 with private bathroom; Free House with real ale; Children welcome; Bar food; Car park (40); Exeter 6 miles, Moretonhampstead 4; £.

Enjoy a friendly welcome in our traditional Country Pub in the picturesque thatched village of Dunsford. Quiet en suite bedrooms are available in the tastefully converted cob barn. An ideal base for touring Dartmoor, Exeter and the coast, and the beautiful Teign Valley. Real ale and home-made meals are served. Well behaved children and dogs are welcome. The accommodation is suitable for disabled guests and non-smokers. Please ring Mark or Judy Harrison for further details. *Tourist Board Listed Approved, CAMRA, Good Pub Guide.*

THE ROLLE ARMS,
Lower Budleigh, East Budleigh,
Devon EX9 7DL
Tel: 01395 442012

3 bedrooms; Whitbread House with real ale; Historic interest; Children and pets welcome; Bar and restaurant meals; Car park (12); Budleigh Salterton 2 miles; £.

Lying between Exeter and Sidmouth, this attractive, 250 year-old coaching inn is a magnet for tourists and holidaymakers anxious to make the most of lovely East Devon. The bar thrummed with convivial conversation and we were most impressed by the menu, an exciting miscellany of pastas, pizzas, steaks, seafood and sweets, all at most competitive prices. There are real ales to appeal to the connoisseur (or just plain thirsty!) and those in holiday mood may indulge in several pub games. One may well be tempted to linger longer in such delightful surroundings. Very little persuasion will be needed for very comfortable, if limited, accommodation is available. Book early if possible.

THE GLOBE HOTEL,
Topsham, Near Exeter,
Devon EX3 0HR
Tel: 01392 873471
Fax: 01392 873879

17 bedrooms, all with private bathroom; Free House with real ale; Historic interest; Bar and restaurant meals; Car park (20); Exeter 4 miles; ££.

Dark oak panelling, comfortable leather settles and period prints all contribute to the traditional character of this sixteenth century coaching inn which stands on the main street of the ancient town of Topsham, on the estuary of the River Exe. Those seeking overnight accommodation will find comfortable bedrooms, all with private bathrooms, colour television, direct-dial telephone, and tea and coffee making facilities. For an extra touch of luxury, rooms are available with four-poster or half-tester beds. The good value range of bar meals includes all the traditional favourites, and in the restaurant a full à la carte menu is served with courtesy and efficiency. *South West Tourist Board* ☗ ☗ ☗ *Commended.*

Devon 45

THE NOBODY INN,
Doddiscombsleigh, Near Exeter, Devon EX6 7PS

Tel: 01647 252394
Fax: 01647 252978

7 bedrooms, 5 with private bathroom; Free House with real ale; Historic interest; Bar food, restaurant Tuesday to Saturday evenings only; Car park; Exeter 7 miles, Dunsford 4; ££.

There is always somebody in the quaintly named Nobody Inn, for it is extremely popular with visitors and locals alike. A typical Devonshire hostelry, the inn originated in the sixteenth century as an ale and cider house for miners working nearby. Today it provides more sophisticated facilities, but still in a warm, traditional style. A well-stocked bar with a cheerful log fire offers over 230 whiskies, including a large selection of malts; bar meals are a popular order. Would-be gourmets are recommended to the à la carte restaurant where well-cooked and attractively presented food, supported by 800 fine wines, satisfies the most obdurate palate. Real old world charm is epitomised in accommodation which skilfully incorporates the most modern amenities, including showers, without spoiling the effect. All the Torbay resorts are within easy reach by car, and the edge of Dartmoor National Park is only half a mile away.

THE OLD THATCH INN,
Cheriton Bishop, Near Exeter, Devon EX6 6HJ

Tel: 01647 24204
Fax: 01647 24584

3 bedrooms, all with private bathroom; Free House with real ale; Historic interest; Bar meals; Guide dogs only; Car park (25); Crediton 6 miles; ££.

Justifiably proud of its reputation for the quality, choice and value for money in respect of the substantial home cooked meals served in the bar, lounge and Travellers Nook, this 16th century one-time coaching house stands on the eastern fringe of the Dartmoor National Park. Now a Grade II Listed building with beamed ceilings and an open stone fireplace where a log fire crackles a welcome in winter, the old hostelry retains an ambience seasoned by time and enhanced by high standards of friendly service. For touring the area, comfortable overnight accommodation is available in the form of double bedrooms, all with en suite facilities, colour television, radio/alarm and tea and coffee-makers. ♛♛♛ *Commended.*

THE GLOBE INN,
Frogmore, Near Kingsbridge,
Devon TQ7 2NR

Tel: 01548 531351

6 bedrooms, 3 with private bathroom; Free House with real ale; Children and pets welcome; Bar and restaurant meals; Car park; Kingsbridge 3 miles; £.

Situated in the pretty village of Frogmore which lies between Dartmouth and Kingsbridge and surrounded by magnificent coastal scenery, uncrowded beaches, and historic towns and villages, The Globe is an ideal base for all holiday activities. Accommodation comprises six comfortable bedrooms (three en suite), all with razor points, colour television and tea/coffee making facilities. Two bars provide the setting for the enjoyment of fine cask-conditioned ales and other refreshments, while the intimate candlelit barn restaurant serves menus to suit all pockets and palates, from traditional pub fayre to more exotic specialities, including locally caught seafood. ❦❦, *AA QQ Recommended*.

GEORGE HOTEL,
Market Street, Hatherleigh,
Devon EX20 3JN

Tel: 01837 810454
Fax: 01837 810901

11 bedrooms, 9 with private bathroom; Free House with real ale; Historic interest; Children and pets welcome; Bar meals, restaurant evenings only (not Sunday); Car park (75); Torquay 40 miles, Bude 20; £££.

Built in 1450 as a monks' retreat, this cob and thatch pub still provides something of a quiet haven in which to refresh the spirit and calm the senses, as well as offering all the modern comforts and amenities most would be hard put to forgo today. Telephone and colour television are supplied in all the pleasantly decorated guest rooms, most of which also have en suite facilities; some have the added luxury of a four-poster bed. Meals may be taken informally in the well stocked bar, or selected from the à la carte menu available in the George's rather nice restaurant. ❦❦❦❦, *AA/RAC* **

BRIDGE INN,
Bridge Street, Hatherleigh,
Devon EX20 3JA

Tel: 01837 810947

6 bedrooms, all with private bathroom; Free House with real ale; Historic interest; Children and pets welcome; Bar and restaurant meals; Car park (25); Okehampton 7 miles; ££.

An unspoiled country market town of true Devonian character, Hatherleigh is worth a place on any touring itinerary of the area. Not least of its attractions is this charming 16th century inn on the banks of the River Lew. Homely overnight accommodation is available at most reasonable rates and the Letheren family extend a warm welcome to visitors of all ages. The inn has a beer garden and a skittle alley and is especially noteworthy for its high standard of home cooking; the à la carte menu will probably surprise and delight diners expecting less sophisticated fare. Good bar snacks are available in the attractive stone-faced bar.

Devon 47

ROCK INN,
Haytor Vale, Newton Abbot,
Devon TQ13 9XP

Tel: 01364 661305
Fax: 01364 661242

10 bedrooms, 8 with private bathroom; Free House with real ale; Children welcome; Bar meals, restaurant evenings only; Car park (20); Ashburton 5 miles; £££/££££.

In a sheltered and secluded setting on the fringe of Dartmoor, this charming, 18th century coaching inn has a friendly welcome for all and is recommended for its excellent accommodation and refreshment. Who would "o'er the moors so free"? Above rises Haytor Rock, 1490 feet above sea level and beyond lie Dartmoor's heathy slopes and wooded valleys teeming with wildlife. Free fresh air promotes hearty appetites that the splendid Rock Inn is well qualified to cater for, the imaginative and varied, chef-inspired dishes temptingly presented. With brasswork, oak furniture and log fires, the bars are full of character; invariably they buzz with convivial conversation and on fine days one may enjoy a glass of one's fancy outside and take in the panorama of a verdant, rolling countryside. Guest rooms are delightfully furnished; all have en suite facilities, colour television with satellite channel, in-house video, radio, direct-dial telephone, mini-bar and tea and coffee-makers. Special weekend and seasonal breaks are organised. There are numerous sporting and leisure opportunities in the area quite apart from walking the moors. These include horse riding, river fishing, especially for Dart salmon, and golf, whilst the south coast resorts with all their attractions are within easy reach. ♛♛♛♛, *AA/RAC***.

JOURNEY'S END INN,
Ringmore, Near Kingsbridge, Devon
Tel: 01548 810205

4 bedrooms, 2 with private bathroom; Free House with real ale; Historic interest; Bar and restaurant meals; Car park; Plymouth 17 miles, Bigbury 2.

Dating from 1300, the Journey's End was prescribed a New Inn in the reign of Elizabeth I, and R.C. Sherriff wrote part of his play Journey's End here. Set in a beautiful and unspoilt thatched village amidst the rolling South Hams countryside, and only 15 minutes from quiet National Trust coast, this hostelry is a haven for the thirsty, hungry or weary traveller. In the oak-panelled bar a wide range of cask-conditioned ales may be supped, and there is an extensive and inviting food menu. The charming cottage-style bedrooms provide an exceptionally high standard of comfort, two with beautifully appointed private bathrooms. There is also a family suite. All rooms have colour television, personal radio, and tea-making facilities. In winter, a blazing log fire provides warmth in the bar, and individually controlled central heating ensures comfort in the bedrooms. This ancient inn is an ideal centre for holidaymaking at all times of the year. Golf, sea and river fishing, numerous coves and unspoilt beaches, the moors, Plymouth and Kingsbridge are all within easy reach.

MASONS ARMS INN,
Knowstone, South Molton, Devon EX36 4RY
Tel: 01398 341231

4 bedrooms, all with private bathroom; Free House with real ale; Historic interest; Children and pets welcome; Bar meals, restaurant evenings only plus Sunday lunch; South Molton 7 miles; £/££.

To escape to this delightful, 13th century thatched inn tucked away in the foothills of Exmoor is hardly obeying the call of the wild for this is largely a conservation area in picturesque and tranquil countryside known for such gentle rural pursuits as fishing, walking, riding and even painting. Under the kind supervision of the friendly resident owners, David and Elizabeth Todd, the inn offers high quality home-cooked food, fine wines, well-kept real ales and charming accommodation. Light meals are served in the bar at lunchtime and evening with log fires glowing a warm welcome in autumn and winter. Formal meals are available in the dining room in the evenings and Sunday lunchtime.

Devon 49

THE ARUNDELL ARMS,
Lifton,
Devon PL16 0AA

Tel: 01566 784666
Fax: 01566 784494

29 bedrooms, all with private bathroom; Free House with real ale; Historic interest; Children welcome, pets allowed except in restaurant; Car park (80); Launceston 4 miles; ££££.

Deep in the heart of the Devon countryside, where only the haunting calls of wildlife disturb the tranquillity, lies the Arundell Arms. One of the country's premier sporting hotels, it offers superb opportunities for traditional country pursuits of all kinds — hill walking, golf, birdwatching, horse riding and, of course, fishing. Relaxation comes easily here, the deep, comfortable easy chairs and blazing log fires a cosy backdrop to animated discussion about "the one that got away". Accolades have deservedly been heaped upon the superb cuisine which betrays the touch of a master chef, and the elegant en suite bedrooms show the same attention to detail that is the mark of a truly first-rate establishment. ♛♛♛♛ Highly Commended, AA *** and Three Rosettes for Restaurant.

RISING SUN HOTEL,
Harbourside, Lynmouth,
Devon EX35 6EQ

Tel: 01598 753223
Fax: 01598 753480

16 bedrooms, all with en suite shower/bathroom; Free House; Historic interest; Bar and restaurant meals; Barnstaple 20 miles, Minehead 17; ££££.

This fourteenth century smugglers' inn overlooking the harbour and river is steeped in history, with oak panelling, crooked ceilings, thick walls, and uneven oak floors. All the bedrooms have recently been refurbished to a very high standard and the roof re-thatched. The excellent restaurant specialises in local game and seafood. It is claimed that R.D. Blackmore wrote part of his novel *'Lorna Doone'* whilst staying at The Rising Sun. The poet Shelley spent his honeymoon in 1812 in a cottage, now named after him, which is part of the hotel. It has a four-poster bed and a comfortable sitting room, and is ideal for a special holiday occasion. Guests can relax in the beautifully landscaped garden and free fishing is available on the hotel's private stretch of salmon river. ♛♛♛♛ Highly Commended, AA** and Two Rosettes for Food, RAC** and Merit Awards, Johansens "Inn of the Year 1991", Egon Ronay, Les Routiers Casserole Award, Good Hotel Guide Recommended, Good Pub Guide.

The £ symbol when appearing at the end of the italic section of an entry shows the anticipated price, during 1997, for single full Bed and Breakfast.

Under £25	£	Over £36 but under £45	£££
Over £25 but under £36	££	Over £45	££££

This is meant as an indication only and does not show prices for Special Breaks, Weekends, etc. Guests are therefore advised to verify all prices on enquiring or booking.

EXMOOR SANDPIPER INN,
**Countisbury, Near Lynmouth,
Devon EX35 6NE**

Tel: 01598 741263
Fax: 01598 741358

16 bedrooms, all with private bathroom; Free House with real ale; Historic interest; Children and pets welcome; Bar and restaurant meals; Car park; Lynton 2 miles; £££.

This fine old coaching inn, reputedly dating in part from the 13th and 15th centuries, lies in a beautiful setting amidst rolling moors, high above Lynmouth on the coastal road with the dramatic backdrop of Exmoor. Bedrooms are designed for your every comfort, with tea-making, colour television and bathroom en suite. After a traditional English breakfast, discover the magic of Exmoor by car or on foot, along Doone Valley following the river to the majestic Watersmeet, or further to the Valley of Rocks and beyond to the Devon/Somerset borders. Delicious five-course dinners include smoked salmon, seafood platters with lobster, steaks and a delicious selection of sweets. Brochure on request. *Commended, RAC**.*

WHITE HART INN,
**The Square, Moretonhampstead,
Dartmoor, Devon TQ13 8NF**

Tel: 01647 440406
Fax: 01647 440565

20 bedrooms, all with private bathroom; Free House with real ale; Children over 10 years welcome; Bar and restaurant meals; Car park (10); Exeter 11 miles; ££.

"The Most Famous Inn on Dartmoor". Moretonhampstead is the "gateway" to 365 square miles that make up Dartmoor National Park, ideal for walking and relaxing. The White Hart, an historic coaching inn, has stood in the town square for over 350 years. It has 20 de-luxe bedrooms en suite, with colour television, courtesy trays, hairdryers and telephones; bathrooms have power showers, big fluffy towels and complimentary toiletries. Our restaurant is famous for good food (and plenty of it!), using local meat, fresh fish, vegetables, and cream from Devon farms. Bar snacks are served in the cosy lounge and the oak-beamed bar which also has a selection of real ales. "The most famous coaching inn on Dartmoor". *Highly Commended, AA and RAC **, Egon Ronay, Minotel.*

BLACKCOCK INN,
Molland, South Molton,
Devon EX36 3NW

Tel: 01769 550297
Fax: 01769 550297

Accommodation in 2 cottages; Free House with real ale; Children and pets welcome; Bar and restaurant meals; Car park (65); South Molton 6 miles; ££.

On the southern fringe of Exmoor and romantically remote, this old acquaintance of ours continues to lure those with a will to get away from it all. The effort is well worth while for this homely, stone-built inn, set in a picturesque valley, extends a real Devon welcome to families. Excellent real ales and home-cooked bar and restaurant meals are served seven days a week. Children are welcome and there is a beer garden, an indoor heated swimming pool and a family and games room; free live entertainment is provided on Saturday evenings. Accommodation is provided in delightfully equipped cottages situated just behind the pub where there is a caravan and camping site. An idyllic rural retreat with coarse fishing available nearby.

HIGHER WESTERN RESTAURANT,
Oakford, Tiverton,
Devon EX16 9JE

Tel: 01398 341210

3 bedrooms, all with private bathroom; Free House with real ale; Historic interest; Children and pets welcome; Bar and restaurant meals; Car park (15); Bampton 6 miles; £.

Small licensed country restaurant situated on the B3227, three miles west of Oakford in Greater Exmoor, an area of outstanding natural beauty. We offer a quiet retreat to those wanting to "get away from it all", and a relaxing base for touring Exmoor and the North Devon coast. The excellent food is cooked to order, specialising in imaginative menus using local and own produce, with a carefully chosen wine list. Accommodation comprises one twin and two double rooms, all en suite. There is ample parking. The restaurant is open all year round.

THE HUNTERS' INN,
Heddon's Mouth, Parracombe,
Devon EX31 4PY

Tel: 01598 763230

10 bedrooms, 8 with private bathroom; Free House with real ale; Historic interest; Children welcome; Bar and restaurant meals; Car park; Lynton 4 miles; £.

This unique inn with the "pub-like" atmosphere is situated in one of the most beautiful valleys in North Devon, lying between Lynton and Combe Martin. Wildlife abounds and peacocks roam free. There are many lovely walks, particularly the one mile walk to the rocky cove at Heddon's Mouth. The inn offers a well-stocked bar with a fine selection of real ales, a Buttery catering for hot or cold meals, and comfortable accommodation. Bedrooms have bathrooms en suite, colour television, hospitality trays and electric blankets; some have four-poster beds. The inn is completely centrally heated, so you can be sure of a welcome as warm as that offered by the resident proprietor and his caring, courteous staff.

THE FOX AND GOOSE,
Parracombe, Exmoor,
Devon EX31 4PE
Tel: 01598 763239

6 bedrooms, all with shower; Free House with real ale; Historic interest; Children welcome, pets by arrangement; Bar meals; Car park; Lynton 4 miles; £.

An excellent centre from which to explore Exmoor and the North Devon coast, this old coaching inn is a country lover's dream. Apart from a profusion of wildlife, the area offers opportunities for fishing, clay pigeon shooting and horse riding. As a base for such activities, this friendly hostelry on the River Heddon we can heartily recommend for its cosy comforts, delicious home cooking, real ales and rural conviviality. Off the beaten track but well worth finding, the inn provides good Bed and Breakfast accommodation and the chance to relax in picturesque surroundings and appreciate nature's bounties and the worthwhile things in life. Terms are very reasonable with children under 5 free and those from 5 to 14 at half-price.

MILDMAY COLOURS INN,
Fore Street, Holbeton, Plymouth,
Devon PL8 1NA
Tel: 01752 830302
Fax: 01752 830540

9 bedrooms, all with private bathroom; Free House with real ale; Pets by arrangement; Bar meals, restaurant weekends only; Car park (30); Yealmpton 3 miles; £.

A magnet for real ale buffs and racing enthusiasts, this old inn was built in 1617 and is set in a beautiful village near superb beaches and with Dartmoor and the fine city of Plymouth within easy reach. Golf, fishing, horse riding, sailing and walking the Devon Coastal Path are local activities to be enjoyed. Renamed in memory of the steeplechasing legend, the late Anthony Mildmay, today, it is famed for brewing its own beer by the traditional method — whatever the choice, a magnificent tipple! There are two friendly bars with an extensive snack menu (including 'Nosebag Nibbles') and a popular à la carte restaurant known for its delicious home cooking. Excellent en suite accommodation is available in two converted cottages opposite.

STAG INN,
Rackenford, Near Tiverton,
Devon EX16 8DT
Tel: 01884 881369

2 bedrooms, 1 with private bathroom; Free House with real ale; Historic interest; Children welcome; Bar meals, restaurant evenings only; Car park; Witheridge 4 miles; £.

Quietly slumbering in deepest Devon, the thatched Stag is a long-established acquaintance. It is one of the oldest hostelries in the country, having been built in 1232 and one of its interesting features is an old tunnel, said to have been used by the notorious highwayman, Tom King. Enter the cosy bar with its low beams and Jacobean panelling and relax, if it be winter, before a blazing log fire in the inglenook. The intrepid challenger at the dart board or skittle alley will be accommodated by the locals with a knowing but appreciative smile. Home-cooked meals are served in the bar or Well Room Restaurant; children have their own special menu. This is a superb place in which to stay with Exmoor, Dartmoor and both coasts within easy reach.

THE ANCHOR INN,
Beer, Near Seaton,
Devon EX12 3ET

Tel: 01297 20386

8 bedrooms, all with private bathroom; Free House with real ale; Bar food, restaurant evenings only; Exeter 22 miles, Honiton 11, Seaton 2.

Happily free from the razzamatazz of the big Devon resorts, the little fishing village of Beer retains a sense of harmony and tranquillity that is most conducive to a relaxing and refreshing break. And these are qualities one finds in abundance at the Anchor, owned and managed by David Boalch to offer quiet, comfortable accommodation and good, wholesome food. The pretty restaurant, like many of the bedrooms, has glorious sea views and specialises in locally caught sea food; lighter meals are available in the bars, together with traditional ales. A delightful bonus is the splendid cliff-top garden where visitors may eat and drink in the long sunny Devon days. *AA**, Egon Ronay Recommended.*

THE THREE HORSESHOES,
Branscombe, Seaton,
Devon EX12 3BR

Tel: 01297 680251

Accommodation; Real ale; Historic interest; Sidmouth 5 miles; £.

A lovely 16th century coaching house with log fires and brasses, set in an area of outstanding natural beauty. Central for sea or country; footpaths lead through woodland and cliff walks. Wonderful wildlife in the area. Honiton, which has many antique shops and is noted for lace making, is nearby, as is historic Exeter; Sidmouth is just ten minutes away. All bedrooms are centrally heated and have tea/coffee making facilities. There is "trad" jazz every Saturday night in the function room, and there is a lounge bar for those who want a quiet drink. Jan and John Moore will give you the warmest of welcomes and help you plan your outings if you wish.

THE OXENHAM ARMS,
South Zeal, Okehampton,
Devon EX20 2JT

Tel: 01837 840244
Fax: 01837 840791

8 bedrooms, all with private bathroom; Free House with real ale; Historic interest; Children and pets welcome; Bar and restaurant meals; Car park (8); Exeter 17 miles; £££.

The fascinating history of this most ancient inn dates back even further than 1477, when it was first licensed. Among the many intriguing architectural features to be found at almost every turn is a prehistoric monolith set in a wall in one of the small lounges: this is believed to be part of the original site, with the inn actually constructed around it by the 12th century lay monks who were the original builders. Unobtrusive modernisation has brought the standard of amenities right up to date, without losing any of the inn's timeless charm. Food here is regarded as being of prime importance (and rightly so!), with the emphasis on fine local produce and seasonal specialities. All in all, a most splendid establishment. ♛♛♛ Commended.

BARN OWL INN,
Aller Mills, Kingskerswell, Near Torquay,
Devon TQ12 5AN

Tel: 01803 872130
Fax: 01803 875279

6 bedrooms, all with private bathroom; Free House with real ale; Historic interest; Children over 14 welcome; Bar meals, restaurant evenings only; Car park (40); Torquay 2 miles; £££.

This 16th century inn boasts no less than three bars, all retaining many period features such as oak beams, stone-flagged floors and inglenook fireplaces. A separate à la carte restaurant under the personal supervision of French chef, M. Denis Lejette, provides a charming venue. Nationally acclaimed bar meals are on offer lunchtimes and evenings. The six delightfully decorated en suite bedrooms all have television, direct-dial telephone, hairdryer and tea-making facilities. The Barn Owl Inn is conveniently situated between Torquay and Newton Abbot, making it an ideal centre for exploring all the local tourist attractions. ♛♛♛ Commended, AA QQQQ Selected, Logis Two Fireplaces, Egon Ronay and Johansens.

"WHO'D HAVE THOUGHT IT" INN,
Milton Combe, Near Yelverton,
Devon PL20 6HP

Tel: 01822 853313

No accommodation; Free House with real ale; Pets welcome, children in beer garden only; Bar meals; Car park (30); Tavistock 6 miles.

This 16th century inn is steeped in tradition and proud of its association with Sir Francis Drake whose home, Buckland Abbey, is only a quarter of a mile away. There are many tales told of the ghosts that haunt this historic hostelry and also of the event that gave the inn its name. A local artist was commissioned to depict this event and it is now portrayed on the outside sign. A wide range of real ales and a comprehensive menu is on offer at lunchtimes and in the evening and this is a delightful setting in which to relax and put the world (somewhere out there!) to rights. Homely accommodation may be arranged nearby.

PLEASE MENTION THIS GUIDE WHEN YOU WRITE
OR PHONE TO ENQUIRE ABOUT
ACCOMMODATION.
IF YOU ARE WRITING, A STAMPED,
ADDRESSED ENVELOPE IS ALWAYS APPRECIATED.

SEA TROUT INN,
Staverton, Near Totnes,
Devon TQ9 6PA

Tel: 01803 762274
Fax: 01803 762506

10 bedrooms, all with private bathroom; Free House with real ale; Children and pets welcome; Bar and restaurant meals; Car park (50); Totnes 2 miles; £££.

Over the years, this old friend, so conveniently placed for Dartmoor and the pleasures of Torbay and the South Devon coast, has served countless happy holidaymakers. Hidden away in the tranquil Dart Valley, the inn dates back to to the 15th century, and until thirty or so years ago was known as the Church House, an inn name that abounds in the county. Visually the archetypal traditional English inn, the Sea Trout has two attractive bars with oak beams, log fires, brasses and prize specimens of fish in showcases. With an excellent selection of bar meals, cask-conditioned ales and a wide range of wines, spirits and especially malt whiskies, relaxation is easy, and the friendly locals in the adjoining Village Bar will be happy to accept challenges at pool and darts. The spruce and neatly-decked restaurant is an elegant place in which to enjoy an imaginative and intriguing choice from the à la carte and set dinner menus in the evenings, with vegetarian dishes always available. Delightful bedrooms in cottage style await the overnight guest; all are delectably furnished and appointed with private bathroom, individually controlled central heating, colour television, and direct-dial telephone. Permits for trout, sea trout and salmon fishing are available from the Inn, the unofficial headquarters of the Dart Angling Association. For a real taste of rural Devon, the Sea Trout has it all! *Commended, Good Pub Guide, Egon Ronay.*

Dorset

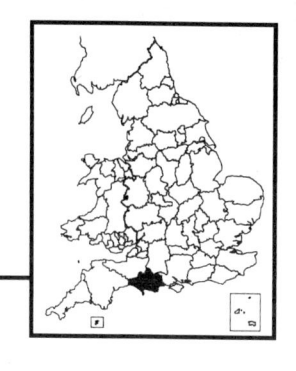

ANVIL HOTEL,
Salisbury Road, Pimperne,
Blandford, Dorset DT11 8UQ

Tel: 01258 453431
Tel and Fax: 01258 480182

10 bedrooms, all with private bathroom; Free House; Historic interest; Children and pets welcome; Bar and restaurant meals; Car park (30); Bournemouth 26 miles, Salisbury 24, Poole 16; £££/££££.

A long, low thatched building set in a tiny village deep in the Dorset countryside two miles from Blandford — what could be more English? And that is exactly what visitors to the Anvil will find — a typical old English hostelry dating from the sixteenth century, set in an English country garden and offering good old-fashioned English hospitality. A mouthwatering full à la carte menu with delicious desserts is available in the charming beamed and flagged restaurant and a wide selection of bar meals in the attractive, fully licensed bar. All bedrooms have private facilities. Ample parking. Clay pigeon shooting and tuition for individuals. *ETB* 👑👑👑 *Commended, Good Food Pub Guide, Les Routiers.*

COPPLERIDGE INN,
Motcombe, Shaftesbury,
Dorset SP7 9HW

Tel: 01747 851980
Fax: 01747 851858

10 bedrooms, all with private bathroom; Free House with real ale; Children welcome; Bar and restaurant meals; Car park (100); Shaftesbury 2 miles; £££.

A real gem in the heart of dreamy Dorset, this 17th century farmhouse has been tastefully transformed into 10 spacious bedrooms with wonderful views across the Blackmore Vale. All have en suite bedrooms, television, radio, telephone, mini-bar and tea and coffee-makers. A wide range of home-cooked bar meals includes game and fresh fish; adjacent is a beautiful flagstoned lounge with a log fire and a cosy, candlelit à la carte restaurant which also offers a variety of well-presented dishes. This delightful retreat stands in 15 acres of meadow, woodland and garden, incorporating two hard tennis courts and a cricket pitch. Dorset may be tranquillity personified but there is plenty to do and see in the area. Leisure facilities in the village include an equestrian centre, clay pigeon shoot, and a sports centre with swimming pool; trout fishing may be arranged. *ETB* 👑👑👑 *Highly Commended.*

Durham

including Hartlepool, Middlesbrough, Stockton, Redcar and Cleveland (formerly Cleveland).

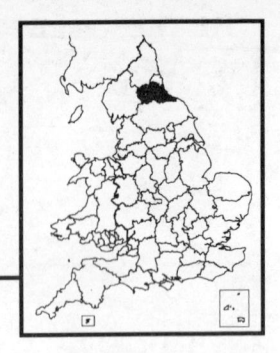

THE CROXDALE INN,
Front Street, Croxdale, Near Durham,   Tel: 01388 815727/420294
Co. Durham DH6 5H   Fax: 01388 815368

12 bedrooms, all with private bathroom; Bar and restaurant meals; Durham 3 miles; £££.

Situated south of Durham just off the A167 and within a few minutes' drive of the A1M, this is an ideal base for touring the many attractions of North East England, such as Durham's magnificent Cathedral and Castle, Beamish Open Air Museum, Hadrian's Wall and the unspoiled coastline. The Inn has recently been refurbished, and all bedrooms are en suite with tea/coffee making facilities, telephone and remote-control television. The restaurant provides delicious à la carte menus, and there is an excellent choice of mouth-watering bar meals. Additional amenities include a jacuzzi, sauna, and a luxurious four-poster honeymoon suite with whirlpool bath. **See also Colour Advertisement on page 4.**

MORRITT ARMS HOTEL,
Greta Bridge, Near Barnard Castle,   Tel: 01833 627232
Co. Durham DL12 9SE   Fax: 01833 627392

19 bedrooms, all with private bathroom; Free House with real ale; Historic interest; Bar and restaurant meals; Children and pets welcome; Car park; Barnard Castle 3 miles; £££.

In an area rich in scenic and historic interest, the 17th century Morritt Arms offers traditional coaching inn hospitality to residents and travellers alike. Built on a Roman settlement, still visible today, it gained its reputation through the Dickensian era as the second overnight stop for the London-Carlisle mail coach. Dickens himself stayed at Greta Bridge in 1839 whilst researching *Nicholas Nickleby*. He is remembered in the Dickens Bar with its remarkable murals of Pickwick characters and it is a challenge identifying them whilst enjoying a glass of one's fancy. Real ales and a fine selection of bar food are served in the Green Room with splendid à la carte dining available in the Copperfield Restaurant, fine fare complemented by an award-winning wine list. This is a fascinating area to explore, with unspoilt countryside and numerous historic castles and houses to visit. The hotel's excellent accommodation makes this an extremely viable proposition; en suite bedrooms all have remote-control television and hospitality trays, whilst some have four-poster or brass beds. Sporting opportunities in the locality include golf, shooting, fishing and walking as well as a number of racecourses. Hosts, Peter Phillips and Barbara-Anne Johnson, assure guests of a warm welcome and also use their expertise in organising conferences, business meetings and other social functions for which the hotel is well-equipped. ☆☆☆☆ *Commended*

THE TEESDALE HOTEL,
Middleton-in-Teesdale, Near Barnard Castle,
Co. Durham DL12 0QG

Tel: 01833 640264
Fax: 01833 640651

10 bedrooms, all with private bathroom; Free House with real ale; Historic interest; Children and pets welcome; Bar meals, restaurant evenings only; Car park; Barnard Castle 8 miles; ££.

The delightful country village of Middleton-in-Teesdale is a wonderful base for exploring the wooded valleys and rolling moorland of this most northerly Yorkshire dale. Thoughtfully modernised to blend in modern amenities without losing any of its olde worlde charm, the former coaching inn provides comfortable accommodation and real Northern hospitality. Good country cooking can be enjoyed in the spacious dining room and in the cosy lounge bar, and the newly opened Rally Bar and Patio, based on a Spanish cantina, offers a colourful touch of Continental style. Comfortable accommodation is available at rates to suit all budgets, and well appointed Courtyard Cottages offer the alternative of self catering if preferred. Dogs are very welcome, free of charge. ETB ☻☻☻☻ Commended, AA and RAC **, Egon Ronay.

Essex

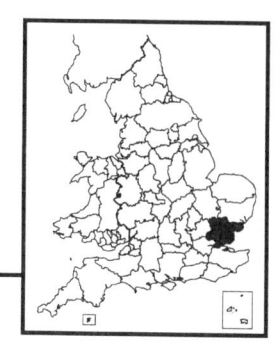

ROSE AND CROWN HOTEL,
East Street, Colchester,
Essex CO1 2TZ

Tel: 01206 866677
Fax: 01206 866616

30 bedrooms, all with private bathroom; Free House with real ale; Historic interest; Children welcome; Bar and restaurant meals; Car park (50); London 51 miles; ££££.

The oldest inn in the centre of Britain's oldest recorded town is the fascinating claim made by this historic posting house. With its black and white timbered facade and old beams, the inn has an attraction enhanced by age and experience. A refurbishment and extension programme recently undertaken has not diminished the ambience of its character-filled bars and the superb guest rooms and suites represent a charming blend of ancient and modern, epitomised by four poster rooms with jacuzzi, bath and shower. Popular as a meeting place for dining well at reasonable cost, the Rose and Crown is also well in vogue as a conference and function venue. ☻☻☻☻ Commended, AA and RAC ***.

THE PELDON ROSE INN,
Mersea Road, Peldon,
Essex CO5 7QJ

Tel and Fax: 01206 735248

3 bedrooms; Free House with real ale; Historic interest; Children and pets welcome; Bar meals, restaurant Friday and Saturday evenings; Car park (100); Colchester 5 miles; £.

One's lasting memory of this attractive, pink-washed pub is usually the friendly welcome one has received, for whether calling in for just meal or drink, or staying a few nights in one of the comfortable guest rooms, every effort is made by the Everett family and their staff to ensure that all one's requirements are cheerfully and efficiently catered for. Single and double rooms are available, all delightfully decorated and equipped with television and coffee making facilities. Throughout the week top quality fare is supplied lunchtime and evenings in the beamed bar and in the more formal setting of the intimate restaurant.

THE FARMHOUSE INN,
Monk Street, Thaxted,
Essex CM6 2NR

Tel: 01371 830864
Fax: 01371 831196

11 bedrooms, all with private bathroom; Free House with real ale: Historic interest; Children welcome; Bar and restaurant meals; Car park (50); Saffron Walden 6 miles; £££.

Set in over an acre of gardens with lovely countryside views, yet only eight miles from Stansted Airport, this outstandingly comfortable inn dates, in part, from the 16th century. Recently extended and refurbished, it presents a fine range of beers, bar snacks and "daily specials" seven days a week. The 60-seater restaurant created from the conversion of the adjoining barn and stables is full of character; the à la carte menu is chef-supervised and features fresh local and seasonal produce. Completed in July 1990, the excellent guest rooms contain bathrooms en suite, colour television with remote-control, direct-dial telephone and tea and coffee making facilities. *ETB* ☻☻☻, *Egon Ronay.*

Taking a pet on holiday? Then buy
"PETS WELCOME"
THE ANIMAL LOVERS' HOLIDAY GUIDE
Details of Hotels, Guest Houses, Furnished Accommodation, Caravans, etc, where holiday makers and their pets are made welcome.
Available from most newsagents and bookshops price £4.60
or from Publishers (£5.50 including postage, UK only).
FHG PUBLICATIONS LTD
Abbey Mill Business Centre, Seedhill, Paisley, Renfrewshire PA1 1TJ

Gloucestershire

including South Gloucester, and Bristol (formerly Avon).

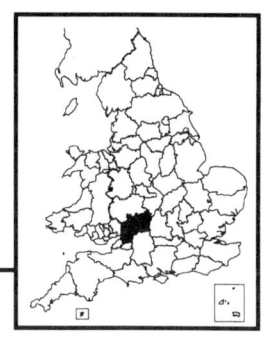

THE COMPASS INN,
Tormarton, Near Badminton,
Gloucestershire GL9 1JB

Tel: 01454 218242
Fax: 01454 218741

28 bedrooms, all with private bathroom; Free House with real ale; Historic interest; Children welcome; Bar meals, restaurant evenings only; Car park (250); Chipping Sodbury 3 miles; ££££.

The area's sea-faring traditions are celebrated in the name of this sturdily constructed 18th century former coaching inn —- a former landlord decorated the bar with memorabilia from Bristol's docks, though, sad to say, all that remains is a pair of ship's lanterns and some stout wooden beams. Standing in six acres of well-tended grounds, The Compass offers easy access to the major cities of the south-west, the Cotswolds, the Wye Valley and the Forest of Dean. The excellent restaurant offers a good choice of traditional cooking, with the emphasis on local fresh vegetables and game in season, and a full range of wines, spirits and beers, including a choice of real ales and some intriguing country wines, is available in the friendly bar. Prettily decorated en suite bedrooms offer good value overnight accommodation ☻☻☻☻ Commended, AA and RAC**.

BROCKWEIR COUNTRY INN,
Brockweir, Near Chepstow,
Gloucestershire NP6 7NG

Tel: 01291 689548

3 bedrooms; Free House with real ale; Historic interest; Children welcome, dogs on lead only; Bar meals; Car park (12); Chepstow 5 miles; £.

Popular with the many walkers who enjoy rambles up the steep pastures to Offa's Dyke and the Devil's Pulpit, this friendly 17th century inn on the banks of the River Wye offers hospitality to all. Real ales and farm ciders are supplemented by regularly changing guest brews, and good wholesome bar food can be enjoyed in the snug main bar, where in winter a log fire blazes a welcome to all. In fine weather, refreshments can be enjoyed outside in the sheltered garden. Those inclined to try local pastimes such as salmon fishing, canoeing or horse riding can be comfortably accommodated in cosy bedrooms, one of which has a four-poster bed and is reputed to be haunted.

CROWN INN AND HOTEL,
High Street, Blockley, Moreton-in-Marsh, Gloucestershire GL56 9EX

Tel: 01386 700245
Fax: 01386 700247

21 bedrooms, all with private bathroom; Free House with real ale; Historic interest; Well-behaved children welcome, pets allowed in bars and bedrooms; Bar and restaurant meals; Car park; Moreton-in-Marsh 3 miles; £££.

Radiating warmth from the very stones of its honey-coloured facade, this lovely, 16th century inn on Blockley's High Street seems to have grown in stature and appeal over the years we have known it. A traditional hostelry in one of the most picturesque and unspoilt of all Cotswold villages, it is now very much in the hotel class without losing its intimate ambience, as may be witnessed in the convivial bars where real ale and light meals may be appreciated in company with friendly concourse with the locals before a blazing log fire. For first-rate dining, the Fish and Grill Restaurant is one of the finest in the area, whilst the very best in English and French cuisine will titillate the palate when dining by candlelight in the Coach House Restaurant, so attractively furnished in contemporary style. For visits to Cheltenham and touring the Cotswolds, there are few better places in which to stay and Stratford-upon-Avon, Warwick, Worcester, Kenilworth and Oxford are also within easy reach. Modern conveniences of the highest calibre blend perfectly with old beams and mellow stone walls in the en suite guest rooms, all of which have colour television, radio, hair dryer and tea and coffee-making facilities. Several charming suites are also available, some resplendent with beautiful four-poster beds. Special breaks in co-ordination with Naunton Downs Golf Club are organised at reasonable rates with starting times guaranteed. ☙☙☙☙ *Highly Commended, AA*** and Rosette, RAC ***, Which? Hotel Guide Best Hotel in Gloucestershire 1996.*

THE EIGHT BELLS INN,
Church Street, Chipping Campden,
Gloucestershire GL55 6JG
Tel: 01386 840371

3 bedrooms, all with private bathroom; Free House with real ale; Historic interest; Bar and restaurant meals; Stratford-upon-Avon 8 miles; ££.

Built in the 14th century to house the stonemasons and store the bells whilst the church was being built, the Eight Bells has a fascinating history and, even now, is an integral part of the old wool town. It is known that the inn played host to royalty in the past; today, Proprietors, Patrick and Paul Dare, will extend a right royal welcome to visitors who come here seeking sustenance and shelter. Mouth-watering lunchtime and evening meals will reward the search, menus being varied and frequently changed, and there is a selection of real ales. En suite twin and double bedrooms provide comfortable accommodation and for a Cotswold base full of character, the inn is well worth consideration.

WILD DUCK INN,
Drakes Island, Ewen, Near Cirencester,
Gloucestershire GL7 6BY
Tel: 01285 770310/770364

10 double bedrooms, all with private bathroom; Historic interest; Free House with real ale; Bar and restaurant meals; Car park (50); Chippenham 18 miles, Cheltenham 16, Swindon 16, Tetbury 9, Cirencester 3, Kemble Station 1; ££££.

Nestling in delightful, unspoilt Gloucestershire countryside, this is an old inn of outstanding character, with original beams and inglenook open fires giving a traditional atmosphere of warmth and friendliness. Food is of the highest quality, with an extensive menu operating at lunchtime and in the evenings. Bar lunches are also available. Three bedrooms have four-posters and overlook the delightful, award-winning garden. All ten rooms have private bath en suite, colour television, tea/coffee making facilities and telephone, making this a desirable overnight or weekly holiday base, in addition to being an enchanting place to quench one's thirst. Access, Visa, Amex accepted.🍴🍴🍴, *RAC****, *Les Routiers Inn of the Year 1994*, *Ashley Courtenay*, *Egon Ronay*. **See also Inside Back Cover.**

DOG AND MUFFLER INN,
Joyford, Near Coleford,
Gloucestershire GL16 7AS
Tel: 01594 832444

5 bedroooms, all with private bathroom; Free House with real ale; Children and pets welcome; Bar and restaurant meals; Car park (30); Coleford 2 miles; ££.

Why an inn with such an intriguing name should have a Stable Bar is not clear but, be that as it may, this fine hostelry is certainly one for the traditionalist. Pool, darts and a skittle alley provide diversions whilst enjoying a glass of real ale or local cider. In good weather, the call of the beer garden may take precedence, especially for those with children in tow; the play area will be well appreciated. Also popular with tourists of the Royal Forest of Dean and nearby Wye Valley is the splendid à la carte cuisine. The inn has a markedly high linger factor and those submitting to its influence will find first-rate en suite accommodation at their disposal.

Gloucestershire 63

WYNDHAM ARMS HOTEL,
Clearwell, Near Coleford, Gloucestershire GL16 8JT

Tel: 01594 833666
Fax: 01594 836450

7 bedrooms, all with private bathroom; Free House with real ale; Historic interest; Children welcome; Bar and restaurant meals; Car park (50); Coleford 2 miles; ££.

In a gentle valley on the edge of the verdant, fairy-tale Royal Forest of Dean, the splendid 600-year-old Wyndham Arms is a recommended centre for a plethora of country pleasures. It is full of old-world charm and although still an inn at heart, now offers inspired hotel facilities, the delicious food served in the busy restaurant and bar being renowned for miles around, home-grown produce figuring prominently. The Rivers Severn and Wye provide fresh salmon in the summer and the chefs are justly proud of their wonderful home-made desserts. Special diets are catered for and children rave about their own "small persons" menu. Deserving the fullest praise for this happy state of affairs are Proprietors, John, Robert and Rosemary Stanford, who fell in love with the place in 1973 and whose West End experience has since served them (and their guests) so well. Elegant guest rooms are delightfully furnished; all have bathrooms en suite, colour television, direct-dial telephone and beverage making facilities amongst their thoughtful appointments. There are six ground floor rooms for the less physically able and flat access to the bar and restaurant. For children there are cots, high chairs and baby-listening intercom. After dining memorably, quiet evenings may be spent, pint or malty dram in hand, chatting with the locals in the cosy bar, perhaps after an excursion to the Wye Valley or Slimbridge Wildfowl Trust, a day's shooting or golf or, hopefully, a winning day at Cheltenham or Chepstow races. ♛♛♛♛ Highly Commended, AA/RAC ***, Les Routiers, Logis.

THE LAMB,
Great Rissington, Cheltenham,
Gloucestershire GL54 2LP

Tel: 01451 820388
Fax: 01451 820724

14 bedrooms, all with private bathroom; Free House with real ale; Children and pets welcome; Bar and restaurant meals; Car park (15); Burford 5 miles; £/££.

Set in a peaceful Cotswold valley village, this is a comfortable, cosy inn where the whole family will be welcomed by hosts Richard and Kate Cleverly. A pretty garden with play area will attract the younger members of the family whilst parents refresh themselves in the attractive main bar. Real ale is available, along with farm cider and a most reasonable wine list, and bar food can claim to be truly home-made and includes delicious soups, sandwiches and pies; a wider choice may be enjoyed in the separate dining room. Bedrooms are decorated in pretty, chintzy style, and among six lovely suites is one with a king-size bed, another with a four-poster, Millie's House and Jemima's House. ❦❦❦ *Commended, Egon Ronay Pub of the Year 1994.*

OSTRICH INN,
Newland, Near Coleford,
Gloucestershire GL16 8NP

Tel: 01594 833260

2 bedrooms; Free House with real ale; Historic interest; Pets by arrangement; Bar and restaurant meals; Monmouth 4 miles; £.

With a good range of cask ales and bar meals, the Ostrich is delightfully situated between the Royal Forest of Dean and the Wye Valley, both areas of outstanding natural beauty. The inn's history has been lost in the mists of time but it probably dates back to the late 16th century. Spared the ravages of brewers' 'improvements', this friendly retreat retains its old-world charm and is a recommended port of call for a casual visit or even as a touring base. Accommodation is limited so prior booking is strongly advised; a double and a twin-bedded room are comfortably appointed, each having a television and tea-making facilities. Terms are moderate and guests have the use of a residents' lounge.

Gloucestershire 65

OLD STOCKS HOTEL,
The Square, Stow-on-the-Wold, Gloucestershire GL54 1AF

Tel: 01451 830666
Fax: 01451 870014

18 bedrooms, all with private bathroom; Free House; Historic interest; Bar and restaurant meals; Car park (14); London 84 miles, Stratford-upon-Avon 21, Cheltenham 18; ££.

The charming old town of Stow-on-the-Wold lies in the heart of the Cotswolds and is an ideal base for touring this beautiful area. Those seeking accommodation here could do no better than the Old Stocks Hotel, whose tasteful guest rooms are in keeping with the hotel's old world character. Cotswold stone walls and oak beams contrast magnificently with modern amenities of colour television, tea/coffee facilities, radio, hairdryer, direct-dial telephone and en suite bathroom. Five superior rooms are also available, providing an even greater range of comforts. Although the hotel concentrates on providing excellent value for money, no corners are cut in providing mouth-watering menus offering a wide range of choices. Special bargain breaks are also available and the resident proprietor, Alan Rose, or indeed any of the caring staff will be happy to provide advice on exploring this enchanting area. *ETB* 👑👑👑👑, *AA**, Les Routiers.*

RAGGED COT INN,
Hyde, Chalford, Near Stroud, Gloucestershire GL6 8PE

Tel: 01453 884643/731333
Fax: 01453 731166

10 bedrooms, all with private bathroom; Free House with real ale; Historic interest; Bar and restaurant meals; Car park (55); Cirencester 9 miles; ££.

Furnished in traditional style with a strong ambience of a mellow past, this lovely inn has warm and friendly bars which are full of character. Bar snacks may be obtained here but for more formal dining, the intimate restaurant offers superb food from an award-winning à la carte menu. Vegetarian dishes are also available. Set in unspoilt countryside, this is an ideal touring centre for the Cotswolds and nearby are the country estates of HRH The Princess Royal and HRH Prince Charles. Beautifully appointed accommodation is a feature of the Ragged Cot, all rooms having en suite facilities, colour television, telephone and hospitality tray, and there is a suite with a four-poster bed. 👑👑👑 *Commended.*

CROWN HOTEL,
Frampton Mansell, Stroud, Gloucestershire GL6 8JG

Tel: 01285 760601
Fax: 01285 760681

12 bedrooms, all with private bathroom; Free House with real ale; Historic interest; Children and pets welcome; Bar meals; Car park (60); Stroud 5 miles; ££.

In a quiet Cotswold village equidistant from Stroud and Cirencester, this is a delectable little inn-cum-hotel; unpretentious, homely and of good solid worth. Nowhere is this more apparent than in its wide range of appetising home-made snacks and main meals — and at most reasonable prices, too! A good Cotswold holiday centre, easily accessible yet somewhat off the beaten track, the Crown provides well appointed accommodation in double, twin and single rooms, all with en suite bath and shower, colour television, direct dial telephone and tea and coffee-making facilities. Rates represent very good value for money. 👑👑👑, *Egon Ronay.*

THE PLAISTERERS ARMS,
Abbey Terrace, Winchcombe, Near Cheltenham,
Gloucestershire GL54 5HH   Tel and Fax: 01241 602358

5 bedrooms, all with private bathrooms; Free House with real ale; Pub food; Cheltenham 8 miles; £.

Set in the heart of historic Winchcombe (the capital of Mercia in the Middle Ages), and close to Sudeley Castle, the Plaisterers Arms is an unusual split-level Cotswold stone inn with oak-beamed ceilings and a wonderful traditional atmosphere. The inn serves a varied selection of hand-pulled real ales and a wide range of meals, including delicious home-made pies, daily specials and a traditional roast lunch on Sundays. Upstairs are five well appointed and attractively decorated en suite bedrooms, all with colour television and tea/coffee facilities. At the rear is a large beer garden with attractive patios which overflow with spectacular floral displays during spring and summer. ☆☆ Commended.

FOR THE MUTUAL GUIDANCE OF GUEST AND HOST

Every year literally thousands of holidays, short breaks and overnight stops are arranged through our guides, the vast majority without any problems at all. In a handful of cases, however, difficulties do arise about bookings, which often could have been prevented from the outset.

It is important to remember that when accommodation has been booked, both parties – guests and hosts – have entered into a form of contract. We hope that the following points will provide helpful guidance.

GUESTS: When enquiring about accommodation, be as precise as possible. Give exact dates, numbers in your party and the ages of any children. State the number and type of rooms wanted and also what catering you require – bed and breakfast, full board etc. Make sure that the position about evening meals is clear – and about pets, reductions for children or any other special points.

Read our reviews carefully to ensure that the proprietors you are going to contact can supply what you want. Ask for a letter confirming all arrangements, if possible.

If you have to cancel, do so as soon as possible. Proprietors do have the right to retain deposits and under certain circumstances to charge for cancelled holidays if adequate notice is not given and they cannot re-let the accommodation.

HOSTS: Give details about your facilities and about any special conditions. Explain your deposit system clearly and arrangements for cancellations, charges etc. and whether or not your terms include VAT.

If for any reason you are unable to fulfil an agreed booking without adequate notice, you may be under an obligation to arrange suitable alternative accommodation or to make some form of compensation.

While every effort is made to ensure accuracy, we regret that FHG Publications cannot accept responsibility for errors, omissions or misrepresentations in our entries or any consequences thereof. Prices in particular should be checked because we go to press early. We will follow up complaints but cannot act as arbiters or agents for either party.

Hampshire

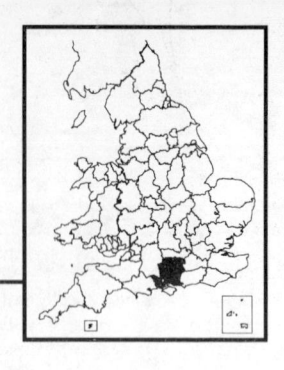

THE ROSE AND CROWN,
Lyndhurst Road, Brockenhurst,
Hampshire SO42 7RH

Tel: 01590 622225
Fax: 01590 623056

11 bedrooms, 5 with private bathroom; Eldridge Pope House with real ale; Historic interest; Bar meals, restaurant Fri/Sat evenings plus Sun. lunch; Children welcome; Car park (50); Lyndhurst 4 miles; £.

In the very centre of the lovely New Forest, this creeper clad old coaching inn in a typically 'olde English' garden, is furnished in keeping with its character. Dating from about 1700, it now presents every modern convenience and guests are bound to appreciate the high standard of the traditional and international cuisine served in the charming Garden Room Restaurant, whilst the Forest Food Parlour is obviously a popular innovation with families. Two spruce bars, toasty warm in winter, we are pleased to say, offer the opportunity for a game or two of pool or darts. Well appointed overnight accommodation is available and Hosts, Brian and Daile Parkin extend a warm welcome to casual or longer stay visitors.

THE COMPASSES INN,
Damerham, Near Fordingbridge,
Hampshire SP6 3HQ

Tel: 01725 518231
Fax: 01725 518880

6 bedrooms, all with private bathroom; Free House with real ale; Historic interest; Children and pets welcome; Bar and restaurant meals; Car park; Fordingbridge 3 miles; ££.

A perfect example of the traditional English country inn, The Compasses offers excellent value for money and a really warm welcome. Superb accommodation is available, with a choice of single, double and family rooms and a four-poster room. All are en suite, with television and tea and coffee making facilities. Great pride is taken in both the quality and variety of food and drink, with freshly produced food, an extensive wine list, a selection of over 60 malt whiskies and 5 real ales. The Compasses is situated in the heart of rural Wessex and offers excellent opportunities for exploring the New Forest, South Coast and many other local attractions. Commended, Egon Ronay.

NEW INN,
Heckfield, Near Hook,
Hampshire RG27 0LE

Tel: 0118 932 6374
Fax: 0118 932 6550

16 bedrooms, all with private bathroom; Free House with real ale; Historic interest; Children and pets welcome; Bar meals; Car park (80); Hook 4 miles; ££££.

Developed from a 15th century inn, still very much there in influence, the extended New Inn brightens up the verdant North Hampshire countryside with its superb facilities. Oak beams and roaring log fires still maintain the classic old-world charm of the bar; a place to meet, chat and refresh in the traditional manner that has existed here for more than 150 years. Adjacent, the restaurant presents an intimate setting for the appreciation of worthy à la carte cuisine. Beautifully decorated throughout in tasteful modern style, this exceptional free house boasts high-grade hotel amenities, the individually-furnished bedrooms all having en suite appointments. For that special occasion, a magnificent four-poster suite with a whirlpool bath provides that little extra luxury. ❧❧❧❧ *Highly Commended, AA**.*

THE INN BY THE SEA,
177 Portsmouth Road, Lee-on-the-Solent,
Hampshire PO13 9AD

Tel: 01705 550303
Fax: 01705 551409

No accommodation; Whitbread House with real ale; Children welcome; Bar and restaurant meals; Car park; Gosport 4 miles.

Lee is a good centre for sea angling, sailing or just watching the shipping in the Solent and the bright and breezy seafront is seldom crowded, even in the season. Walking along the long esplanade is recommended as a pleasant means of inducing a hearty thirst or appetite before visiting the Inn by the Sea where a vast range of reasonably-priced dishes awaits, in accordance with the enlightened policy laid down by the Brewers Fayre organisation. This is very much a happy family venue where children are genuinely welcome and catered for with their own Charlie Chalk menu. Good food and drink where parents can relax in pleasant surroundings. Accommodation may be arranged close by.

HIGH CORNER INN,
Linwood, Near Ringwood,
Hampshire BH24 3QY

Tel: 01425 473973
Fax: 01425 480015

8 bedrooms, all with private bathroom; Free House with real ale; Historic interest; Children and pets welcome; Bar and restaurant meals; Car park; Southampton 18 miles, Bournemouth 17; ££.

A lovely, typically English, early 18th century inn in the very heart of the New Forest, the High Corner Inn gave us a warm feeling of pleasurable anticipation by its very appearance. We were not disappointed; whilst enjoying a leisurely aperitif, we were confronted with a difficult decision in making a lunchtime choice from a wide-ranging bar snacks menu. After a starter, we chose the grilled Avon trout with almonds and a homemade fruit pie to follow. The meal was delicious and we were tempted to return later for an à la carte dinner served in a charming little restaurant. There are rooms for families with children, and a woodland garden, squash court and stables. ❧❧❧ *Commended, Egon Ronay and Les Routiers Recommended.*

NOTE

All the information in this book is given in good faith in the belief that it is correct. However, the publishers cannot guarantee the facts given in these pages, neither are they responsible for changes in policy, ownership or terms that may take place after the date of going to press. Readers should always satisfy themselves that the facilities they require are available and that the terms, if quoted, still apply.

THE GEORGE HOTEL,
High Street, Odiham, Basingstoke,
Hampshire RG29 1LP

Tel: 01256 702081
Fax: 01256 704213

18 bedrooms, all with private bathroom; Courage House with real ale; Historic interest; Bar and restaurant meals; Car park (30); Basingstoke 7 miles; £££.

To step over the threshold of The George is like entering a living history lesson - at every turn one's gaze meets a reminder of its noble past. Here, an Elizabethan wall painting; there, wattle and daub walls and original timber framing; in the oak-panelled Cromwell's Restaurant superbly preserved stone flags and an intricately carved fire surround. The twentieth century finds a place here too — those with a nostalgia for pre-decimal coinage can inspect the examples set in the floor in 1972! Rest assured, however, that all modern amenities are available in the individually styled bedrooms (some with four-posters). Dining here is a particular pleasure, candlelight and attentive service complementing the imaginative menus and excellent wine list. And afterwards, relax in the friendly bar, whose popularity with locals bears testimony to the fine quality of its ales! ❦❦❦ *Commended, AA**, Johansens.*

YE OLDE GEORGE INN,
Church Street, East Meon, Petersfield,
Hampshire GU32 1NH

Tel: 01730 823481
Fax: 01730 823759

6 bedrooms, all with private bathroom; Free House with real ale; Historic interest; Bar and restaurant meals; Car park; Petersfield 5 miles; £.

A lovely hostelry with its restaurant comprising a pair of converted 15th century cottages complete with original inglenook fireplaces and exposed brickwork and beams, the George complements the historic village in which it is situated. The country pub bar invites with its old pine tables, benches, open fires, horse brasses and selection of cask ales and bar food dishes. Night time sees the restaurant at its best with polished tables reflecting the firelight and candleglow as meals chosen from an imaginative à la carte menu and fine wines are given due reverence. Delicious cream teas are served in summer months. The desire may arise to linger longer in this charming place. ❦❦❦, *Egon Ronay Recommended.*

WHITE HART HOTEL,
The Square, Whitchurch,
Hampshire RG28 7DN

Tel: 01256 892900
Fax: 01256 896628

18 bedrooms, 10 with private bathroom; Free House with real ale; Historic interest; Bar and restaurant meals; Car park (20); Andover 6 miles; £££

Steeped in period atmosphere, this traditional coaching inn has been welcoming travellers since 1461. The hospitality and personal service is no less warm and welcoming today. The hotel is widely known for its first-class food, whether it be a tasty home-cooked bar snack, a delicious cream tea or an à la carte dish in the charming Lord Denning Restaurant with its genuine Queen Anne ceiling. Judge for yourself! Catering for the modern businessman and casual traveller alike, the White Hart has a variety of period rooms, mostly of Georgian design. The majority have en suite facilities and all have colour television and tea and coffee makers. Prices, in all respects, are extremely competitive. ♛♛, *Les Routiers*.

THE WOODFALLS INN,
The Ridge, Woodfalls,
Hampshire SP5 2LN

Tel: 01725 513222
Fax: 01725 513220

10 bedrooms, all with private bathroom; Free House with real ale; Children welcome; Bar and restaurant meals; Car park (30); Bournemouth 20 miles, Southampton 15, Salisbury 7.

Nestling on the northern edge of the New Forest, on an old route to the cathedral city of Salisbury, this award-winning inn has provided hospitality to travellers since 1870. Ideal for visiting the New Forest, Stonehenge, Romsey and Winchester. After recent refurbishment, all bedrooms are tastefully and individually decorated, with en suite facilities (some with four-poster beds). There is an award-winning restaurant and a bar serving food and real ales. ETB ♛♛♛ Commended, AA QQQQQ Premier Selected, Johansens, Ashley Courtenay.

Hampshire

Hereford & Worcester

BROADWAY HOTEL,
The Green, Broadway,
Hereford & Worcester WR12 7AA

Tel: 01386 852401
Fax: 01386 853879

18 bedrooms, all with private bathroom; Free House with real ale; Historic interest; Restaurant meals; Car park (40); Worcester 21 miles; ££.

One of the most attractive buildings in what is probably the most photographed village in England, where almost every honey-coloured Cotswold stone echoes the atmosphere of Elizabethan times, the Broadway Hotel is a fine example of how the old and new can be harmonised. All the character and charm of this erstwhile abbot's residence has been retained, while skilfully incorporating the most modern comforts. All the well appointed bedrooms, including the four-poster bedroom, have private bathrooms. The Orchard Suite provides well equipped conference facilities. Recently purchased by Andrew Riley, a local man, this is a family-run business. One "old fashioned" attribute that the hotel is proud to maintain is its friendly and welcoming service, making a stay here a real pleasure. ♛♛♛♛, AA and RAC***.

ANCIENT CAMP INN,
Ruckhall, Near Eaton Bishop,
Hereford & Worcester HR2 9QX

Tel: 01981 250449
Fax: 01981 251581

5 bedrooms, all with private bathroom; Free House with real ale; Historic interest; Bar food, restaurant evenings only (not Mondays); Car park (20); Hereford 4 miles; ££.

This must be one of the loveliest settings of any wayside inn — secluded down a private drive and perched atop an escarpment overlooking a wide bend of the River Wye as it meanders through lush countryside. In fine weather the flower-decked patio is a most pleasant spot for a relaxing drink and quiet contemplation of the distant hills. The inn is fast becoming recognised for the exceptional quality of its menus, which might offer such delights as Home-Smoked Duck Breast, Delice of Salmon and Summer Fruit Terrine, all reflecting the care and imagination which is lavished on preparation and presentation. Accommodation is of the same high standard as every other aspect of this establishment, each guest room having private facilities and a full range of amenities. ♛♛♛ Commended, AA** and Two Food Rosettes.

THE GREEN MAN,
Fownhope,
Hereford & Worcester HR1 4PE

Tel: 01432 860243
Fax: 01432 860207

15 bedrooms, all with private bathroom; Free House with real ale; Historic interest; Children welcome; Bar food, restaurant evenings only; Car park (80); Gloucester 24 miles, Monmouth 22, Ross-on-Wye 9, Hereford 7; ££.

This ancient black and white timbered inn provides an ideal base for exploring the beautiful surrounding countryside and nearby places of interest. There are two bars, an oak-beamed restaurant, a buttery for bar snacks and a large attractive garden. The resident proprietors place great emphasis upon the quality of food and an informal and friendly atmosphere. An extensive bar food menu is available mornings and evenings, and dinners à la carte are served in the restaurant. Bedrooms all have colour television, radio alarm, direct-dial telephone, tea/coffee making equipment, central heating and many extras. ETB ♛♛♛ Commended, AA**, RAC**, Les Routiers, Egon Ronay. **See also Outside Back Cover.**

RHYDSPENCE INN,
Whitney-on-Wye, Near Hay-on-Wye, Hereford & Worcester HR3 6EU
Tel: 01497 831262

7 bedrooms, all with private bathroom; Free House with real ale; Historic interest; Bar and restaurant meals; Car park; Hay-on-Wye 4 miles; ££.

This picturesque black-and-white timbered inn can claim to be both the first and last in England, standing as it does on the border between Herefordshire and Powys. Indeed it can trace its intriguing history back to the time when it offered food and sustenance to Welsh cattle drovers on their way to the English markets. Today it is popular with both locals and visitors, providing an excellent selection of traditional and more unusual bar and restaurant meals, accompanied by an extensive choice of wines, beers and spirits. Those fortunate enough to be able to linger awhile in this captivating spot will find immaculate en suite bedrooms, tastefully furnished and decorated in traditional style. ☙☙☙ *Highly Commended, AA QQQQQ Premier Select.*

THE CROWN INN,
Hopton Wafers, Near Cleobury Mortimer, Hereford & Worcester DY14 0NB
Tel: 01299 270372
Fax: 01299 271127

8 bedrooms, all with private bathroom; Free House with real ale; Historic interest; Children welcome; Bar meals, restaurant evenings only plus Sunday lunch; Car park (40); Cleobury Mortimer 2 miles; £££.

It is difficult to decide whether to concentrate on cuisine, accommodation or indeed the surroundings of this lovely old 16th century coaching inn —for all are appealing enough in themselves to merit the full space allotted here. Open fires add warmth and atmosphere throughout the Crown, in bar, lounge and restaurant; brassware is polished to gleaming perfection; fabrics are bright and freshly laundered; and flowers add their own special charm. Guest bedrooms have received the same loving attention to detail as public rooms, all being furnished and decorated in a delightful country-cottage style well suited to their old beams, and also equipped with remote-control colour television, telephone, trouser press, and tea and coffee facilities. En suite bathrooms are a further feature of each room. Sandwiches, steaks and everything in between can be found on the excellent bar menu, and the light airy restaurant provides such delights as venison, chicken, and lamb, prepared and presented with flair and imagination. Those who have over-indulged will find it no great penance to walk off the extra pounds in the beautiful surrounding countryside. ☙☙☙ *Commended.*

THE TALBOT,
New Street, Ledbury,
Hereford & Worcester HR8 2DX

Tel: 01531 632963
Fax: 01531 633796

7 bedrooms, 5 with private bathroom; Free House with real ale; Historic interest; Children and pets welcome; Bar and restaurant meals; Car park (8); Hereford 12 miles; ££/£££.

Take a step back in time to this owner-run historic inn which offers a warm and friendly welcome. It has an original oak-panelled restaurant and an old world bar with log fire, where guests can enjoy an excellent choice of refreshments, including well-kept ales. A regularly changing menu available lunchtimes and evenings will satisfy most tastes and budgets. Ideally placed for visiting historic Malvern and the Wye Valley, the Talbot makes a good base whether on business or touring, and however long or short your stay you will be assured of warm hospitality and first-class service.👑👑, *Egon Ronay.*

FEATHERS HOTEL,
High Street, Ledbury,
Hereford & Worcester HR8 IDS

Tel: 01531 635266
Fax: 01531 632001

11 bedrooms, all with private bathroom; Free House with real ale; Historic interest; Children and pets welcome; Bar meals, restaurant Thu/Fri/Sat evenings only plus Sun. lunch; Car park (20); Hereford 12 miles; ££££.

This charming old hostelry is very much a landmark on this pleasant little town's main street as it has been since the days of Elizabeth I. A famous coaching inn in its time, its delightful Fuggles Bar has an informal atmosphere in which to appreciate a variety of freshly-cooked dishes with traditional ales and cider in refreshing company. More formal tastes are well catered for in the restaurant which presents interesting à la carte and table d'hôte menus enhanced by a comprehensive wine list. Guest rooms are full of character, contemporary comforts including private bathrooms, remote-control colour television, direct dial telephone and tea-making facilities. A superb conference/function facility is one of the most modern in the area. 👑👑👑👑 *Commended, AA*** and Rosette, Egon Ronay.*

ROYAL OAK HOTEL,
South Street, Leominster,
Hereford & Worcester HR6 8JA

Tel: 01568 612610
Fax: 01568 612710

18 bedrooms, all with private bathroom; Free House with real ale; Historic interest; Children and pets welcome; Bar and restaurant meals; Car park; Hereford 12 miles; ££.

In the heart of verdant Herefordshire countryside, the market town of Leominster with its antique shops is an interesting place for a relaxing holiday. This old coaching inn exhibits a wealth of beams, open fires and original oak panelling in its friendly bars and should come high on any touring itinerary. Features include the Regency Room graced by a minstrels' gallery and beautiful chandeliers and the intimate Cellar Bar with its brick arched alcoves. Fine home-cooked food is served in company with local real ale and the restaurant offers a wide range of tasty dishes. We can understand a reluctance to leave this well-run hostelry, so why not stay for a day or so; first-rate accommodation awaits. ♚♚♚, *AA/RAC **, Egon Ronay.*

MALVERN HILLS HOTEL,
Wynds Point, Malvern,
Hereford & Worcester WR13 6DW

Tel: 01684 540237/540690
Fax: 01684 540327

17 bedrooms, 16 en suite, one with private bathroom; Free House with real ale; Historic interest; Children and pets welcome; Bar meals, restaurant evenings only; Car park (50); Great Malvern 2 miles; ££.

Set amidst the tranquillity of the Malvern Hills to the west of the town centre, this privately owned and run hotel is the ideal place for walking and enjoying the breathtaking views over Elgar's Kingdom and, opposite, the Roman hill fort and ancient earthworks. The hotel has an oak-panelled lounge bar with an open log fire, and serves excellent value snacks and real ales. Nightingales Restaurant, open each evening, serves wholesome English cuisine from a daily table d'hôte menu. The bedrooms are very comfortable and beautifully decorated, with superb views over the hills. Open all year. ♚♚♚♚ *Commended, AA/RAC **.* **See also Colour Advertisement on page 5.**

CHEQUERS INN,
Chequers Lane, Fladbury, Pershore,
Hereford & Worcester WR10 2PZ

Tel: 01386 860276

8 bedrooms, all with private bathroom; Free House with real ale; Historic interest; Bar and restaurant meals; Car park (25); Evesham 3 miles.

A perfect example of the traditional English hostelry, the Chequers Inn stands at the end of a quiet lane in this delightful village in the Vale of Evesham. Those seeking accommodation will find beautifully kept en suite guest rooms, some with balconies, some with open rural views, and all well equipped with colour television, radio, telephone and tea trays. Even if time precludes one staying a while in this charmed area, the Chequers is still worth a flying visit for its fine fare. A carvery is provided Thursday, Friday and Saturday evenings and Sunday lunchtime, while bar meals and an à la carte menu are available daily. Special Weekend Breaks and Golf Breaks — details on request. *ETB* ♚♚♚ *Commended, AA**.*

The **£** symbol when appearing at the end of the italic section of an entry shows the anticipated price, during 1997, for single full Bed and Breakfast.

Under £25	£	Over £36 but under £45	£££
Over £25 but under £36	££	Over £45	££££

This is meant as an indication only and does not show prices for Special Breaks, Weekends, etc. Guests are therefore advised to verify all prices on enquiring or booking.

YE HOSTELRIE,
Goodrich, Near Ross-on-Wye,
Hereford & Worcester HR9 6HX
Tel: 01600 890241

7 bedrooms, all with private bathroom; Free House with real ale; Historic interest; Bar and restaurant meals; Car park (25); Ross-on-Wye 4 miles; £.

Behind the romantic facade of Ye Hostelrie is an intriguing history going back at least three centuries. The oldest surviving parts of the building date from the early 17th century. Major alterations to the original were effected early in the l9th century, since when this charming place has kept pace with the demands of the times. A fine place from which to explore the delights of the Wye Valley, the inn is centrally heated and the accommodation features en suite bathroom or shower in all rooms, each of which also has television. Tempting à la carte and table d'hôte dishes and an extensive selection of home-made bar meals are served every lunchtime and evening and prices are very reasonable. AA**.

YE OLDE SALUTATION INN,
Market Pitch, Weobley,
Hereford & Worcester HR4 8SJ
Tel: 01544 318443
Fax: 01544 318216

4 bedrooms, all with private bathroom; Free House with real ale; Historic interest; Bar and restaurant meals; Car park; Hereford 12 miles, Leominster 9; ££.

This fine timber-framed black-and-white building dates back over 500 years and commands fine views over the medieval village of Weobley, ideally placed for exploring the Welsh Marches, Black Mountains and the Brecon Beacons. Those tempted to linger awhile will find comfortable centrally heated bedrooms, including a luxury en suite four-poster room. And what could be more pleasant of an evening than a relaxing drink in front of the inglenook fireplace in the lounge bar, while contemplating the delights on offer in the Oak Room Restaurant. Chris and Frances Anthony take great pride in the freshness and quality of the carefully planned menus presented here, cooking each dish to order and using only the best of local produce. Major credit cards accepted. ☻☻☻ *Highly Commended, AA** and Two Red Rosettes.* **See also Colour Advertisement on page 4.**

PUBLISHER'S NOTE

While every effort is made to ensure accuracy, we regret that FHG Publications cannot accept responsibility for errors, omissions or misrepresentations in our entries or any consequences thereof. Prices in particular should be checked because we go to press early. We will follow up complaints but cannot act as arbiters or agents for either party.

Hertfordshire

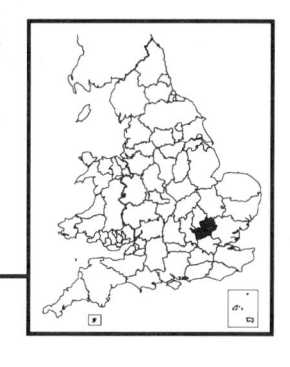

**BROCKET ARMS,
Ayot St Lawrence, Welwyn,
Hertfordshire AL6 9BT**

Tel: 01438 820250
Fax: 01438 820068

7 bedrooms, 3 with private bathroom; Free House with real ale; Historic interest; Children welcome, pets not allowed in bedrooms; Bar meals, restaurant evenings only; Welwyn 2 miles; £££.

The charm of this lovely village, the home of George Bernard Shaw for 40 years, is reflected in the cosy elegance of the Brocket Arms, whose proximity to Central London (just 25 miles) makes it very popular for short breaks. Twin-bedded rooms, comfortably furnished and pleasing to the eye, provide overnight accommodation, and those seeking the romance of a four-poster bed will find their needs catered for. Cuisine is on a par with accommodation, with lunch served daily in the bar and restaurant and later on an extensive à la carte menu available each evening in the candlelit restaurant. Refreshments can also be enjoyed *al fresco* in the pretty gardens, weather permitting. AA/RAC **, Egon Ronay, Good Pub Guide.

**SPORTSMAN HOTEL,
Station Approach, Chorleywood,
Hertfordshire WD3 5NB**

Tel: 01923 285155
Fax: 01923 285159

18 bedrooms, all with private bathroom; Children welcome; Rickmansworth 2 miles; £££/££££.

Dating from the late 19th century, the Sportsman is built on a hillside opposite the Underground station, making it a very convenient base for sightseeing in London and for business trips. The comfortable en suite bedrooms are smartly furnished and equipped with television, direct-dial telephone, radio alarm, tea-making equipment and trouser press. Public areas are light and airy, and the delightful Garden Bar looks out onto the spacious garden, terrace and children's play area. The hotel has a Children's Certificate and provides no-smoking areas and changing facilities. Major credit cards accepted. **See also Colour Advertisement on page 5.**

Please mention
Recommended WAYSIDE & COUNTRY INNS
when seeking refreshment or
accommodation at a Hotel
mentioned in these pages.

Isle of Wight

**SPYGLASS INN,
The Esplanade, Ventnor,
Isle of Wight PO38 1JX**　　　　　　　　　　Tel: 01983 855338

*3 suites; Free House with real ale; Historic interest; Children welcome;
Bar and restaurant meals; Car park; Shanklin 3 miles; £.*

Yo, ho, ho and a bottle of what you fancy — to go with your choice of freshly prepared fare from the extensive menu and served in a nautical environment. This fine seafront hostelry is renowned for its magnificent cuisine with seafood, naturally, a speciality of the house. One of the most famous inns on the delectable island, the Spyglass is a happy, friendly place to visit with entertainments and special events held regularly. Conviviality reigns in the bar, a mood to which a glass or two of the fine real ales contributes not a little. Bed and breakfast accommodation is provided in three self-contained suites comprising a double bedroom with bathroom en suite and a lounge and patio with wide sea views. Your hosts are Neil, Stephanie and Rosie Gibbs. *Egon Ronay Recommended.*

Available from most bookshops, the 1997 edition of THE GOLF GUIDE covers details of every UK golf course – well over 2000 entries – for holiday or business golf. Hundreds of hotel entries offer convenient accommodation, accompanying details of the courses – the 'pro', par score, length etc.

Endorsed by The Professional Golfers' Association (PGA) and including Holiday Golf in Ireland, France, Portugal, Spain and the USA.

**£8.99 from bookshops or £9.80 including postage
(UK only) from FHG Publications,
Abbey Mill Business Centre, Paisley PA1 1JT**

CLARENDON HOTEL AND WIGHT MOUSE INN, Chale,
Isle of Wight PO38 2HA
Tel: 01983 730431

14 bedrooms, 2 family suites, 8 with private bathroom or shower; Free House with 6 real ales; Historic interest; Children most welcome; Bar and restaurant meals; Car park (200); Newport 9 miles, Ventnor 7; ££.

Our Hotel, The Clarendon, is a 17th century Coaching Inn of immense charm and character enjoying an enviable reputation for excellent food, wine, comfort and hospitality. Standing in its own lovely grounds, it overlooks the magnificent West Wight coastline and is surrounded by beautiful National Trust countryside. Children are very welcome, at reduced rates, and we are a few minutes from Blackgang Chine and several beautiful beaches. We have absolutely everything for your comfort, including our first class restaurant and cocktail bar. We are also included in the Egon Ronay guide "AND BABY COMES TOO", and have a yellow duck award for our baby/child care expertise. All rooms including two luxury family suites have colour television and tea and coffee making facilities, and all bathrooms have hairdryers.
Our Pub, The Wight Mouse Inn, which is attached to the hotel, has great atmosphere, open fires, six real ales, 365 different whiskies, excellent meals and live entertainment nightly all year round, and is open all day every day for hot meals and drinks. Our beautiful gardens have swings, slides, climbing frames, pets' corner, plus ballpond, bouncy castle, sandpit, trikes and Shetland pony rides with Arthur. Golf, Shooting, Fishing, Horse Riding and Car Hire can easily be arranged. For a brochure and full details please write to John and Jean Bradshaw. *ETB* 🏵🏵🏵 *Highly Commended, Egon Ronay UK Family Pub of the Year 1990, Coca-Cola/Schweppes/Publican UK Family Pub of the Year Award 1995 and 1996, Good Pub Guide Family Pub of the Year 1996, UK Whisky Pub of the Year 1994, Les Routiers, Ashley Courtenay, AA**, RAC** and Merit Awards for Hospitality, Comfort and Service, CAMRA Recommended.*

Kent

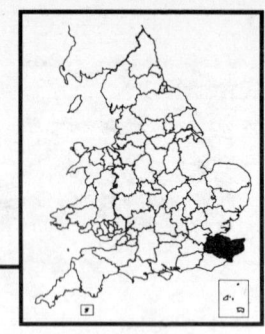

FLYING HORSE INN,
Boughton Aluph, Near Ashford,   Tel. 01233 620914
Kent TN25 4HH   Fax: 01233 661010

5 bedrooms; Free House with real ale; Historic interest; Bar and restaurant meals; Car park; Ashford 4 miles; £/££.

Deep in the fertile 'Garden of England', this 15th century hostelry with its oak beams and crackling log fires in winter is a real gem. The comfortable and romantic Minstrel Bar with its sunken wells is a big attraction, the ideal place to relax in good company with one's choice from a large selection of real ales. Everything is in traditional vein at this happy retreat, even to the cricket played on the village green opposite. There is an excellent range of gourmet meals available seven days a week in both the bar and dining room. A really homely place in which to stay, the inn has centrally heated bedrooms, all with hot and cold water, colour television and tea and coffee-making facilities.

THE ABBOT'S FIRESIDE HOTEL,
Elham, Near Canterbury,   Tel: 01303 840265
Kent   Fax: 01303 840852

5 bedrooms, all with private shower; Free House; Historic interest; Bar and restaurant meals; Car park (15); Folkestone 6 miles, Channel Tunnel 5; ££.

For over 500 years this outstanding Tudor building, complete with lattice windows and huge oak beams, has watched history unfold — and taken its own part in the pageant by offering food, comfort and hospitality to those, from a fugitive king to the footsore traveller, who have sought such within its stout wooden doors. Little wonder then that this quaint old building now leans forward slightly, as if taking its ease a little after so long! And taking one's ease seems so appropriate here, ensconced in front of the great carved fireplace from which the hotel takes its name, contemplating the outstanding five-star à la carte menus for morning coffee, luncheon or dinner. First class facilities and comfort await the visitor in the fully en suite bedrooms — luxury only dreamed of by those long-ago travellers!

THE RINGLESTONE INN,
Harrietsham, Near Maidstone, Kent ME17 1NX

Tel: 01622 859900
Fax: 01622 859966

No accommodation; Free House with real ale; Historic interest; Children welcome; Buffet lunches, restaurant; Car park (50); Leeds Castle 3 miles.

Since the early 1600s this unique inn has offered a "ryghte joyouse and welcome greetynge to ye all", and still today its original brick and flint walls, sturdy oak beams, inglenooks and traditional wooden furniture reflect the relaxed atmosphere of less hurried times. Highly recommended in most good food guides since 1984, the Ringlestone offers superb "help yourself" buffet lunch, cream teas and interesting evening menus, featuring the best of local produce. Those in search of refreshment will savour the selection of well-kept real ales and the interesting range of English country fruit wines — something really different! Set in two acres of peaceful gardens deep in the lush Kent countryside, this truly welcoming inn upholds the finest traditions of English inn-keeping. Amex, Diner, Visa, Mastercard and Switch accepted.

THE HARROW INN,
Warren Street, Near Lenham, Maidstone, Kent ME17 2ED

Tel: 01622 858727
Fax: 01622 850026

13 bedrooms, all with private bathroom; Free House with real ale; Historic interest; Children welcome; Bar and restaurant meals; Car park (100); Lenham 2 miles; £££.

Situated high on the North Downs of Kent amidst lush farmland, The Harrow was once a resting place for pilgrims en route to Canterbury. Now a comfortable country inn, it offers visitors good food and a comfortable night's stay in centrally heated en suite bedrooms, all provided with modern necessities such as telephone, colour television, and clock radio. Eating here is popular with residents and locals alike, either in the lounge bar or in the quieter, secluded restaurant overlooking the garden. The Harrow is conveniently situated for visiting historic Canterbury and the Cinque Ports, as well as being within half an hour's drive of the Channel ports and the Tunnel. ♛♛♛♛, *AA, RAC, Egon Ronay.*

DERING ARMS,
Pluckley, Ashford, Kent TN27 0RR

Tel: 01233 840371
Fax: 01233 840498

3 bedrooms; Free House with real ale; Historic interest; Children and pets welcome; Bar and restaurant meals; Car park (30); Charing 3 miles; ££.

The striking architecture of this former hunting lodge, with its curved Dutch gables and arched windows, makes it well worthy of note, as indeed does the fine selection of real ales to be found within. Good traditional bar food is served daily, including home-made specialities such as pies and puddings, freshly prepared seafood, and game in season. Log fires, solid wood furniture and traditional bar games create a warm and friendly atmosphere, and comfortable accommodation can be obtained at very reasonable rates. The attractive village of Pluckley has many interesting old houses, and the church's 15th century screens are well worth a visit.

CROWN INN,
Sarre, Near Birchington, Kent CT7 0LF

Tel: 01843 847808
Fax: 01843 847914

12 bedrooms, all with private bathroom; Shepherd Neame House with real ale; Historic interest; Children and pets welcome; Bar and restaurant meals (restaurant closed Sunday evening); Car park; Birchington 4 miles; £££.

This neat hostelry has a colourful history stretching back to 1500. Customers have included Charles Dickens, Rudyard Kipling, Douglas Fairbanks and Mary Pickford whilst a montage in one of its three cosy bars commemmorates the fact that the survivors of the Charge of the Light Brigade held their reunion dinners here. Today, sympathetic modernisation has provided a number of comfortable en suite bedrooms. A full à la carte menu is available in a pleasant split-level restaurant with hot and cold snacks served in the bars. A unique cherry brandy made to a secret recipe brought over by the French Huguenots in the 17th century and sold nowhere else, has led to the inn becoming known universally as the Cherry Brandy House. ♛♛♛.

Kent 81

Lancashire

including Greater Manchester, and Merseyside.

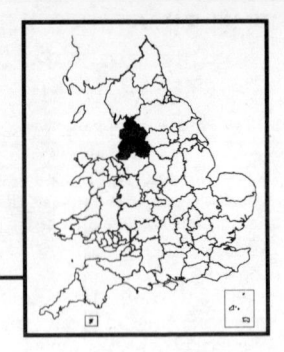

HARK TO BOUNTY INN,
Slaidburn, Near Clitheroe,
Lancashire BB7 3EP

Tel: 01200 446246
Fax: 01200 446361

8 bedrooms, all with private bathroom; Scottish Courage House with real ale; Historic interest; Children and pets welcome; Bar and restaurant meals; Car park (35); Clitheroe 7 miles; ££.

Dating back to the 13th century, this solid old inn was known as 'The Dog' until 1875. Entertaining the local hunt, the entertainment was interrupted by the persistent baying of the favourite dog of the local squire who was heard to exclaim 'Hark to Bounty' and the name has stuck ever since. In the heart of the scenic Forest of Bowland, the inn was once the seat of the Bowland Forest Court and anyone giving it a trial today will pronounce a most favourable verdict in respect of accommodation, cuisine and service. A popular haunt of locals and tourists alike, the oak beamed bar provides excellent bar meals and real ale with more substantial fare served in a highly commended restaurant.

BROWN COW INN,
19 Bridge Road, Chatburn, Near Clitheroe,
Lancashire BB7 4AW

Tel: 01200 441272

No accommodation; Whitbread House with real ale; Historic interest; Children and pets welcome; Bar and restaurant meals; Car park (30); Clitheroe 2 miles.

To the north, the fells of the Forest of Bowland sweep away to the horizon, whilst to the south of this friendly and unpretentious inn lies Pendle Hill, legendary haunt of witches. Haunted itself by escapees from the huddle of industrial towns of Lancashire and West Yorkshire, the Brown Cow is a real breath of fresh air, inviting friends old and new to sample its hospitality and refreshment, the latter in the form of traditional ales and wholesome fare ranging from the extensive bar menu to the popular Barbecue Restaurant. Here, speciality steaks, chicken kebabs and fish dishes come high on the recommended list.

DIGGLE HOTEL,
Diggle, Saddleworth, Near Oldham,
Lancashire OL3 5JZ

Tel: 01457 872741

3 bedrooms; Free House with real ale; Historic interest; Children welcome; Bar meals (not Sun.); Car park; Oldham 6 miles; £.

Commanding lovely views of the surrounding countryside, this family-run free house seems far removed from the urban clamour of Manchester, hence its undoubted popularity with city-orientated folk who appreciate a run out into the country to relax with good sustenance and a variety of real ales. Home-made food is available at lunchtimes and in the evening with children made very welcome and in receipt of their own menu. Refreshment may be taken in the garden of this most pleasant little hotel in clement weather and comfortable accommodation is available at very reasonable rates. *Egon Ronay.*

THE STRAWBURY DUCK HOTEL,
Overshores Road, Entwistle, Near Bolton,
Lancashire BL7 0LU
Tel: 01204 852013

4 bedrooms, all with private bathroom; Free House with real ale; Historic interest; Children welcome; Excellent food (closed Monday lunchtime except Bank Holidays and peak summer period); Car park; Manchester 10 miles; ££/£££.

Small and cosy and bursting with old-fashioned charm, this welcoming free house sits comfortably by the Manchester/Blackburn railway line and offers four nicely furnished guest bedrooms to the weary traveller, three with four-poster bed and all with full en suite facilities and tea/coffee making. Bar fare ranges from sandwiches to genuine Aberdeen Angus steaks served on a hot sizzle plate. Also a choice of vegetarian dishes and a wide range of authentic Indian and Balti cuisine. Pub renowned for fine selection of hand-drawn real ales (weekly guest beers).

Key to Tourist Board Ratings

The Crown Scheme
(England, Scotland & Wales)

Covering hotels, motels, private hotels, guesthouses, inns, bed & breakfast, farmhouses. Every Crown classified place to stay is inspected annually. *The classification*: Listed then 1-5 Crown indicates the range of facilities and services. Higher quality standards are indicated by the terms APPROVED, COMMENDED, HIGHLY COMMENDED and DELUXE.

The Key Scheme
(also operates in Scotland using a Crown System)

Covering self-catering in cottages, bungalows, flats, houseboats, houses, chalets, etc. Every Key classified holiday home is inspected annually. *The classification*: 1-5 Key indicates the range of facilities and equipment. Higher quality standards are indicated by the terms APPROVED, COMMENDED, HIGHLY COMMENDED and DELUXE.

The Q Scheme
(England, Scotland & Wales)

Covering holiday, caravan, chalet and camping parks. Every Q rated park is inspected annually for its quality standards. The more ✔ in the Q – up to 5 – the higher the standard of what is provided.

Lincolnshire

including North Lincolnshire, and North East Lincolnshire, formerly Humberside (Immingham).

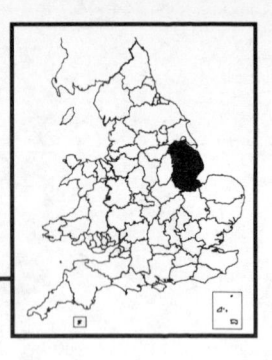

**TALLY HO INN,
Aswarby, Near Sleaford,
Lincolnshire NG34 8SA** Tel: 01529 455205

*6 bedrooms, all with private bathroom; Free House with real ale;
Bar food, restaurant evenings only and Sunday lunch; Car park (40); Sleaford 4 miles; ££.*

It is well worth seeking out this unashamedly rural inn for its refreshingly individual selection of starters, main courses and puddings. Try Kromeskies (bacon rolls stuffed with turkey, ham, mushrooms and herbs, served with a chilli marie rose dip) followed by Lincolnshire Lamb Stew and Dumplings (with rosemary, cider and apples) and you'll certainly know you have had a meal! The bucolic theme is emphasised by the fact that the 17th century building lies in the middle of the Aswarby Estate and is surrounded by parkland on which sheep graze contentedly and that the handful of en suite bedrooms are set away from the house in a carefully converted dairy/cowshed. Friendly and informal, with a cosy log fire, this is an unusually good port of call – a veritable collector's item. *ETB* ✹✹ *Commended, AA QQQ.*

RECOMMENDED SHORT BREAK HOLIDAYS IN BRITAIN

Introduced by John Carter, TV Holiday Expert and Journalist

Specifically designed to cater for the most rapidly growing sector of the holiday market in the UK. Illustrated details of hotels offering special "Bargain Breaks" throughout the year.
Available from newsagents and bookshops for £4.25 or direct from the publishers for £4.80 including postage (UK only).

**FHG PUBLICATIONS LTD
Abbey Mill Business Centre, Seedhill,
Paisley, Renfrewshire PA1 1TJ**

Norfolk

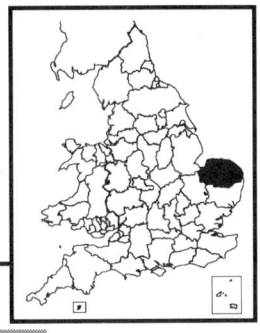

THE HOSTE ARMS,
The Green, Burnham Market, King's Lynn,   Tel: 01328 738777
Norfolk PE31 8HD   Fax: 01328 730103

21 bedrooms, all with private bathroom; Free House with real ale; Historic interest; Children and pets welcome; Bar lunches, restaurant evenings only; Car park; Wells 5 miles; ££££.

In the peaceful heart of Lord Nelson's Norfolk, this 17th century hotel overlooks the green of a beautiful and tranquil Georgian village. Under the careful guidance of proprietor, Paul Whittome, it continues to grow in popularity and has been awarded high accolades for the excellent service it offers, particularly for the imaginative menus served each evening in the restaurant. The same high standards and meticulous attention to detail can be found in the individually styled bedrooms, which are fully en suite and have all modern requirements. An abundance of leisure facilities, an unspoiled coastline, and a rich variety of wildlife make this a delightful spot for a short break at any time of year.

GEORGE AND DRAGON HOTEL,
Cley-next-the-Sea, Near Holt,   Tel: 01263 740652
Norfolk NR25 7RN   Fax: 01263 741275

8 bedrooms, 6 with private bathroom; Free House with real ale; Children and pets welcome; Bar and restaurant meals; Car park (20); Holt 4 miles; £/££.

Built in classic Edwardian style on the site of a former inn, the George and Dragon looks out over the famous North Norfolk salt marshes, so beloved of birdwatchers. Numerous rare birds are protected through the aegis of the Norfolk Naturalists Trust which was actually formed at the hotel. The inn dominates the white-washed cottages and cobbled courtyards that surround it. Gentle breezes sigh through the grasses of this haunting landscape, lamenting the withdrawal of the sea but no wistful spirits exist in this comradely and cosy place where traditional real ales and super fare attracts dyed-in-the-wool inn enthusiasts. Warmly welcoming, this happy hostelry also provides splendid overnight accommodation. *Commended.*

KING'S HEAD HOTEL,
Lynn Road, Great Bircham, King's Lynn,
Norfolk PE31 6RJ
Tel: 01485 578265

5 bedrooms, all with private bathroom; Free House with real ale; Children welcome, pets by arrangement; Bar and restaurant meals; Car park; Docking 3 miles; ££.

This Victorian hotel on the edge of the Sandringham estate has a somewhat refined air about it as well it might for several members of the Royal family have been known to pop in for lunch on the odd occasion. The daily 'specials' place emphasis on fresh local produce whilst the Lodge Restaurant boasts a wide-ranging à la carte menu. There are two comfortable bars cheered by a log fire in cool weather, a cosy residents' lounge and a large garden. With the resort of Hunstanton and the uncrowded North Norfolk coast to explore, this is a charming holiday base set in unspoilt countryside and, for this purpose, five well appointed guest rooms are available. 👑👑👑

THE JOHN H. STRACEY,
West End, Briston, Melton Constable,
Norfolk NR24 2JA
Tel: 01263 860891

3 bedrooms, 1 wih private bathroom; Free House with real ale; Historic interest; Children welcome; Bar and restaurant meals; Car park; Holt 4 miles; £.

Named after a local lad who found fame in the boxing ring a few years ago, this fine old inn, in fact, dates from the 16th century when it was a staging post on the Wells to Norwich road. We were captivated by the time-honoured ambience exuded by its low ceilings, oak beams and copper knick-knacks reflecting the glow of a welcoming log fire. The old hostelry used to be called the Three Horseshoes and synonymous with the change of name, the stables were converted into a splendid, well-patronised restaurant known for its wholesome, home-cooked fare. This is a place of infinite character in tranquil, rural Norfolk with the coast within easy reach. Les Routiers.

SCOLE INN,
Ipswich Road, Scole, Near Diss,
Norfolk IP21 4DR
Tel: 01379 740481
Fax: 01379 740762

23 bedrooms, all with private bathroom; Free House with real ale; Historic interest; Children welcome, pets in annexe rooms only; Bar and restaurant meals; Car park; Diss 2 miles; ££££.

This delightful unspoilt 17th century coaching inn has a wealth of history, and has been thoughtfully and sensitively upgraded to provide all the facilities expected by today's discerning traveller. The bedrooms are individually appointed and stylishly decorated; all have full en suite facilities and some have the added luxury of a four-poster bed. The food in the elegant restaurant is highly regarded in both the immediate area and beyond for its high standards of preparation and presentation, and there are two characterful bars serving real ales. Special terms for short breaks make a stay in this scenic area a most attractive prospect. 👑👑👑👑, AA and RAC **.

ROSE & CROWN INN AND RESTAURANT,
Old Church Road, Snettisham, King's Lynn,   Tel: 01485 541382
Norfolk PE31 7LX   Fax: 01485 543172

4 bedrooms, all with private bathroom; Free House with real ale; Historic interest; Children welcome; Bar lunches, restaurant meals; Car park (80); Hunstanton 4 miles; ££.

Children are well catered for at this nice old pub, having their own special room, a garden to play in, and a separate menu with all their favourites. For adults rather grander fare is on hand, each dish specially prepared to order. Featured in many leading guide books, the Rose and Crown offers a wide choice, ranging from modestly priced steaks and a delicious lamb stew to the simple — and not so simple — sandwich. Conveniently located just off the main A149 coast road, the inn provides comfortable bed and breakfast accommodation with en suite bathrooms, colour television and tea/coffee facilities. ☕☕☕ *Commended, Family Welcome Guide Gold Award 1996.*

THREE HORSESHOES,
The Street, Warham, Fakenham,
Norfolk NR23 1NL   Tel: 01328 710547

5 bedrooms, one with private bathroom; Free House with real ale; Historic interest; Pets welcome; Bar and restaurant meals; Car park; Wells 2 miles; £.

Well worth finding, this is a real old Norfolk pub with no carpet and gas lighting, an integral part of a peaceful village of flint cottages. The secret here is the wonderful home cooking; real country fare (no chips!) with local seafood a speciality. The A149 coast road between Wells next-the-Sea and Stiffkey is just under a mile away, beyond which stretch the famous saltings, haunt of rare birds. In this rare and tranquil backwater, comfortable accommodation is available next door to the inn at Old Post Office Cottage, a lovely old Grade II Listed building with exposed beams and many other period features.

THE LIFEBOAT INN,
Station Road, Wells-next-the-Sea,
Norfolk NR23 1AE   Tel: 01328 710288

Some bedrooms with private bathroom; Free House with real ale; Historic interest; Children welcome; Bar and restaurant meals; Fakenham 9 miles.

The Lifeboat Inn is a Grade II Listed building, formerly a coaching inn, and offers a range of fully en suite rooms, rooms with showers and single rooms. An excellent range of real ales, beers, lagers, wines and spirits is provided, and fresh local produce, including seafood, fish, game, poultry and vegetables in season, is used to produce the delicious menus available in the restaurant and bar. The inn is centrally situated in this quaint old fishing port, a relaxing haven set between the nature reserves of Scolt Head and Blakeney Point, and an ideal base for exploring North Norfolk and the many places of interest in the area. The warmest of welcomes is offered and attractive rates are available for off-season, weekend and mid-week breaks. **See also Colour Advertisement on page 5.**

Norfolk   87

Northamptonshire

THE WINDMILL AT BADBY,
Badby, Daventry,
Northamptonshire NN11 6AN

Tel: 01327 702363
Fax: 01327 311521

8 bedrooms, all with private bathroom; Free House with real ale; Historic interest; Children and pets welcome; Bar and restaurant meals; Car park (25); Daventry 3 miles; £££.

A traditional wayside inn with roses round the door, the eye-catching Windmill is a lively place in tranquil surroundings. Convenient for Silverstone and Towcester with their varieties of horse-power, this tastefully-modernised inn promotes speciality evenings with dancing and entertainment; folk, jazz and quiz nights and other functions. With several real ales, home-cooked meals and bar snacks served at affordable prices daily, it is easy to understand its popularity. Credit is due to John Freestone, the motivating force behind the organisation of accommodation, menus and special events. Stratford-upon-Avon, Oxford, Sulgrave Manor and Blenheim are all within easy reach and several extremely comfortable en suite bedrooms await overnight guests. ♛♛♛ *Approved.*

THE GREYHOUND,
Milton Malsor, Northampton,
Northamptonshire NN7 3AP

Tel: 01604 858449

No accommodation; Chef & Brewer House with real ale; Historic interest; Bar meals; Car park; Northampton 4 miles.

Milton Malsor, hidden away between Towcester and Northampton, is a picturesque English village. This former coaching inn harks back to the 19th century, and with its exposed beams, grandfather clock and log fires still retains a wealth of character as well as plenty of old-fashioned hospitality. The garden with its duck pond and patio is ideal for leisurely summer days. As well as a wide choice of cask conditioned ales, lagers and soft drinks there is an extensive blackboard menu which features imaginative pub food, all beautifully presented at reasonable prices. A wide range of quality wines has been chosen to accompany the food and all are available by both the bottle and glass. There are over 40 main courses to choose from, and an interesting selection of hot and cold snacks and vegetarian meals. The choice of desserts is equally tempting and delicious. The Greyhound is open all day every day for food and drink. Local attractions include Silverstone and Towcester Racecourses, and Towcester itself has many historical connections with the Civil War and Oliver Cromwell.

THE GLOBE HOTEL,
High Street, Weedon, Northampton, Northamptonshire NN7 4QD

Tel: 01327 340336
Fax: 01327 349058

18 bedrooms, all with private bathroom; Free House; Historic interest; Bar and restaurant meals; Car park (40); Daventry 4 miles; £.

Weedon Village, at the very heart of England, was for many years a cavalry training centre, particularly during the Napoleonic Wars. The Globe itself dates from that time and has been totally refurbished by Peter and Penny Walton to a most comfortable standard, whilst still retaining its historic character. All 18 rooms are fully equipped and are en suite. We offer a Weekend Giveaway Break Bed and Breakfast rate of only £21.70 per person per night (double). Situated on the crossroads of the A5/A45, three miles west of Junction 16 of the M1, within easy touring distance of Warwick Castle, Leamington Spa, Stratford-upon-Avon, Naseby Battlefield, Althorp House (Princess Diana's ancestral home), Stoke Bruerne Waterways Centre and Museum, and Silverstone Grand Prix Circuit. Our comprehensive food operation OPEN ALL DAY features a home fayre bar meals menu, pies (our speciality) and a value-for-money à la carte menu. Send for our free tour and information pack. *Commended, RAC**.*

THE RED LION HOTEL,
East Haddon, Northamptonshire NN6 8BU

Tel: 01604 770223
Fax: 01604 770767

5 bedrooms; Traditional House with real ale; Historic interest; Children welcome; Bar and restaurant meals; Car park; Northampton 8 miles.

This traditional, stone-built inn sits snugly in the charming village of East Haddon, just seven miles from Junction 18 on the M1 and eight miles from Northampton. Leisure facilities in the area are excellent — golf, fishing, squash, swimming and snooker are all available locally. Those wishing to make the most of a relaxing weekend break will find comfortable, spick-and-span bedrooms with full en suite facilities, television, etc. Good English cooking is the basis of the carefully balanced à la carte menu and a comprehensive range of gourmet bar food is available at lunchtime and in the evening. Lighter appetites are well catered for in the brass and copper bedecked bars, with a tasty range of gourmet bar food, accompanied by one's choice from the well-kept ales, beers, wines and other refreshments. *Egon Ronay, Good Food Guide.*

Northumberland

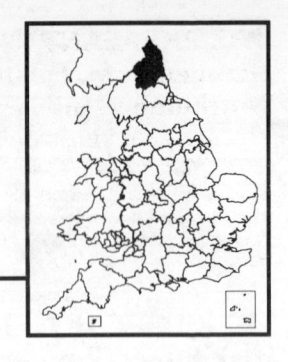

BLUE BELL HOTEL,
Market Square, Belford,
Northumberland NE70 7NE

Tel: 01668 213543
Fax: 01668 213787

17 bedrooms, all with private bathroom; Free House with real ale; Historic interest; Children and pets welcome; Bar meals, restaurant evenings only plus Sunday lunch; Car park (20); Berwick-upon-Tweed 14 miles; £££.

Less than a mile from the A1, this creeper-clad early 18th century hotel enjoys a central position near to the old Market Cross in Belford village. Guest rooms are furnished in elegant Georgian style, and all have bath or shower en suite, colour television, beverage making facilities, telephone and hairdryer. The finest local lamb, seafood and game is complemented by fresh produce straight from the inn's extensive vegetable garden, and meals may be enjoyed in the restaurant or less formally in the buttery. With easy access to stretches of unspoiled coastline, historic houses and castles, and busy market towns, Belford is a wonderful base for a short break or longer stay. ♛♛♛♛ *Highly Commended, RAC Three Merit Awards.*

ANGEL INN,
Main Street, Corbridge,
Northumberland NE45 5LA

Tel and Fax: 01434 632119

5 bedrooms, all with private bathroom; Scottish & Newcastle House with real ale; Historic interest; Children welcome, pets by arrangement; Bar and restaurant meals; Car park; Hexham 3 miles; £££.

Tastefully refurbished to enhance its period appeal, the 17th century Angel, the oldest hostelry in the village, offers excellent value for money and good old-fashioned hospitality. Accommodation vies with the very best, all guest rooms having en suite facilities, colour television, radio alarm, direct-dial telephone, and hairdryer. Fresh local produce features prominently on the menus available in the bar and restaurant, with traditional favourites and imaginative specialities vying for attention. Founded in Saxon times, Corbridge is located on the B6530 on the north side of the famous 17th century bridge over the River Tyne. ♛♛♛♛ *Commended, Egon Ronay, AA, RAC.*

THE PHEASANT INN,
Stannersburn, Falstone, Hexham, Northumberland NE48 1DD

Tel and Fax: 01434 240382

8 bedrooms, all with private bathroom; Free House with real ale; Historic interest; Bar food, restaurant evenings only, plus Sunday lunch; Car park (35); Newcastle-upon-Tyne 20 miles; ££.

Over its 400 years of history at one time a farm, then a staging post for mail and tax collection, The Pheasant now offers hospitality and good cheer to visitors to this most lovely part of Northumberland. Just one mile from Kielder Water, Europe's largest landscaped reservoir, which offers an unrivalled choice of water sports, it makes an excellent base for a holiday in the area, whether active or more leisurely. Old farming implements and country bric-a-brac decorate the walls of the bars and dining room, where traditional country cooking has gained an excellent reputation, both locally and farther afield. Cosy bedrooms, all en suite, provide overnight acccommodation at most reasonable rates. ❦❦❦ Commended, AA QQQ, Logis.

OLDE SHIP HOTEL,
Seahouses, Northumberland NE68 7RD

Tel: 01665 720200
Fax: 01665 721383

16 bedrooms, all with private bathroom; Free House with real ale; Children over 10 welcome; Bar lunches, restaurant meals; Car park (16); Berwick-upon-Tweed 22 miles, Alnwick 14; ££.

Old-fashioned in a sense, this homely old inn was originally built as a farmhouse in the mid-eighteenth century. The Olde Ship stands above the picturesque harbour and has a long established reputation for excellent food and drink. Because of the nautical theme throughout one may be tempted to linger in this fascinating hostelry. All guest rooms, including two with four-poster beds, are en suite and have telephone and satellite colour television. Mr and Mrs A.C. Glen personally supervise the well-being of their guests, and for a holiday break in convivial surroundings this little place has much to commend it. Courtesy coach from local station. The local Rotary Club meets at the Olde Ship on Tuesday evenings. ❦❦❦❦ Commended.

Other specialised
FHG PUBLICATIONS

- Recommended COUNTRY HOTELS OF BRITAIN £4.25

- PETS WELCOME! £4.60

- BED AND BREAKFAST IN BRITAIN £3.50

- THE GOLF GUIDE (PGA) Where to Play / Where to Stay £8.99

Published annually; Please add 55p postage (UK only) when ordering from the publishers.

FHG PUBLICATIONS LTD
Abbey Mill Business Centre, Seedhill,
Paisley, Renfrewshire PA1 1TJ

Oxfordshire

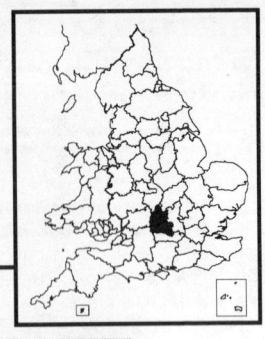

PEAR TREE INN,
Scotland End, Hook Norton, Banbury, Oxfordshire OX15 5NU
Tel: 01608 737482

One bedroom; Hook Norton House with real ale; Historic interest; Children and pets welcome; Bar meals (not Tues. or Sun. evening); Car park (13); Chipping Norton 5 miles; £.

This attractive, old-world pub has the distinction (and undoubted advantage!) of being just about 300 yards from its parent (Hook Norton) brewery. A real village inn with few ideas above its station, this is a friendly port of call and very much one for the collector. Apart from the well-known ale, a surprisingly comprehensive range of home cooked dishes is on offer in the bar with the menu varied enough to suit most tastes. For a quiet break in idyllic and unsophisticated surroundings, the little inn has a double room with its own lounge/dining room and en suite shower room. Rates are very reasonable. The ideal 'away from it all' location. ✹✹ *Commended.*

BLEWBURY INN,
London Road, Blewbury, Oxfordshire OX11 9PD
Tel: 01235 850496

3 bedrooms, all with private bathroom; Free House with real ale; Children welcome, pets by arrangement; Bar and restaurant meals; Car park (15); Didcot 3 miles; ££.

The undulating countryside between Newbury and Oxford has enjoyed fame as a racehorse training area. A salient feature of a picturesque village, the Blewbury Inn also has its share of acclaim, primarily on account of its highly creative and highly appreciated cuisine. What is more, there is no need to take out a mortgage to pay for one's indulgence. The non-smoking restaurant changes daily and the use of a microwave or deep fryer is devoutly spurned. There is a snug bar justly popular with the locals and accommodation is simple but extremely comfortable; all rooms are fully en suite and have colour television. *Egon Ronay, Good Food Guide.*

THE KING'S HEAD INN AND RESTAURANT,
Bledington, Near Kingham, Tel: 01608 658365
Oxfordshire OX7 6HD Fax: 01608 658902

12 bedrooms, all with private bathroom; Free House with real ale; Historic interest; Children welcome; Bar food, restaurant evenings only; Car park (70); Stow-on-the-Wold 4 miles; ££.

Facing Bledington's village green with its brook and ducks stands the 15th century King's Head Inn, an establishment which has echoed with the sounds of convivial hospitality for over four centuries. Bledington nestles in the heart of the Cotswolds and is within easy reach of all top tourist attractions. The charming accommodation is in keeping with the atmosphere, all bedrooms (en suite) having television, telephone and hot drinks facilities. High quality and inventive bar fare is served, with full à la carte and table d'hôte menus in the award-winning restaurant in the evenings. A selection of real ales and interesting whiskies is served in the bar which has original old beams and an inglenook fireplace. ETB ☆☆☆ *Commended, Egon Ronay *, AA QQQQ Selected, Good Pub Guide Dining County Pub of the Year, Logis.*

THE LAMB AT BUCKLAND,
Buckland, Faringdon, Tel: 01367 870484
Oxfordshire SN7 8QN Fax: 01367 810475

4 bedrooms, all with private bathroom; Free House with real ale; Historic interest; Children welcome; Bar lunches and restaurant meals; Car park (60); Faringdon 4 miles; ££/£££.

When one thinks of the Lamb one automatically thinks of food, for its tempting range of bar meals and dinners are worth coming a long way to marvel at and enjoy. This friendly inn offers an extensive range of food calculated to suit all palates and purses, and has won many accolades for its imaginative approach. Set in a peaceful village on the edge of the Cotswolds, it is a welcoming port of call, with a convivial bar serving real ale, and a pleasant garden where refreshment may be taken in good weather. Excellent overnight accommodation is available, also at moderate rates.

LAMB INN,
Sheep Street, Burford, Tel: 01993 823155
Oxfordshire OX18 4LR Fax: 01993 822228

15 bedrooms, all with private bathroom; Free House with real ale; Historic interest; Children and pets welcome; Bar lunches, restaurant evenings only plus Sunday lunch; Car park (8); Witney 7 miles; ££££.

Step into the bars of this lovely 15th century inn and step back into history with its flagged floors and gleaming copper, brass and silver reflecting the flicker of log fires. Everyone's idea of what the ancient English inn should be, the Lamb has a lot to live up to and it succeeds almost without effort. Like many buildings in this charming Cotswold town, the hostelry has a facade of honeyed stone: a place in which to wind down and enjoy the good and unhurried things of life — not that there are any shortcomings in the standards of service, particularly when dining by candlelight in the pretty pillared restaurant. Guest rooms are delightfully cottagey in style, some having four-poster or half tester beds. *Johansens "Inn of the Year" 1995.*

THE PLOUGH AT CLANFIELD,
Clanfield,
Oxfordshire OX18 2RB

Tel: 01367 810222
Fax: 01367 810596

6 bedrooms, all with private bathroom; Free House; Historic interest; Bar lunches and restaurant meals; Car park (25); London 60 miles, Oxford 15; ££££.

This lovingly restored 16th century country house sits on the crossroads of a typically quiet Cotswold village. One of the finest examples of the Elizabethan manor house, the Plough is a comfortably furnished haven where you can relax and forget about the cares of the world. From the traditional appeal of the bar and lounge one passes to its crowning glory, the award-winning Tapestry Room Restaurant where the imaginative blend of dishes celebrate classic English and French cuisine that is renowned far and wide. The charm of this ancient hostelry extends to its skilfully modernised en suite accommodation: each room has a colour television, telephone and a host of thoughtful extras; rooms with jacuzzis are also available. 👑👑👑 *Highly Commended, AA*** and two Restaurant Rosettes, RAC***, Johansens.*

MASON ARMS,
South Leigh, Near Witney,
Oxfordshire OX8 6XN

Tel: 01993 702485

2 bedrooms, both with private bathroom; Free House with real ale; Historic interest; Bar lunches and restaurant meals; Car park; Witney 3 miles; £££.

Chocolate boxes and jigsaw puzzles have long been decorated by pictures similar to that made by this delectable 15th century thatched inn between Oxford and the Cotswolds. Close by is the 12th century church where John Wesley preached his first sermon. The interior resembles a country house or gentleman's club, with antiques, starched white cloths and candles providing an atmosphere of intimate elegance (not suitable for babies and children). Open fires, flagstone floor and gleaming copper and brass add character to the cosy bar where there is an interesting selection of real ales, malt whiskies and wines. Steaks and fish dishes are cooked to order in an intimate restaurant (cover charge £1!). De luxe en suite accommodation is available.

SHEPHERDS HALL INN,
Witney Road, Freeland,
Oxfordshire OX8 8HQ
Tel: 01993 881256

5 bedrooms, all with private bath or shower and toilet; Free House with real ale; Children welcome; Bar food; Car park (50); Oxford 12 miles, Witney 4, Woodstock 4; £.

One of the finest houses for miles, the welcoming Shepherds Hall stands on the A4095 Woodstock to Witney road, in an area famed for its sheep rearing, hence its name. Rooms are now modernised, with colour television, direct-dial telephones and tea/coffee making facilities, yet retain the atmosphere of a true country inn, and proprietors Liz and David Fyson present a comprehensive selection of appetising meals and snacks in the bar every day. This is a good place to bring the family (perhaps after visiting Woodstock and Blenheim Palace) for there is an attractive beer garden and children's play area. Wholesome accommodation is available at reasonable rates and this includes a full English breakfast. *HETB* ☻☻.

Shropshire

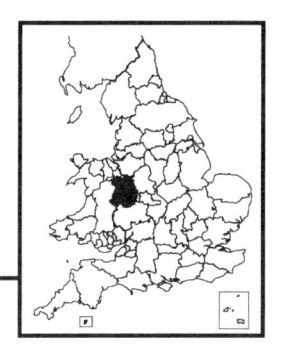

THE ROEBUCK,
Brimfield, Ludlow,
Shropshire SY8 4NE
Tel: 01584 711230
Fax: 01584 711654

3 bedrooms, all with private bathroom; Free House with real ale; Historic interest; Children and pets welcome; Bar and restaurant meals; Car park (20); Tenbury Wells 4 miles; ££££.

In a pretty village between Ludlow and Leominster, the Roebuck is widely renowned for its superb Poppies Restaurant (open Tuesday to Saturday inclusive) which dispenses imaginative set luncheons and à la carte dinners lovingly prepared by Chef/Proprietor, Carole Evans and a dedicated staff, whilst the bar menu is no less worthy. This is an ideal venue for a rewarding break in tranquil surroundings. There are numerous sporting activities available in the area and Ludlow National Hunt races are held regularly during the season. Excellent en suite accommodation is available. Ludlow is a picturesque market town steeped in history with an impressive Norman castle, whilst Leominster, with its origins in the wool trade, has numerous antique shops.

THE RAGLETH INN,
Little Stretton, Near Church Stretton,
Shropshire SY6 6RB
Tel and Fax: 01694 722711

2 bedrooms, Free House with real ale; Historic interest; Children welcome, pets in bar only; Bar and restaurant meals; Car park (30); Church Stretton 1 mile; £.

Over the past three hundred years many wayfarers have crossed the threshold of the Ragleth Inn in search of comfort, good cheer and hospitality, and still today the old traditions are faithfully upheld. Good, freshly prepared meals are provided both at lunchtimes and in the evenings, along with fine real ales and other refreshments which can be enjoyed in the bars or in the relaxed atmosphere of the Ragleth dining room. A traditional Sunday lunch is offered too in this lovely old inn, where in the winter log fires cast a glow against the old oak beams and handsome antique furniture, and where in summer the attractive beer garden invites visitors to sit outside and contemplate the peaceful surroundings.

RED LION INN,
Llanfair Waterdine, Near Knighton,
Shropshire LD7 1TU
Tel: 01547 528214

3 bedrooms, one with private bathroom; Free House with real ale; Historic interest; Bar and restaurant meals; Car park; Knighton 4 miles; ££/£££.

Dating from the 16th century (if not earlier), the Red Lion Inn is centrally located in some of the most beautiful countryside of the English/Wesh Border country. A wide variety of interesting places can easily be reached along uncrowded, sometimes almost deserted, highways and byways, and the hills immediately around offer great mountain bike excursions or excellent walking trails. Chris and Judy Stevenson, the proprietors, are justly proud of running a traditional country inn and restaurant, offering good old-fashioned courtesies to their guests, alongside a selection of cask-conditioned ales, fine wines and an excellent bar and restaurant menu featuring English and Italian specialities with a few international favourites appearing as blackboard specials. Whatever the weather, outside or in, this is an ideal place to visit.

TALBOT INN,
Much Wenlock,
Shropshire TF13 6AA

Tel: 01952 727077

6 bedrooms, all with private bathroom; Free House with real ale; Historic interest; Bar and restaurant meals; Car park (6); Bridgnorth 9 miles; £££.

Once part of Wenlock Abbey, this charming 13th century inn is entered through an archway which opens into a quiet courtyard garden; inside the exposed beams, open log fires and fresh flowers create a mood of relaxed contentment. Guest rooms with private facilities are in a converted malthouse in the courtyard, which also houses a comfortable residents' lounge and breakfast room; all are attractively furnished. A good choice of home-cooked dishes is available lunchtime and in the evening and even those on the strictest of diets should give in for once and sample the famous Bread and Butter Pudding, a speciality of the house. ♛♛♛ Commended, Egon Ronay Recommended.

CROWN INN,
Wentnor, Near Bishop's Castle,
Shropshire SY9 5EE

Tel: 01588 650613
Fax: 01588 650436

4 bedrooms, Free House with real ale; Historic interest; Bar lunches, restaurant meals; Children welcome, no pets in public rooms; Car park; Bishop's Castle 5 miles; £.

David and Jane Carr run this charming 16th century country inn and are doing a great job in upgrading its accommodation and amenities. A real find amongst the rolling Shropshire hills, the Crown has old beams, open fireplaces and horse brasses to create the mood in which to savour the excellent à la carte cuisine, featuring a mouth-watering variety of home-cooked fare as well as real ales. Menus change regularly and include at least three vegetarian dishes; lunchtime specials are served in the bar and prices are very reasonable. With good walking, horse riding, fishing, golf and even gliding available nearby plus the historic appeal of Ludlow and Shrewsbury, this homely and tranquil place is well worth close acquaintance. *Tourist Board Listed Commended.*

The **£** symbol when appearing at the end of the italic section of an entry shows the anticipated price, during 1997, for single full Bed and Breakfast.

Under £25	£	Over £36 but under £45	£££
Over £25 but under £36	££	Over £45	££££

This is meant as an indication only and does not show prices for Special Breaks, Weekends, etc. Guests are therefore advised to verify all prices on enquiring or booking.

Somerset

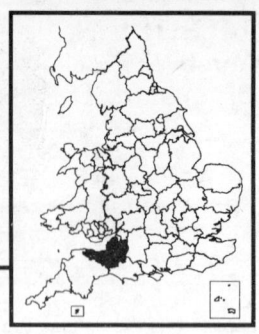

including Bath and North East Somerset, and North West Somerset.

BOWL INN & RESTAURANT,
Lower Almondsbury, Bristol, Somerset BS12 4DT

Tel: 01454 612757
Fax: 01454 619910

8 bedrooms, all with private bathroom; Scottish & Newcastle House with real ale; Historic interest; Children welcome; Bar and restaurant meals; Car park (50); Bristol 7 miles; ££/££££.

One has a certain sympathy with the ghost of the Grey Lady which is said to haunt this hostelry — for anyone would be reluctant to leave the white-washed Bowl Inn which overlooks the Severn Estuary from its quiet corner of the Vale. Bar food here includes home-made soup and sandwiches, fresh or toasted, together with a wide range of snacks and other meals, such as lasagne, mixed grills and fish; more formal cuisine is available in the restaurant which boasts an extensive à la carte menu with some exotic specialities. The cosy guest accommodation has been thoughtfully refurbished to highlight the many historic features, and is fully equipped to meet the needs of travellers. ♛♛♛ *Commended, Egon Ronay.*

THE WALNUT TREE HOTEL,
North Petherton, Bridgwater, Somerset TA6 6QA

Tel: 01278 662255
Fax: 01278 663946

32 bedrooms, all with private bathroom; Free House with real ale; Historic interest; Children welcome; Bar and restaurant meals; Car park (72); Bridgwater 3 miles; ££.

In appearance a classic wayside hostelry on the A38 (M5 Exit 24 one mile), this delightfully renovated 18th century inn today has many of the attributes of a first-class hotel. One may still relax with a pint of real ale and rub shoulders with the locals in the bar and contemplate a menu offering excellent fare ranging from a well-filled granary roll to a succulent steak in the Cottage Room. For memorable à la carte dining, the tastefully decorated Sedgemoor Restaurant is justly popular and prices are very reasonable. Accommodation is of an extremely high standard, suiting the needs of holidaymakers and businessmen alike. Rooms, all en suite, are furnished in bright modern style and there are outstanding facilities for meetings and social events. ♛♛♛♛ *Highly Commended, AA*** 72%, Egon Ronay, Ashley Courtenay.*

THE WHEELWRIGHTS ARMS,
Monkton Combe, Near Bath, Somerset BA2 7HD

Tel: 01225 722287
Fax: 01225 723029

8 bedrooms, all with private shower; Free House with real ale; Historic interest; Bar food; Car park (20); Bath 3 miles; £.

With excellent accommodation housed in the converted barn and stables, this is a lovely base from which to visit the numerous houses, gardens and places of interest which lie within a few miles, including of course the city of Bath itself. The hostelry stands in the peace and quiet of the lovely Midford valley. A large selection of home cooked food is served, with the addition of a grill menu in the evening. In addition there is a choice of four real ales. The bedrooms (mostly beamed) are equipped with shower, toilet, washbasin, colour television, central heating, tea and coffee making facilities, direct-dial telephones and hairdryers. Terms are very reasonable. The inn is also a lovely base for walking, fishing, riding or just relaxing. In the summer guests are free to use the pleasant garden and patio, and in winter cosy log fires warm the bar.

THE MALT SHOVEL INN,
Blackmoor Lane, Cannington, Bridgwater, Somerset TA5 2NE

Tel: 01278 653432

4 bedrooms, one with private bathroom; Free House with real ale; Historic interest; Children welcome; Bar and restaurant meals; Car park; Taunton 9 miles; ££/£££.

Those who follow the Malt Shovel signpost near Cannington on the A39 west of Bridgwater will be amply rewarded. In addition to well-kept real ale and a most cheering welcome from licensees Robert & Frances Beverley and Philip & Sally Monger they will find a tempting array of reasonably priced bar food, ranging from a freshly cut sandwich to more substantial homemade pies, and succulent fillet and sirloin steaks. Comfortable bed and breakfast accommodation is available, and residents who would dine in style are recommended to the very good restaurant which attracts both local and passing trade. Children are welcomed.

THE HORSE POND INN AND MOTEL,
The Triangle, Castle Cary, Somerset BA7 7BD

Tel: 01963 351762/350318
Fax: 01963 351764

4 motel rooms and 2 bedrooms, all en-suite; Free House with 5 real ales; Historic interest; Children welcome; Bar and restaurant meals; Car park (20); Bournemouth 35 miles, Lyme Regis 32, Weymouth 30, Bristol 29, Weston-super-Mare 28, Bath 25; £££.

This beautifully renovated old coaching inn dates back to the sixteenth century and today, under its welcoming hosts, Charlie and Fiona Anderson, specialises in good home cooking. In such a convivial atmosphere relaxation comes easily, with lively chatter with the locals and unspoilt countryside to walk and enjoy within a stone's throw from the inn. Castle Cary is delightfully placed for half-day visits to numerous places of geographic and historic interest, with day excursions including the coast which may be reached by car within one hour. The inn has very comfortably appointed accommodation and the terms represent excellent value, with reductions for a stay of one week or more. Six golf courses within half an hour's drive.

YORK INN,
Honiton Road, Churchinford, Taunton,
Somerset TA3 7RF
Tel: 01823 601333

4 bedrooms, all with private bathroom; Free House with real ale; Historic interest; Children and pets welcome; Bar and restaurant meals; Car park (20); Taunton 8 miles; ££.

"Environmentally sensitive" is the latest politically correct phrase to describe an area of "outstanding natural beauty". Be that as it may, the latter adequately (and less clumsily) portrays the delightful setting of this exquisite little hostelry. The traditional, well-kept English village inn, it has a colourful appearance, thanks to the hanging baskets and tubs of flowers that greet visitors. Inside, oak beams and an open fireplace give a hint of origins in the 16th century. Improvements have been introduced in subtle style and the spacious guest bedrooms are now blessed with modern appointments. A fine touring base with numerous sporting opportunities nearby, the inn is also worth a visit to confirm its high reputation for classic cuisine. ☜☜, AA QQQ.

THE BULL TERRIER,
Croscombe, Wells,
Somerset BA5 3QJ
Tel: 01749 343658

3 bedrooms, 2 with private bathroom; Free House with real ale; Historic interest; Children and pets welcome; Bar and restaurant meals; Car park; Wells 3 miles; ££.

Good food and plenty of choice — that is very much the order of the day at this friendly country inn where menus range from freshly cut sandwiches to generous helpings of home-made traditional dishes — and don't forget to leave space for one of the wickedly tempting desserts! The three cosy bars serve a good range of refreshments including well-kept real ales, lager and cider. Should overnight accommodation be required, there are three prettily decorated bedrooms (two with en suite bath or shower), all comfortably furnished and complete with colour television and tea/coffee making facilities. There are many lovely walks in the area and the village itself has a fine church with Jacobean carvings.

THE LUTTRELL ARMS,
36 High Street, Dunster,
Somerset TA24 6SG
Tel: 01643 821555
Fax: 01643 821567

27 bedrooms, all with private bathroom; Free House with real ale; Children and pets welcome; Bar and restaurant meals; Garages (3); Minehead 2 miles; ££££.

Built as the guest house to Cleeve Abbey, this ancient establishment adopted its present name in 1779 to honour the Lords of the Manor of Dunster, whose castle overshadows the pretty Exmoor village. Attractively decorated en suite bedrooms pamper overnight guests with colour television, tea and coffee facilities, radio and telephone, and several offer a sumptuous four-poster bed to provide that extra touch of luxury. Lunch and dinner may be enjoyed in the popular Luttrell Restaurant, and both the hotel bar and the Ostlers Bar offer an excellent range of refreshments including real ales. Pleasant and well-tended gardens surround the hotel, and the views of coast and moorland are guaranteed to enchant. AA ***.

THE REST AND BE THANKFUL INN,
Wheddon Cross, Exmoor,
Somerset TA24 7DR
Tel and Fax: 01643 841222

5 bedrooms, all en suite; Free House with real ales; Historic interest; Children welcome; Bar and restaurant meals; Car park; Dunster 5 miles; ££.

After an exhilarating day exploring the wild and picturesque moorland, one's first thought on catching sight of this neat cream-painted inn must surely be "what an appropriate name!". Rest is assured in the comfortable, well-appointed bedrooms, each with en suite shower and enjoying sweeping views of Dunkery Beacon, the highest point in Somerset. The hungry or thirsty traveller will be thankful too for the traditional home-cooked meals and snacks served in the restaurant and bar, accompanied perhaps by a glass of well-kept ale or a selection from the carefully chosen wine list. In finer weather patrons can relax in the charming garden patio, while the more actively inclined can make use of the games room and skittle alley. Credit cards accepted. *Highly Commended, RAC Acclaimed, AA QQQQ.*

CROSSWAYS INN,
West Huntspill, Near Highbridge,
Somerset TA9 3RA
Tel: 01278 783756

3 bedrooms, all with private bathroom; Free House with real ale; Historic interest; Children and pets welcome; Bar and restaurant meals; Car park (60); Burnham-on-Sea 3 miles; £.

Conveniently located on the A38 (Exits 22 and 23 from the M5), this spacious 17th century inn is very popular with families, whether on a day out or staying overnight. Children sharing a room with their parents are accommodated free and there is a special family room for meals and refreshments. In fine weather meals can be taken on picnic tables under the trees in the spacious garden. A good range of real ales is available, including a weekly-changing guest beer, and service is cheerful and efficient. The Crossways is ideally situated for exploring the West Country and is just a short drive from the lively holiday resort of Weston-super-Mare. *Egon Ronay, Good Pub Guide.*

PLEASE MENTION THIS GUIDE WHEN YOU WRITE

OR PHONE TO ENQUIRE ABOUT

ACCOMMODATION.

IF YOU ARE WRITING, A STAMPED,

ADDRESSED ENVELOPE IS ALWAYS APPRECIATED.

THE ROYAL OAK OF LUXBOROUGH,
Luxborough, Near Watchet,
Somerset TA23 OSH

Tel and Fax: 01984 640319

5 bedrooms, 3 with private bathroom; Free House with real ale; Children and pets welcome; Bar lunches and restaurant meals; Car park; Dunster 4 miles; £/££.

Following a visit to Dunster Castle, after about six miles we came upon the delightful village of Luxborough lying in a fold of the gentle Brendon Hills. The homely Royal Oak was a welcome sight and on closer acquaintance, we were captivated by its quiet and confident character — no gimmicks, no false pride or brewer's plastic, just good solid worth in its unspectacular bars where a moderately priced selection of wholesome dishes was on offer; true country fare and real ale which was suitably appreciated. With breathtaking Exmoor scenery beckoning walkers, this is an idyllic spot in which to pass an hour or so or even a few days. A tip — walk first, eat and drink later!

MANOR ARMS,
North Perrott,
Somerset TA18 7SG

Tel: 01460 72901

5 bedrooms, all with private bathroom; Free House with real ale; Historic interest; Children welcome; Bar and restaurant meals; Car park (26); Crewkerne 2 miles; £.

A focal point in a village of lovely hamstone cottages, this handsome 16th century Grade II Listed building displays abundant character through its exposed stonework, inglenook fireplace and original oak beams, the bar warmed by a log fire in cool weather. Lovingly restored and having acquired a reputation for its superb (and reasonably-priced) English fare, this typical wayside inn overlooks the green. This is a tranquil area of picture-book villages and verdant, undulating countryside with the Dorset coast within 20 minutes' drive and a number of historic houses close at hand. Bed and breakfast accommodation is available in the Coach House situated in the gardens in a quiet setting behind the inn. All five guest rooms have en suite shower rooms and are comfortably furnished, the ideal venue for a quiet and rewarding break. ♛♛ *Commended, AA QQQ.*

THE PECKING MILL INN,
Evercreech, Near Shepton Mallet, Somerset BA4 6PG

Tel: 01749 830336
Fax: 01749 831316

6 bedrooms, all with private bathroom; Free House with real ale; Historic interest; Bar and restaurant meals; Car park (26); Shepton Mallet 4 miles; ££.

History, legend and breathtaking scenery combine in the Mendip area of Somerset to make it the perfect setting for a short break or longer stay, and at the Pecking Mill you will find added to these attractions warm hospitality and a friendly welcome for all. Bedrooms have everything one could wish for to make one's stay comfortable, including private bathrooms, colour television, direct-dial telephone, hairdryer and trouser press; the most attractive room rate includes a full English breakfast. The bar and restaurant retain the traditional atmosphere of the inn's 16th century origins and offer an excellent choice of good food, well kept ales and other refreshments. Short Breaks. 🍺🍺🍺, AA**, RAC Two Tankards.

CROSSWAYS INN,
North Wootton, Near Shepton Mallet, Somerset BA4 4EU

Tel: 01749 890237
Fax: 01749 890476

17 bedrooms, all with private bathroom; Free House with real ale; Children welcome, pets by arrangement; Bar and restaurant meals; Car park (100); Wells 3 miles; ££.

Just a few miles from the romantic town of Glastonbury and overlooking the Vale of Avalon, this delightful inn serves well as either a touring base or tranquil retreat from worldly care, providing comfortable and cosy overnight accommodation at a moderate cost. Bars are friendly and relaxing, and here one may eat inexpensively and most satisfactorily from a wide menu. Grills, roasts and fish dishes are served in the Crossways Restaurant, where advisability of booking is an indication of its immense popularity. Nearby tourist attractions include the beautiful cathedral at Wells, historic Bath and the Cheddar Gorge. 🍺🍺🍺, AA and RAC **.

LETHBRIDGE ARMS,
Bishops Lydeard, Taunton, Somerset TA4 3BW

Tel: 01823 432234

7 bedrooms; Whitbread House with real ale; Historic interest; Children and pets welcome; Bar and restaurant meals; Car park; Taunton 5 miles; £.

We were drawn to this traditional, 16th century former coaching inn both by its overweening character but also, on a more practical note, by its first-rate food and beer, plus good service and the warmest of welcomes. We were particularly impressed by the wide choice of real ales and home-made dishes on offer. There is a large beer garden, a skittle alley and a convivial bar where various pub games may invoke a challenge or two, but beware — the locals are playing 'at home'! We learnt the hard way! This is a fine centre from which to explore the nearby Quantocks, Exmoor and the Somerset and Devon coasts and for this purpose very comfortable Bed and Breakfast accommodation is available.

SPARKFORD INN,
Sparkford, Yeovil,
Somerset BA22 7JN

Tel: 01963 440218
Fax: 01963 440358

3 bedrooms, all with private bathroom; Free House with real ale; Historic interest; Children welcome, dogs allowed in bar on leads; Bar and restaurant meals; Car park (50); Castle Cary 4 miles; ££.

We knew this fine 15th century coaching inn long before the A303 was re-routed round the village, one would think occasioning a loss of casual trade. However, those in the know still turn off the few yards to enjoy superb carvery and home-made dishes and a choice of at least four real ales. This old inn, one of our favourites, has spacious bars with interesting alcoves and is full of character. In the evening, a full à la carte menu is on offer in the candlelit restaurant. Now a free house run by Nigel and Suzanne Tucker, the inn has vitality and a twinkle in its eye in catering for the whole family. Entertainments are held regularly and children will be in their element here (which means that so will their parents!) with a Snakes and Ladders playroom complete with bouncy castle, trampoline, slide, see-saw and much, much more. This enlightened amenity is available for kiddies' parties with catering provided if required. Outside is a fully enclosed garden and a separate adventure trail. The inn also has a large function room equipped with its own bar and toilets and also a smaller meeting room. This, as visitors will discover, is a difficult place to leave, so why not stay overnight? Excellent bed and breakfast accommodation is available, all rooms having en suite facilities, television, radio and tea and coffee makers and rates are very reasonable.

THE HATCH INN,
Hatch Beauchamp, Taunton,
Somerset TA3 6SG

Tel: 01823 480245

6 bedrooms; Free House with real ale; Children welcome; Bar and restaurant meals; Car park; Taunton 5 miles; £.

A friendly, family-owned and operated village inn, offering bed and breakfast; families catered for. All bedrooms have colour television and tea and coffee making facilities, and there is a pleasant dining room and a comfortable, well-stocked bar serving real ales. Home-cooked meals, including vegetarian dishes, are a speciality. The inn also has a very nice garden, a skittle alley, a spacious function room and a large car park. It is situated in a quiet village only a few minutes' drive from the M5 (Junction 25) and the county town of Taunton, amidst spectacular Somerset countryside. It makes a very good base for visiting the many attractions in South and West Somerset.

Staffordshire

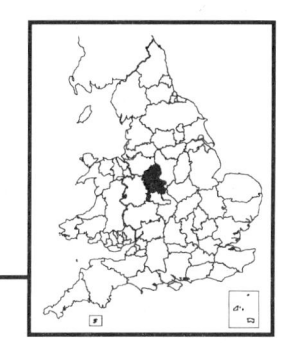

RIVERSIDE HOTEL,
Branston, Burton-upon-Trent,
Staffordshire DE14 3EP

Tel: 01283 511234
Fax: 01283 511441

22 bedrooms, all with private bathroom; Free House; Children and pets welcome; Bar snacks and restaurant meals; Car park (130); Burton upon Trent 2 miles; ££££.

In a garden setting overlooking open countryside and the River Trent, this elegant and well-tended hotel has a truly delightful old-English style panelled bar. To dine in the almost jungle-like splendour of the Garden Room Restaurant is to confirm its reputation for superb cuisine — the comprehensive menu is both imaginative and extensive. Apart from the nearby Meadowside Sports Complex, there are three local golf courses, horse racing at Uttoxeter and Nottingham, and good opportunities for coarse and fly fishing. The hotel provides comfortable and stylish accommodation, all rooms having bath, shower, colour television, radio, direct-dial telephone and tea and coffee makers. ♛♛♛♛ *Commended, AA ***, RAC *** and Food Award, Egon Ronay and Ashley Courtenay Recommended.*

Suffolk

THE PLOUGH INN,
Brockley Green, Hundon, Sudbury,
Suffolk CO10 8DT

Tel: 01440 786789
Fax: 01440 786710

8 bedrooms, all with private bathroom; Free House with real ale; Children welcome; Bar and restaurant meals; Car park; Haverhill 3 miles; ££££.

Combining the best of both worlds, this splendid establishment offers the tranquillity of the countryside, while being just a short drive from the lively bustle of market towns such as Sudbury and Bury St Edmunds and the sporting pleasures of Newmarket. The University city of Cambridge is also within a short drive. All that is finest in the time-honoured traditions of English inn-keeping can be found here — good, home-cooked food, well-kept ales and comfortable accommodation. Bedrooms are of a particularly high standard and offer all the facilities expected by today's discerning traveller, including en suite facilities, Teletext television and telephone. ♛♛♛♛, *Good Pub Guide, Good Beer Guide.*

CROWN HOTEL,
High Street, Bildeston,
Suffolk IP7 7EB

Tel: 01449 740510
Fax: 01449 740224

15 bedrooms, 11 with private bathroom; Free House with real ale; Historic interest; Children and pets welcome; Bar and restaurant meals; Car park (40); Hadleigh 5 miles; ££/£££.

Built in 1495 and probably a wealthy merchant's house for some time after, there is later proof of the Crown's existence as an inn in the mid-17th century because tokens were issued here to overcome the almost total absence of small change. We have only known and appreciated its appeal for the past 20 years or so, during which time this former coaching inn has been restored to former glory. The timbered facade and a wealth of old beams in the bar still take the eye although first-rate modern amenities have been introduced. The restaurant boasts an extensive à la carte menu featuring some intriguing speciality dishes and an extensive range of lighter meals and snacks may be enjoyed in the bar. Bedrooms are individually decorated in romantic style and most have private facilities and colour television. A four-poster and some king-sized beds are available. All rooms have tea-making facilities. This fascinating and relatively unexplored part of East Anglia has much to recommend it both architecturally and historically, this splendid hostelry in particular. Sheltered gardens to the rear provide a tranquil setting for relaxation and for the more energetic, there are opportunities for tennis, golf and swimming nearby. Two and three-day breaks are organised, terms for Bed, Breakfast and Evening Meal representing excellent value. *BTA, Les Routiers.*

ANGEL INN,
Stoke-by-Nayland, Near Colchester,
Suffolk CO6 4SA

Tel: 01206 263145

6 bedrooms, all with private bathroom; Free House with real ale; Historic interest; Bar and restaurant meals, lunch and evenings; Car park (25); Hadleigh 5 miles; ££££.

Advice to make a prior booking shows the local popularity enjoyed by the Angel's restaurant — but if one has omitted to do so and is denied the delights of the à la carte dinner menu, all is not lost. Meals on offer in the homely bar prove a worthy alternative and are exceedingly good value as well as being wholesome, satisfying and well presented. Those seeking accommodation in Constable country will be well pleased with what is on offer at this sixteenth-century village inn. En suite guest bedrooms are both attractive and comfortable, and colour television, tea and coffee facilities and telephone are provided in all. ♛♛♛ *Highly Commended.*

SHIP INN,
Dunwich, Near Saxmundham,
Suffolk IP17 3DT

Tel: 01728 648219
Fax: 01728 648675

3 bedrooms, all with private bathroom; Free House with real ale; Historic interest; Children and pets welcome; Bar lunches, restaurant evenings only; Car park; Southwold 4 miles; ££.

On a grey, stormy day, Dunwich can be a melancholy place, especially if one pays heed to the legend of the old town inundated by the relentless sea. Stand on the shore and listen to the ghostly sound of the Bells of Dunwich tolling sadly beneath the waves. A far better place to be is the cosy main bar of this hospitable inn, itself a one-time haunt of smugglers. A cheerful fire adds to the warmth of welcome in chilly weather but on bright days enjoy the delightful garden, the focal point of which is a wonderful old fig tree. One may reflect over good refreshment here that Dunwich is a fascinating and historic place of great charm. The famous Bird Reserve of Minsmere is only a short walk along the coast.

THE SWAN,
Low Street, Hoxne, Eye,
Suffolk IP21 5AS

Tel: 01379 668275
Fax: 01379 668168

No accommodation; Free House with real ale; Historic interest; Children and pets welcome; Bar meals, restaurant Saturday evening and Sunday lunch; Car park (40); Eye 3 miles.

It was in this Suffolk village that St Edmund was captured and slain by the Danes in 869AD, but any Scandinavian encountered today is likely to be of the more peaceable tourist variety, for there is much of interest in this historic area. Those in need of refreshment while exploring it are recommended to the Swan, where an excellent range of bar food is served, including freshly cut sandwiches, omelettes etc as well as daily specials, all of which can be enjoyed outside in fine weather, perhaps while spectating at a leisurely game of croquet. This Grade II* Listed building has been carefully preserved and retains many original features.

THE CROWN INN,
Snape,
Suffolk IP17 1SL

Tel: 01728 688324

3 bedrooms, all with private bathroom; Adnams House with real ale; Historic interest; Bar lunches, restaurant evenings only; Car park (40); Saxmundham 3 miles; ££.

A friendly little country pub, the Crown dates back to the fifteenth century and lies just a short distance from the world-renowned concert hall at Snape Maltings. The traditional character of an English country inn has been maintained, with an abundance of beams, open fires and an inglenook fireplace. Guest accommodation is fully en suite, with central heating. The food emphasis is very much on fresh produce, carefully prepared and imaginatively presented, and as well as a range of well-kept ales, the bar offers a superb selection of wines by the glass and bottle. *Which? Pub Guide, Good Pub Guide.*

BULL HOTEL,
Market Hill, Woodbridge,
Suffolk IP12 4LR

Tel: 01394 382089
Fax: 01394 384902

29 bedrooms, 26 with private bathroom; Free House with real ale; Historic interest; Bar food, restaurant evenings only; Car park (10); Ipswich 8 miles; £££.

The River Deben was the artery of Woodbridge's commercial success for a thousand years. The town built ships for the Royal Navy in the Stuart era and the river was a haven for the more infamous smugglers of the following century. Today, the river is alive with leisure craft whilst the town's picturesque old houses slumber peacefully in their dotage. Present-day visitors to this 16th century former posting house may relax and choose fine food from an extensive à la carte or table d'hôte menu in the charming Gallery Restaurant or try the comprehensive bill of fare available in the bars. Well-appointed guest rooms have bath/showers and WCs en suite as well as television, direct-dial telephones and central heating. ETB 🛏🛏🛏.

THE OLD BULL HOTEL AND RESTAURANT,
Church Street, Sudbury,
Suffolk CO10 6BL

Tel: 01787 374120
Fax: 01787 379044

10 bedrooms, all with private bathroom or shower; Historic interest; Children welcome; Restaurant meals; Car park (17); Cambridge 23 miles, Ipswich 16, Colchester 13; £/££££.

Originally a 16th century beamed coaching inn, now lovingly converted and restored into a guest house and restaurant, the Old Bull Hotel retains that olde worlde charm with a relaxed atmosphere. Each bedroom has a unique character and charm and offers colour television, satellite, telephone and tea and coffee facilities; most are fully en suite. The intimate beamed restaurant offers a bistro-style menu with a wide selection of dishes prepared by the chef proprietor. It is situated in the ancient market town of Sudbury, birthplace of Gainsborough, and is surrounded by many places of interest. Ideal centre for touring the area. Most credit cards accepted. *ETB* 🌙🌙🌙, *AA and RAC Listed.*

Surrey

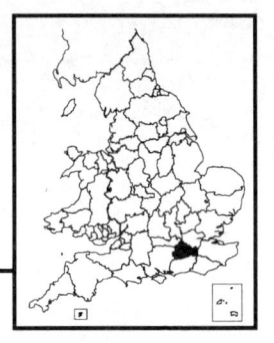

PRINCE OF WALES,
West End, Esher,
Surrey KT10 8LA

Tel & Fax: 01372 465483

No accommodation; Chef & Brewer House with real ale; Historic interest; Bar meals; Car park; Kingston 5 miles.

West End, hidden away between Esher and Cobham, is a truly charming English village. This picturesque English pub is situated directly opposite the village green and duckpond. Dating back to the mid 19th century, with exposed beams, grandfather clock and log fires, this ex-malting house and pub still retains a wealth of character as well as plenty of old-fashioned hospitality. The garden and patio are ideal for leisurely summer days. As well as a wide choice of cask conditioned ales, lagers and soft drinks, there is an extensive blackboard menu which features imaginative pub food, all beautifully presented at reasonable prices. A wide range of quality wines has been chosen to accompany the food, and all are available by the bottle or glass. There are over 40 main courses to choose from, and an interesting selection of hot and cold snacks is also available. Desserts are all equally tempting and delicious. The Prince of Wales is open all day every day for food and drink. Local attractions include Hampton Court Palace, Sandown Racecourse and Claremont Landscaped Gardens.

108   *Suffolk / Surrey*

CHASE LODGE,
10 Park Road, Hampton Wick,
Kingston-upon-Thames, Surrey KT1 4AS

Tel: 0181-943 1862
Fax: 0181-943 9363

11 bedrooms, all with private bathroom; Free House; Children and pets welcome; Bar and restaurant meals; London 10 miles; ££££.

An award-winning hotel with style and elegance set in tranquil surroundings at affordable prices. Quality en suite bedrooms. Full English breakfast and à la carte menu. Licensed bar. Wedding receptions catered for; honeymoon suite available. Natural health therapies offered. Easy access to Kingston town centre and all major transport links; 20 minutes from Heathrow Airport. All major credit cards accepted. ❄❄❄❄ *Highly Commended, AA QQQQ Selected, RAC Highly Acclaimed, Les Routiers.*

RED LION INN,
Shamley Green, Near Guildford,
Surrey GU5 0UB

Tel: 01483 892202
Fax: 01483 893404

4 bedrooms, all with private bathroom; Carlsberg Tetley House; Historic interest; Children welcome; Bar and restaurant meals; Car park (30); Guildford 4 miles; £££.

Surrounded by verdant Surrey countryside, this unpretentious village inn stands on the green, offering a remarkable range of reasonably priced dishes in its restaurant and carvery, while the bistro menu presents a wide selection of interesting home-made dishes. It is little wonder that this friendly pub, which has its origins in the 18th century when it was a coaching inn, has become so popular with the citizens of nearby Guildford who come here regularly, with traditional ales from the barrel in great demand. This is a lovely place in which to spend a few days, and comfortable en suite accommodation is available with a full English breakfast included in the most reasonable room rate. *Egon Ronay, Good Food Guide.*

ANCHOR HOTEL,
Church Square, Shepperton-on-Thames, Surrey TW17 9JY

Tel: 01932 221618
Fax: 01932 252235

29 bedrooms, all with private bathroom; Free House with real ale; Bar food, restaurant evenings only; Car park (20); London 15 miles; ££££.

One of our most famous and traditional inns, this fascinating hostelry has opened its great oak doors to welcome guests for 400 years and still retains its old world charm. Real ale and a selection of other beers and lagers makes this a popular meeting place, whilst dining here in such a relaxed atmosphere is a joy of its own. A tempting range of bar meals is on offer every lunchtime and in the evening. First-class and admirably modernised accommodation is available in the form of bedrooms with en suite facilities, colour television, direct-dial telephone, and tea and coffee makers. As the inn's impressive brochure states: "Through the portals of this Inn have passed the Rich, the Famous, Prime Ministers, Statesmen, Pugilists, Notorious Personages of Dubious Character, Wenches, Visitors from the Colonies (including the Americas), Sporting Gentry, Vagabonds, Glamorous Artists from the World of Motion Pictures, but the most important of all is You!" *Egon Ronay Recommended.*

East Sussex

BULL HOTEL,
2 High Street, Ditchling, East Sussex BN6 8SY

Tel: 01273 843147

4 bedrooms, all with private bathroom; Real ale; Historic interest; Children welcome, dogs on lead only; Bar and restaurant meals; Car park; Burgess Hill 3 miles; ££.

An attractive old black-and-white hostelry on the corner of the High Street of an attractive downland village, the Bull dates from the 16th century and retains much of its original character, a virtue of which the present licensee is obviously enthusiastically aware, as witness the splendid main bar with its open fireplace, beams and pillars. In good weather, refreshment may be enjoyed outside, either on the terrace or at bench tables on the spacious lawns. An ideal base for a country holiday with the sea within easy driving distance, the hotel has single and double en suite bedrooms at most reasonable rates.

THE CRICKETERS ARMS,
Berwick Village, Polegate, East Sussex BN26 6SP

Tel: 01323 870469

No accommodation; Harveys of Lewes House with real ale; Bar meals; Car park; Eastbourne 5 miles, Alfriston 1.

Created in the dim and distant past from a row of flint cottages, this charming and popular inn lies just off the A27 in a tranquil rural setting. From the attractive gardens there are open views of the Downs, whilst, within the bar, the views are both of an aesthetic and practical nature — and delightful ones too. There are three separate rooms with two open log fires and, wonder of wonders, beer is drawn straight from the barrel. Bar meals are available, with home-made specials and fresh fish served each lunchtime and evening. A lovely country hostelry with a traditional atmosphere, the Cricketers is still a favourite venue with coast-bound family parties and also with downland walkers. The pub that is still a *pub*.

THE ROSE AND CROWN INN,
Mayfield,
East Sussex TN20 6TE
Tel and Fax: 01435 872200

4 bedrooms, all with private bathroom; Free House with real ale; Historic interest; Children welcome; Bar and restaurant meals; Tunbridge Wells 8 miles; ££/£££.

This famous inn sits on the village green of the historic and picturesque village of Mayfield. Dating back to 1546, it has unspoilt oak-beamed bars with log fires. Excellent real ales and quality bar meals are served, or you may choose to dine in the informal candlelit restaurant which serves award-winning food and excellent wines. The luxury period bedrooms have en suite bathrooms, central heating, colour television, radio alarms, hairdryers, tea and coffee making facilities and trouser presses. ❦❦❦❦ Commended, AA QQQQ Selected and Rosette for Food, Egon Ronay, Good Pub Guide.

THE HORSESHOE INN,
Windmill Hill, Herstmonceux,
East Sussex BN27 4RU
Tel: 01323 833265
Fax: 01323 832001

15 bedrooms, all with private bathroom; Free House with real ale; Children welcome, pets allowed in non-food areas; Bar and restaurant meals; Car park (100); Hailsham 5 miles, Herstmonceux 1; £/££.

This Elizabethan-style coaching inn is set in a rural location and enjoys picturesque views over the surrounding countryside. Both of the oak-beamed bars have the same friendly atmosphere — Squires with its wood-burning stove or the Long Bar which is very popular with the locals. Families are welcome in the restaurant which is open lunchtimes and evenings, and bar meals and snacks are also available. The cosy bedrooms are well equipped and are offered at most reasonable rates, should you wish to explore the many attractions of the area. Weddings, conferences and other functions can be expertly catered for. Major credit cards accepted. ❦❦❦. **See also Colour Advertisement on page 5.**

West Sussex

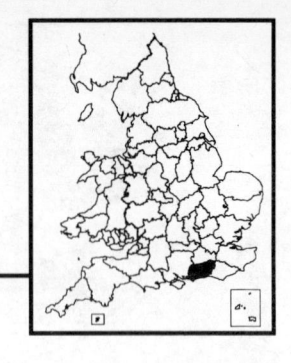

THE ANGEL HOTEL,
North Street, Midhurst,
West Sussex GU29 9DN

Tel: 01730 812421
Fax: 01730 815928

25 bedrooms, all with private bathroom; Free House with real ale; Historic interest; Children welcome; Bar and restaurant meals; Car park (40); Chichester 11 miles; ££££.

In the heart of the lush and leafy West Sussex countryside, this 16th century coaching inn extends a high standard of traditional English hospitality in a lovely English setting. Centrally situated in a historic market town, the Angel invites guests to drink, dine and dally awhile. The informal brasserie features fresh seafoods and hearty roasts in its daily-changing menu, and the elegant Cowdray Room restaurant has won many accolades for its high standards of presentation and service, its imaginative menus supported by an intriguing and unusual wine list. Popular for meetings and social functions, the hotel has individually furnished bedrooms, some with four-posters, all with bathrooms en suite, colour television and direct-dial telephone. ♛♛♛♛ Commended, AA Three Rosettes, Cesar Award 1995, Good Hotel Guide.

THE BAT AND BALL,
Newpound Lane, Wisborough Green,
West Sussex RH14 0EH

Tel: 01403 700313

No accommodation; King & Barnes House with real ale; Historic interest; Children welcome; Bar and restaurant meals; Car park (50); Billinghurst 2 miles.

It is with some pride that Jenny and Roger Hunt have developed such a happy family atmosphere at this friendly, rural West Sussex inn. The fact that children are really welcomed enables parents to relax to the full whilst the youngsters discard (wolf!) their coke and crisps to disport themselves in the play area in the garden. The inn stands in some six acres of grounds, some of which is let off for caravans and camping. Within the convivial bar there is a comfortable seating area for eating. The menu is simple but offers a more than reasonable choice of dishes, including those that invariably appeal to children. A pool room is a popular feature.

NOTE

All the information in this book is given in good faith in the belief that it is correct. However, the publishers cannot guarantee the facts given in these pages, neither are they responsible for changes in policy, ownership or terms that may take place after the date of going to press. Readers should always satisfy themselves that the facilities they require are available and that the terms, if quoted, still apply.

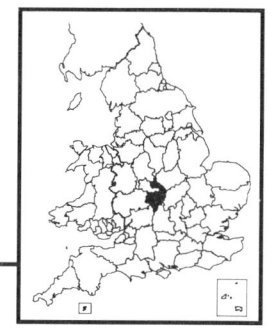

Warwickshire

HALFORD BRIDGE INN,
Fosseway, (A429) Halford, Shipston-on-Stour, Warwickshire CV36 5BN
Tel and Fax: 01789 740382

6 bedrooms, 3 with showers; Free House; Historic interest; Bar and restaurant meals; Car park (40); NEC and Airport 25 miles, Banbury 12, Stratford-upon-Avon 6; M40 (Junction 12) 7.

On the principle that you can't have too much of a good thing Tony and Greta Westwood, proprietors of this charming sixteenth century inn, keep their kitchens open seven days a week to provide sustenance to regulars, residents and hungry passers-by. A wide range of good hot and cold bar food is available, in addition to the excellent fare offered at reasonable prices in the restaurant. Good home cooking is the speciality here, with home-made pickles, sauces, pies etc, as well as fresh vegetables whenever possible. All the comfortably furnished bedrooms have colour television, and tourists who must keep an eye on their budgets as well as the scenery will find them good value for money. Ample parking. ETB ✹✹, *Les Routiers, AA QQ, RAC Recommended, CAMRA, Association of Catering Excellence.* **See also Colour Advertisement on page 6.**

THE WHITE BEAR,
High Street, Shipston-on-Stour, Warwickshire CV36 4AJ
Tel and Fax: 01608 661558

10 bedrooms, all with private bathroom; Bass House with real ale; Historic interest; Children and pets welcome; Bar and restaurant meals; Car park (20); Banbury 12 miles; £.

A recommended port of call in a beautiful touring area, this charming hostelry offers simple and friendly bar service. A wide range of food is available daily in both the bars and the bistro-style restaurant, accompanied by an extensive range of refreshments including real ales and a thoughtfully selected wine list. The friendly staff will do everything possible to ensure that a stay here, however long or short, is a real pleasure. With ten well-appointed guest rooms, all with en suite bath or shower, colour television, telephone and tea/coffee making facilities, this is an ideal base for exploring the many places of interest within easy reach. ✹✹✹, *Bass Best Pub Food National Award*

Stratford-upon-Avon, Warwickshire

WHITE HORSE INN,
Banbury Road, Ettington, Near Stratford-upon-Avon, Warwickshire CV37 7SU
Tel: 01789 740641

4 bedrooms, all ensuite; Real ale; Historic interest; Bar and restaurant meals; Car park (30); Oxford 34 miles, Birmingham 30, Stratford-upon-Avon 6; ££.

What could be more delightful for a holiday or short break in Shakespeare country than a stop-over in this lovely old inn, already conjuring up the atmosphere of days gone by with its furnishings, oak beams, and the warmth of its welcome. Guests can enjoy a glass of real ale with their lunch, and for those who choose to stay longer, the Inn's restaurant serves fine fare in the evening. There is a sun patio and beer garden in which to take advantage of warmer weather. The White Horse's accommodation means that tired visitors may take full advantage of its location, six miles from Stratford and close to Warwick Castle and the Cotswolds. Also near to NEC Birmingham and the Royal Showground at Stoneleigh. All rooms are tastefully furnished and en suite, with colour television, central heating and tea/coffee making facilities. Weekend break reductions from November to April. Proprietors Roy and Val Blower. *ETB* 👑👑.

Wiltshire

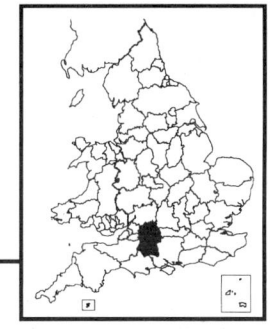

THE CROWN AT ALDBOURNE,
The Square, Aldbourne, Near Marlborough, Wiltshire SN8 2DU
Tel: 01672 540214

2 bedrooms, both with private bathroom; Courage House with real ale; Historic interest; Children welcome; Bar and restaurant meals; Car park (20); Marlborough 6 miles; ££.

Few would dispute Aldbourne's claim to be one of the prettiest villages in Wiltshire, and the Crown's location in the village square, overlooking the duckpond, affords patrons ample opportunity to appreciate fully its charming surroundings. Well kept real ales on handpump and a first-rate bar food menu are served with friendly efficiency, and a genuinely warm welcome is accorded to locals and visitors alike. Just a few minutes from the M4 and just over an hour from central London, the Crown is ideal as a base for touring or as a home-from-home for the business person who wants to avoid the inflated prices and pretentiousness of many modern chain hotels. *Egon Ronay.*

CASTLE INN,
Castle Combe, Chippenham, Wiltshire SN14 7HN
Tel: 01249 783030
Fax: 01249 782315

7 bedrooms, all with private bathroom; Free House with real ale; Historic interest; Children welcome; Bar meals, restaurant evenings only; Car park; Bath 9 miles, Chippenham 4; ££££.

Standing proudly in the market place of what is regarded by many as England's prettiest village, the Castle Inn typifies all that is finest in the hallowed traditions of English inn-keeping. Under the expert guidance of a talented and imaginative chef, it has gained an enviable reputation for its fine English cooking based on the freshest of ingredients, meals being taken in the elegant restaurant or in the informal surroundings of the bar. Needless to say, the range of refreshments on offer includes some excellent real ales, plus a good selection of lagers, spirits and wines. Accommodation is of the same high standard, two of the seven tastefully furnished bedrooms featuring private whirlpool baths, and all having a full range of modern conveniences. *AA*** and 2 Rosettes, RAC Credit to Industry Award 1995.*

HORSE AND GROOM INN,
The Street, Charlton, Near Malmesbury, Wiltshire SN16 9DL
Tel: 01666 823904
Fax: 01666 823390

3 bedrooms, all with private bathroom; Free House with real ale; Historic interest; Children and pets welcome; Bar and restaurant meals; Car park (50); Malmesbury 2 miles; ££££.

Set in an extensive garden dominated by great lime trees, this 16th century coaching inn built of mellow Cotswold stone paints a pretty picture, with its colourful window boxes and hanging baskets. Quite unspoilt, it has a cosy bar cheered by the hospitality shown by proprietors, Philip Gilder and Nichola King, (and a roaring log fire in winter), where simple meals and a selection of local real ales is served. In the matter of food, a high reputation has been acquired for the comprehensive à la carte menu. Three guest rooms are luxuriously appointed with great attention given to detail, particularly to harmonious colour schemes and such thoughtful touches as toiletries, bathrobes and mineral water. *AA QQQQ, Johansens, Egon Ronay.*

METHUEN ARMS HOTEL,
Corsham,
Wiltshire SN13 0HB

Tel: 01249 714867
Fax: 01249 712004

24 bedrooms, all with private bathroom; Gibbs Mew House with real ale; Historic interest; Children and pets welcome; Bar and restaurant meals; Car park; Chippenham 4 miles; £££.

As a centre from which to explore the Cotswolds and Bath or as a delightful spot to stop for refreshment on a day out, the welcoming Methuen Arms is well worth acquaintance. A combination of 14th century and Georgian architecture, it is highly recommended for its cuisine and its comfortable accommodation; the latter comprising beautifully decorated bedrooms, all with en suite facilities, colour television, direct-dial telephone, and tea and coffee makers. The Lounge Bar and Long Room offer a tempting variety of meals and snacks, and in the Winter's Court Restaurant guests may choose from an inspired collection of simple and classical dishes. ❦❦❦❦, *AA and RAC* **.

THE WHITE HART AT FORD,
Ford, Near Chippenham,
Wiltshire SN14 8RP

Tel: 01249 782213
Fax: 01249 783075

11 bedrooms, all with private bathroom; Free House with real ale; Historic interest;Children and pets welcome; Bar and restaurant meals; Car park (100); Chippenham 5 miles; ££££.

"INN OF THE YEAR". Reputedly built in 1553 and listed as being of architectural and historical interest, this lovely old stone-built pub rests beside a trout stream which meanders through the surrounding meadow and looks serenely over the lush Weavern Valley. With a wealth of beams, log fires and old-world charm, the bar has one of the largest selections of real ales in Wiltshire and traditional 'scrumpy' is also served. The cuisine is of first-rate standard and the Riverside Restaurant is widely acclaimed. Luxurious four-poster rooms are included in the guest accommodation at this idyllic retreat and all rooms are provided with bathrooms en suite,colour television, radio and tea-making facilities. ❦❦❦, *AA* **, *Les Routiers, Johansens.*

PUBLISHER'S NOTE

While every effort is made to ensure accuracy, we regret that FHG Publications cannot accept responsibility for errors, omissions or misrepresentations in our entries or any consequences thereof. Prices in particular should be checked because we go to press early. We will follow up complaints but cannot act as arbiters or agents for either party.

THE LAMB AT HINDON,
Hindon, Near Salisbury, Wiltshire SP3 6DP

Tel: 01747 820573
Fax: 01747 820605

13 bedrooms, all with private bathroom; Free House with real ale; Historic interest; Children and pets welcome; Bar and restaurant meals; Car park (20); Bath 28 miles, Salisbury 16; ££.

The fascinating history of this ancient inn is related in its brochure, which reveals among other intriguing facts that it was once the headquarters of a notorious smuggler. No such unlawful goings-on today — just good old-fashioned hospitality in the finest traditions of English innkeeping. Charmingly furnished single, double and four-poster bedrooms provide overnight guests with cosy country-style accommodation, and the needs of the inner man (or woman!) will be amply satisfied by the varied, good quality meals served in the bar and restaurant. Real ales can be enjoyed in the friendly bar, where crackling log fires bestow charm and atmosphere as well as warmth. ♛♛♛♛, AA** and Courtesy & Care Award, RAC **.

THE OLD MILL AT HARNHAM,
Town Path, Salisbury, Wiltshire SP2 8EU

Tel: 01722 322364/327517
Fax: 01722 333367

11 bedrooms, all with private bathroom; Free House with real ale; Historic interest; Children welcome; Bar and restaurant meals; Car park (20); Southampton 21 miles; ££.

With delightful riverside gardens, this tranquil hostelry has immense character and an interesting history. It originates from the early 18th century when it was built as a warehouse attached to an ancient papermaking mill with three water wheels taking water from the River Nadder. The three races can be seen today coursing through the restaurant, the setting for the presentation of superb meals in the distinctive English tradition. Snacks, real ales and malt whiskies are served in a typical country pub bar. Salisbury is conveniently near and, indeed, there are fine views of the cathedral from the inn. A peaceful and rewarding place in which to stay, the Old Mill has excellently appointed bedrooms, all with private bathroom. ♛♛♛ *Commended, AA**.*

THE COMPASSES INN,
Chicksgrove, Tisbury, Near Salisbury, Wiltshire SP3 6NB
Tel: 01722 714318

3 bedrooms, 2 with private bathroom; Free House with real ale; Historic interest; Children welcome; Bar and restaurant meals; Car park (25); Salisbury 11 miles, Tisbury 2; £.

If a visit to the historic city of Salisbury is on your itinerary, then make a slight detour to the pretty village of Chicksgrove where this Grade II Listed thatched freehouse provides rest and refreshment. The inn's history can be traced as far back as the 14th century, and while facilities have been brought right up-to-date, traditional furnishings and good old-fashioned hospitality remind one of a more leisurely age. A fine selection of ales, wines and spirits are the perfect accompaniment to one's choice from the tasty and nutritious menus available at lunchtime and in the evenings. Bed and breakfast accommodation is available at rates guaranteed to keep one's bank manager happy. *Egon Ronay.*

THE BECKFORD ARMS,
Fonthill Gifford, Tisbury, Salisbury, Wiltshire SP3 6PX
Tel: 01747 870385

8 bedrooms, all with private bathroom; Real ale; Historic interest; Bar and restaurant meals; Car park (40); Shaftesbury 7 miles; ££.

This delightful 18th century country inn is highly recommended for its beautiful setting, stylish interiors, gardens, friendly atmosphere and excellent restaurant featuring local produce, imaginatively prepared. Completely refurbished and extended, the Beckford Arms offers a relaxing and comfortable location for walks through an area of outstanding natural beauty or a superb base for many tourist spots including Salisbury, Stonehenge, Bath, New Forest and the South Coast. There are eight tastefully decorated bedrooms, all with colour television and en suite facilities. The Beckford Arms is conveniently situated halfway between London and Plymouth, two miles off the A303 and two miles from Tisbury station. *Highly Commended, Egon Ronay Recommended.*

QUEEN'S HEAD,
Broad Chalke, Near Salisbury, Wiltshire SP5 5EN
Tel and Fax: 01722 780344

4 bedrooms, all with private bathroom; Free House with real ale; Historic interest; Bar and restaurant meals; Car park (40); Bournemouth 30 miles, Salisbury 7; ££.

Just seven miles from Salisbury yet in a lovely rural setting, the old world charm of this inn has been in no way marred by its careful upgrading. En suite guest rooms are spacious and well designed, and each is equipped with colour television, tea-making facilities and telephone. A comprehensive menu operates throughout the inn plus daily "specials". The quality and variety of the food offered is excellent and you can take your meal in the quaintly traditional bar or in one of the separate dining lounges, one of which is non-smoking. The inn is personally run by Michael and Norma Craggs. *WCTB*. **See also Colour Advertisement on page 6.**

OLD BELL INN,
2 Saint Ann Street, Salisbury,
Wiltshire SP1 2DN

Tel: 01722 327958
Fax: 01722 411485

10 bedrooms, all with private bathroom; Free House; Bar lunches; Southampton 23 miles, Amesbury 8; £.

The fourteenth and twentieth centuries meet well at this enchanting hostelry — the former offering old timber beams, huge log fires and medieval atmosphere, the latter providing the comfort of full central heating and spacious guest rooms with en suite facilities. Double and twin rooms are available, and two especially charming rooms have stately four-poster beds. The Old Bell stands adjacent to Salisbury Cathedral, offering extensive views of the Cathedral Close and conveniently situated for all the amenities of the town. Lunch is served in the bar between 12 noon and 3.30pm, when a good range of hot and cold dishes is offered; the wine bar is open all day.

ROSE AND CROWN HOTEL,
Ashbury, Swindon,
Wiltshire SN6 8NA

Tel: 01793 710222
Fax: 01793 710029

11 bedrooms; Arkell's House with real ale; Children welcome; Bar and restaurant meals; Car park; Swindon 7 miles; ££.

In the centre of a picturesque village, this welcoming inn possesses the facilities of a first-class hotel. Beautifully decorated throughout, it has friendly bars, one with a log fire, where appetising snack meals are served at lunchtime and in the evening, whilst the jewel in the Rose and Crown is undoubtedly its fine restaurant which is well recommended for its excellent à la carte menu, service and surroundings. However this happy retreat has many other attributes: guest rooms represent the acme of modern comfort, superb conference facilities exist, and for recreation there is a games room.

East Yorkshire

THE FLEECE INN,
Bishop Wilton, Near York,
East Yorkshire YO4 1RU

Tel: 01759 368251

7 bedrooms; Free House with real ale; Bar food, restaurant evenings only; Car park (20); York 10 miles; ££.

Set in the picturesque and unspoilt village of Bishop Wilton on the edge of the Yorkshire Wolds, the Fleece Inn is a fine touring base, with much to see locally including the City of York and the East Coast. And after a long day's walk on the moors, what could be more relaxing than to return to a satisfying, freshly prepared meal and a glass of good traditional hand-pulled beer? The Fleece has a wide range of good beers and fine wines to be enjoyed on their own or with your bar meal — served at lunchtimes and in the evenings — or your dinner in the dining room. Overnight accommodation is available in seven cheerful and spotlessly clean bedrooms, to be followed by a hearty breakfast to set you up for the next day.

North Yorkshire

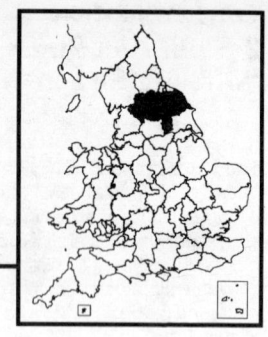

**THE TRADDOCK HOTEL,
Austwick, Near Settle,
North Yorkshire LA2 8BY**

Tel and Fax: 015242 51224

11 bedrooms, all with private bathroom; Free House; Historic interest; Children welcome; Restaurant meals; Car park (22); Settle 4 miles; ££.

"Sit back, relax and be pampered!" is the motto of Frances and Richard Michaelis, hosts at this delightful hotel in the Yorkshire Dales National Park. Set in a picturesque, unspoilt Dales village, The Traddock offers a real Yorkshire welcome, with open fires, and delectable food and wine served in its pretty, oak-beamed dining room. All the comfortable bedrooms are en suite, with colour television, direct-dial telephone, electric blankets and tea and coffee making facilities. The Traddock day starts with a good breakfast, which includes local farm sausages, free-range eggs and home-made marmalade. Afterwards, you could either enjoy the lovely countryside or visit a local attraction. There's a Falconry Centre and two spectacular caves nearby, and the Lake District and coast are also easily reached. Golf, fishing and pony trekking are available in the area."This is a highly recommended Yorkshire gem!". ♛♛♛ *Commended,* AA/RAC**.

Please mention
Recommended WAYSIDE & COUNTRY INNS
when seeking refreshment or
accommodation at a Hotel
mentioned in these pages.

THE BUCK INN,
Thornton Watlass, Near Bedale, Ripon, North Yorkshire HG4 4AH

Tel: 01677 422461
Fax: 01677 422447

7 bedrooms, 5 with private facilities; Free House with real ale; Children welcome; Bar food and dining area; Car park (25); Ripon 11 miles, Northallerton 9; ££.

Friendly country inn overlooking the delightful cricket green in a peaceful village just five minutes away from the A1. Newly refurbished bedrooms, most with en suite facilities, ensure that a stay at The Buck is both comfortable and relaxing. Delicious freshly cooked bar meals are served lunchtimes and evenings in the cosy bar and dining area. On Sundays a traditional roast with Yorkshire pudding is on the menu. Excellent hand-pulled Theakstons, John Smiths, Black Sheep and Tetley cask beer is available, as is a regular guest ale. This is an ideal centre for exploring Herriot country. There is a children's playground in the secluded beer garden where quoits are also played. Private fly fishing available on River Ure and five golf courses within 20 minutes' drive. ☙☙☙ Commended, *Good Pub Guide, AA*, CAMRA Good Pub Food Guide, Beer, Bed and Breakfast, Room at the Inn.*

NEW INN,
Clapham, Near Settle, North Yorkshire LA2 8HH

Tel: 015242 51203
Fax: 015242 51496

13 bedrooms, all with private bathroom; Free House; Historic interest; Bar and restaurant meals; Kendal 21 miles, Skipton 21.

Keith and Barbara Mannion invite you to their friendly eighteenth century residential coaching inn in the picturesque Dales village of Clapham. Ideal centre for walking the three peaks of Ingleborough, Pen-y-Ghent and Whernside. All rooms have full en suite facilities, colour television and tea/coffee facilities. Enjoy good wholesome Yorkshire food in our restaurant, or bar meals in either of our two bars. Dogs welcome. Ring Barbara for details of special mid-week breaks. *ETB* ☙☙☙ *Commended.*

THE NEW INN,
Cropton, Near Pickering,
North Yorkshire YO18 8HH

Tel: 01751 417330
Fax: 01751 417310

7 bedrooms, all with private bathroom; Free House with real ale; Historic interest; Children welcome; Bar and restaurant meals; Car park (50); Pickering 4 miles; £.

Close to the Moors, this small, relaxed, family-run inn prides itself on offering quality food and accommodation in an informal atmosphere. Guests are encouraged to visit the inn's very own brewery which is located in the grounds and provides some excellent real ales and stout including the legendary "Cropton 2 Pints". Accommodation is available in attractively furnished double or twin rooms, each with en suite bathroom, central heating and tea/coffee making facilities. The elegant Victorian Restaurant serves tradtional Yorkshire dishes, while good-value bar meals are available in the newly restored village bar and conservatory. This is superb walking country, and the Inn is within easy travelling distance of many places of interest. 👑👑👑 Commended, Rural Pub of the Year 1995.

TEMPEST ARMS HOTEL & RESTAURANT,
Elslack, Skipton,
North Yorkshire BD23 3AY

Tel: 01282 842450
Fax: 01282 843331

10 bedrooms, all with private bathroom; Jennings House with real ale; Historic interest; Children welcome; Bar and restaurant meals; Car park; Skipton 4 miles; ££££.

Situated just off the A56 Earby-Skipton road, and originally a coaching inn, the Tempest Arms has been greatly extended but retains much of its original character. The traditional bar offers a wide range of Jennings cask ales, and is firmly established as a well-used local. In the intimate surroundings of the restaurant choose from the extensive à la carte menu featuring many English and Continental dishes, or why not dine in the comfortable bar where fish "specials" are listed on a blackboard, or enjoy the chef's recommendations which take advantage of fresh seasonal produce and local specialities. The wine list has been carefully selected to complement the menu, with a wide range in terms of price and product. The 10 well appointed bedrooms provide the overnight guest with comfort and warmth. 👑👑👑.

TENNANT ARMS,
Kilnsey, Near Grassington,
North Yorkshire BD23 5PS
Tel: 01756 752301

10 bedrooms, all with private bathroom; Free House with real ale; Historic interest; Children welcome; Bar and restaurant meals; Grassington 3 miles; £.

Friendly 17th century country inn hotel nestling under the famous Kilnsey Crag in the heart of Wharfedale, between the picturesque villages of Grassington and Kettlewell. All ten bedrooms are en suite. The cosy bars with log fires and beams serve delicious, individually prepared bar meals and hand-pulled ales; or dine in our beautiful pine-panelled dining room and choose from our extensive à la carte menu. Ideal for exploring the Dales. New proprietors, Mr and Mrs N. Dean will give you a warm welcome. ☆☆☆ *Commended.*

THE FORESTERS ARMS,
20 Main Street, Grassington, Skipton,
North Yorkshire BD23 5AA
Tel: 01756 752349

7 bedrooms, one with private bathroom; Free House with real ale; Historic interest; Children and pets welcome; Bar meals; Car park (3); Skipton 8 miles; £.

Once an old coaching inn, the Foresters Arms is situated in the heart of the Yorkshire Dales, and is an ideal centre for walking or touring. It has been a family-run business for over 25 years and offers comfortable accommodation in bedrooms with TV and tea/coffee making facilities. Hand-pulled Tetley and Theakstons beer is available in the friendly bar, where a good selection of food is served at lunchtimes and in the evenings. Please contact Rita Richardson for details. Tourist Board Listed Approved. **See also Colour Advertisement on page 6.**

LONG ASHES INN,
Threshfield, Grassington, Near Skipton,
North Yorkshire BD23 5PN
Tel: 01756 752434
Fax: 01756 752876

4 bedrooms, all with private bathroom; Real ale; Children welcome; Bar food and dining area; Car park; Skipton 9 miles, Grassington 3; £££.

This traditional old Dales inn set in picturesque Wharfedale in the Yorkshire Dales National Park has recently been extensively and sympathetically refurbished to a very high standard, with completely refitted bedrooms and central heating. Each of the bedrooms is elegantly furnished and has its own en suite bathroom, trouser press, hairdryer, tea and coffee making tray, direct-dial telephone, fresh flowers and a bowl of fruit. The beds are extremely comfortable and the honeymoon suite has a lovely four-poster. Overnight guests have free use of the adjacent leisure centre with heated indoor swimming pool, jacuzzi , solarium, sauna, etc. It is ideally situated for exploring the Dales. There is a full menu of interesting dishes prepared by our own chef, which you can enhance with a bottle of wine from our rather special wine list.

MILBURN ARMS HOTEL,
Rosedale Abbey, Pickering,
North Yorkshire YO18 8RA
Tel and Fax: 01751 417312

11 bedrooms, all with private bathroom; Free House with real ale; Historic interest; Bar food, restaurant evenings only; Car park; Kirkbymoorside 6 miles; £££.

Performing a dual function as country hotel and village pub, the charming Milburn Arms is a haven of comfort in the tranquil heart of the North Yorkshire Moors, amidst rambling footpaths and beautiful scenery. Particular pride is taken in the excellent cuisine, with the emphasis on British cooking presented with flair and imagination by chef, Richard Guitton. In the convivial bar one may enjoy good ale (and perhaps a bar meal or snack), a chat with the locals and maybe a game of darts or dominoes The hotel is attractively furnished throughout, en suite guest rooms being appointed with colour television, telephone, beverage making facilities and complimentary toiletries. Owners, Terry and Joan Bentley,will be happy to help plan activities and sightseeing. ☆☆☆☆ *Commended,* AA Two Rosettes.

MAYPOLE INN,
Long Preston, Skipton,
North Yorkshire BD23 4PH
Tel: 01729 840219

6 bedrooms, all with private bathroom; Whitbread House with real ale; Historic interest; Children welcome; Bar and restaurant meals; Car park (25); Settle 4 miles; £.

With a menu to suit all tastes and pockets, from freshly cut sandwiches, salads and filled baked potatoes to traditional favourites such as fish, lasagne and steaks, this friendly inn is understandably popular at lunchtimes and in the evenings. It has been providing hospitality and good cheer for over 300 years, and prides itself on maintaining the high standards which has gained it such a fine reputation over the centuries. Hand-pulled traditional ales are a speciality here, and can be enjoyed beside a crackling open fire, or outside overlooking the village green in finer weather. Spick-and-span bedrooms of varying sizes offer overnight accommodation at extremely attractive rates. ♕♕♕ *Commended, CAMRA.*

THE WHITE SWAN AT PICKERING,
Market Place, Pickering,
North Yorkshire YO18 7AA
Tel: 01751 472288
Fax: 01751 475554

12 bedrooms, all with private bathroom; Free House with real ale; Historic interest; Children and pets welcome; Bar and restaurant meals; Car park (25); Scarborough 16 miles; £££.

One of Yorkshire's oldest coaching inns, the White Swan is a recommended base for a tour of moorland, coast or the city of York. Its attributes are many with its wine list a 'Mecca' for connoisseurs. Worthy of the fine cellar is the daily changing menu in the impressive restaurant, famed for its immaculate presentation of real food, the chefs making skilful use of local produce in the memorable cuisine — and those puddings! In the cosy bar with its log fire, a large selection of dishes is available to complement excellent Black Sheep ale. First-rate accommodation comprises rooms with en suite facilities, colour television, direct-dial telephone and tea and coffee tray whilst the exquisite Ryedale Suite provides that extra touch of luxury. ♕♕♕♕ *Commended, RAC and AA **, Johansens, Egon Ronay.*

FALCON INN,
Whitby Road, Cloughton, Near Scarborough,
North Yorkshire YO13 0DY
Tel: 01723 870717

8 bedrooms, all with private bathroom; Free House with real ale; Bar and restaurant meals; Car park; Scarborough 4 miles; ££.

Standing in its own seven acres of pasture and woodland with its southerly aspect towards the sea, this former coaching inn has recently been refurbished. The old coach house has been converted into the Carvery, leaving the original inside stonework and most of the beams exposed. A wide selection of home-cooked English fare is served either here or in the bar lounge. This is a fine touring centre with several coastal resorts within easy reach. To the rear of the inn, a number of delightful bedrooms are furnished to a very high standard with full central heating, colour television and facilities for making hot drinks. *Les Routiers.* **See also Colour Advertisement on page 6.**

TAN HILL INN,
Keld, Richmond,
North Yorkshire DL11 6ED
Tel: 01833 628246

7 bedrooms, all with private bathroom; Free House with real ale;
Bar food; Car park; Shap 1 mile; ££.

At 1,732 feet above sea level, this is the highest inn in England. Isolated and cut off by drifting snow in severe weather with beer freezing in the pipes, this oasis has been a welcome sight to many a weary traveller over the centuries. An account of 1586 records "a solitary inn" on the site and it probably served the needs of drovers, pack ponies and pedlars long before that date. Today, it is walkers on the Pennine Way, which passes the door, and motorists who take advantage of the wholesome shelter and sustenance. Revitalised since Alec and Margaret Baines took over in 1985, the inn (open 11am to 11pm weekdays; noon to 3pm and 7pm to 10.30pm Sundays) has changed little over the years. The open beams and stone-flagged floor remain and a fire blazes in the grate every day of the year, first arrivals claiming the coveted seats by the hearth. Theakston's excellent hand-pulled ales are on tap, including the palatable and potent Old Peculier. Alec and Margaret have greatly expanded the bar food menu and offer delicious meals to satisfy the most avid appetite. Recent alterations have provided comfortable en suite bedrooms with television and facilities for making hot drinks. Bed and breakfast terms are very reasonable.

THE SPORTSMAN'S ARMS,
Wath-in-Nidderdale, Pateley Bridge, North Yorkshire HG3 5PP

Tel: 01423 711306
Fax: 01423 712524

7 bedrooms, 2 with private bathroom; Free House; Bar meals, restaurant Mon.-Sat. evenings plus Sunday lunch; Car park (30); Pateley Bridge 2 miles; £££.

With the Yorkshire Dales and a plethora of historic castles and abbeys within easy reach, this charming, 17th century inn has the added bonus of being situated in some of the loveliest scenery the county has to offer. In its own grounds and with private fishing in the River Nidd available, the Sportsman's Arms is attractively decorated to a high standard with very comfortable bedrooms to serve overnight guests. A convivial bar is a relaxing place in which to consider pleasures to come in the fine restaurant, known for its wide selection of fresh foods. Gouthwaite Reservoir, famous for its abundant birdlife is just a short stroll away whilst, by way of change, the marvellous shopping facilities of Harrogate beckon.

THE NEW INN MOTEL,
Main Street, Huby, York, North Yorkshire YO6 1HQ

Tel: 01347 810219

8 rooms, all en suite, with shower; Restaurant meals; Car park; York 9 miles.

Nine miles north of York in the village of Huby in the Vale of York, the Motel is an ideal base for a couple of nights away to visit York (15 minutes to the nearest long-stay car park), or a longer stay to visit the East Coast of Yorkshire, the Dales, the Yorkshire Moors, Herriot Country, Harrogate and Ripon. The Motel is situated behind the New Inn (a separate business) which, contrary to its name, is a 500-year old hostelry, originally an old coaching inn, and full of character. All rooms are en suite (singles, doubles, twin and family rooms), and have colour television and tea-making facilities. Good home cooking is served, including vegetarian meals, and a full English breakfast is a speciality. PETS ARE WELCOME. The accommodation is suitable for the disabled. Licensed. Special three-day breaks always available. Telephone for brochure. *AA Listed.*

West Yorkshire

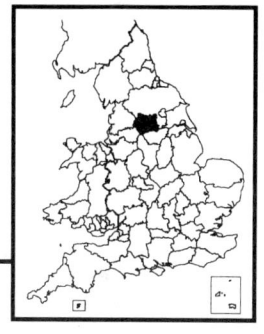

HAREWOOD ARMS HOTEL,
Harrogate Road, Harewood, Near Leeds, Tel: 0113 288 6566
West Yorkshire LS17 9LH Fax: 0113 288 6064

24 bedrooms, all with private bathroom; Samuel Smith House; Bar and restaurant meals; Car park (60); Leeds 7 miles.

Solid and sturdy without, gracious and appealing within, this welcoming hostelry boasts an enviable reputation for both fine home-cooked fare and comfortable overnight accommodation in luxuriously appointed bedrooms, some overlooking gardens and terrace and the rolling hills beyond. All guest rooms are graced with private bath or shower, have tea and coffee facilities and colour television, and are furnished with as much care and concern as the public rooms. Snacks and hot and cold meals are cheerfully served lunchtime and evening in the bar which remains open all day, and the elegant surroundings of the restaurant are a fitting tribute to the à la carte cuisine on offer there. ♕♕♕♕, RAC Comfort Merit Award, AA ***.

OLD WHITE LION HOTEL,
Haworth, Keighley, Tel: 01535 642313
West Yorkshire BD22 8DU Fax: 01535 646222

14 bedrooms, all with private bathroom; Free House with real ale; Children welcome; Bar meals, restaurant evenings only; Car park (8); Keighley 2 miles; £££.

Centrally situated close to the Bronte Museum, Parsonage and Church, this friendly inn was dispensing cheer and hospitality over a century and a half before the remarkable sisters penned their enduring prose. Today the well-stocked bar serves an extensive range of home-made meals and snacks at lunchtime and in the evening, and very fine à la carte and table d'hôte menus are offered in the candlelit restaurant to residents and non-residents alike. Overnight visitors are accommodated in cosy, centrally heated guest bedrooms, all with en suite facilities and most enjoying panoramic views of the village and surrounding countryside. ♕♕♕♕ Commended, AA**, Johansens, Ashley Courtenay.

THE DUKE OF YORK INN,
West Street, Shelf, Halifax, Tel: 01422 202056
West Yorkshire HX3 7LN Fax: 01422 206618

12 bedrooms, all with private bathroom; Whitbread House with real ale; Historic interest; Bar and restaurant meals; Car park (30); Bradford 4 miles; ££.

If you are planning to walk the Calderdale Way or visit the unspoiled moors and dales, then make a note of this 17th century former coaching inn, which is the perfect place to stop for rest and refreshment. An above average choice of real ales, plus a comprehensive selection of beers, wines and spirits guarantees that thirsts will be fully quenched, while a glance at the menu is sure to bring a gleam to the eye of the hungry traveller. From sandwiches to steaks, all appetites are catered for, including an intriguing selection of home-made Indian dishes which will delight more exotic palates. Twelve neat bedrooms offer en suite bathrooms and colour television should overnight accommodation be required. *Les Routiers, Egon Ronay, CAMRA.*

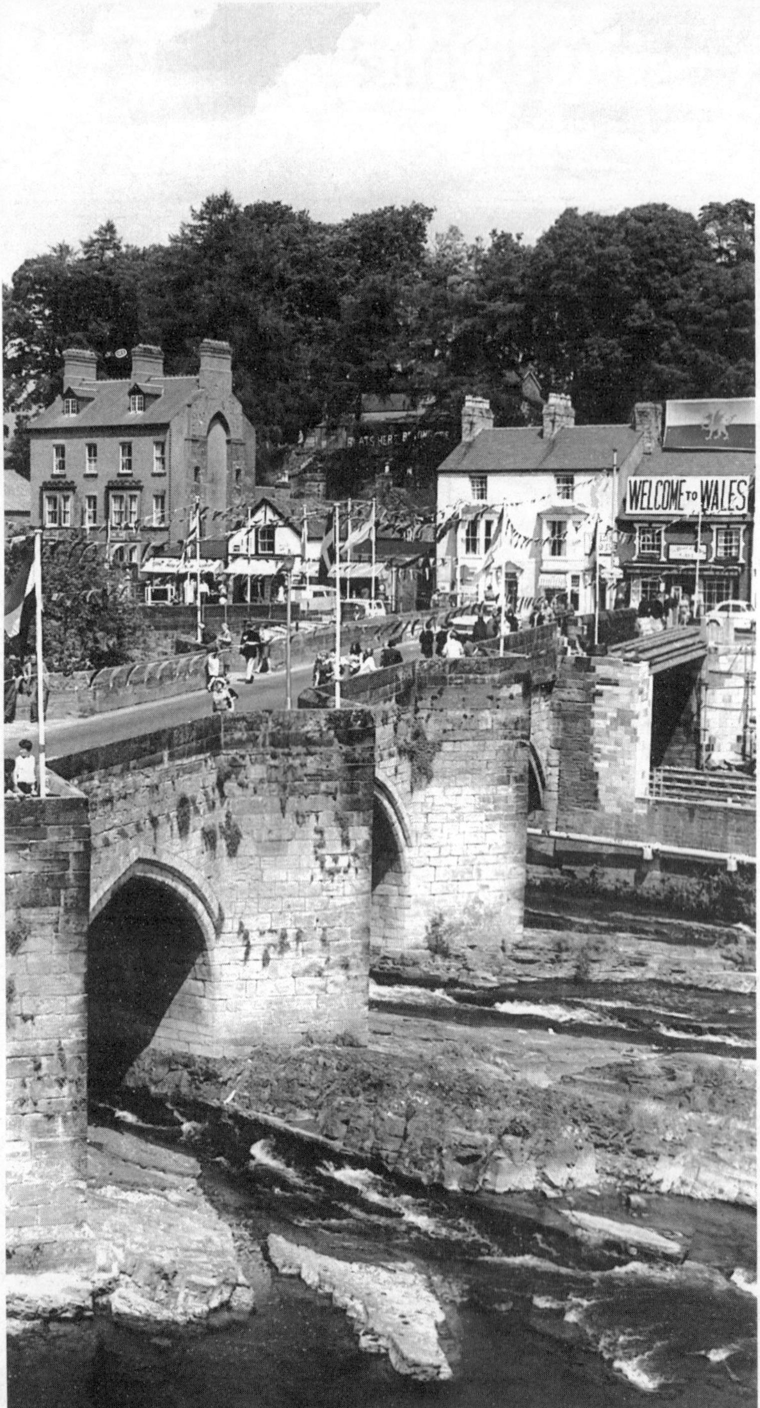
WELCOME TO WALES

WALES

North Wales

(formerly Clwyd and Gwynedd)

Aberconwy & Colwyn, Anglesey, Denbighshire, Flintshire, Gwynedd and Wrexham.

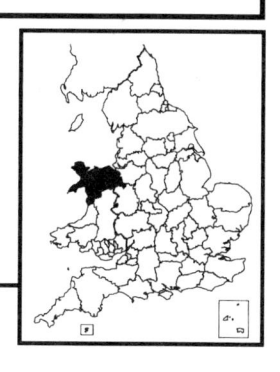

THE GRAPES HOTEL,
Maentwrog, Blaenau Ffestiniog,
North Wales LL41 4HN

Tel: 01766 590365/590208
Fax: 01766 590654

9 bedrooms, all with private bathroom; Free House with real ale; Historic interest; Children and pets welcome; Bar food; Car park; Ffestiniog 3 miles; ££.

Seventeenth century in origin, although dating back in part another four centuries, The Grapes retains many reminders of the past — original stone-work, gleaming brass memorabilia, and in the bar, a wide fireplace supported by a massive slate beam. The extensive bar menu (everything freshly cooked to order) features traditional favourites, plus some specialities to delight more adventurous palates, and includes an imaginative vegetarian selection and a fresh fish "specials" board. The recently refurbished letting bedrooms feature every modern convenience including neat en suite bathrooms, and the old brewhouse has been converted into two family units, both with en suite facilities. ❦❦❦, *Good Pub Guide, CAMRA.*

HARP HOTEL,
Llandwrog, Caernarvon,
North Wales LL54 5SY

Tel: 01286 831071

4 bedrooms, all with private bathroom; Free House with real ale; Historic interest; Children welcome; Bar meals; Car park (20); Caernarvon 5 miles; £.

Traditionally Welsh right down to its foundations, although it is run by Scots, Colin and Madeleine Downie, this solid, stone-built inn has innate character and is a good place for family parties to enjoy an authentic taste of Wales in food and custom. Children under 14 are welcome in the parlour, restaurant and games room and there is also a large beer garden and patio with beautiful views of the mountains. As a contrast from the lofty attractions of Snowdonia, the beach at Dinas Dinlle is only a mile away and the Lleyn Peninsula is within easy reach. The Harp is well worthy of a casual or extended visit to experience good food in some variety, good company and accommodation at moderate outlay. ❦❦, *Welcome Host.*

THE HAWK AND BUCKLE INN,
Llannefydd, Near Denbigh,
North Wales LL16 5ED

Tel: 01745 540249
Fax: 01745 540316

10 bedrooms, all with private bathroom; Free House; Historic interest; Bar lunches and restaurant meals; Car park (20); Colwyn Bay 7 miles; ££.

Every 20th century comfort is to be found at this welcoming seventeenth-century village inn. All the en suite guest rooms in the tasteful extensions are equipped with telephone, tea/coffee making facilities and television; trouser press and hairdryer are available. Furnishings are comfortable and pleasing to the eye. Local game, pork, lamb and freshly caught salmon and trout are imaginatively served in the Inn's popular restaurant, and varied and substantial bar snacks are offered at lunchtime from May 1st to September 30th, and every Wedesday and weekends. Hosts Robert and Barbara Pearson will happily supply a wealth of information on the area. Visa and Access are accepted. *WTB* ❦❦❦❦ *Highly Commended, Egon Ronay, Ashley Courtenay.*

GEORGE III HOTEL,
Penmaenpool, Dolgellau, Meirionnydd,
North Wales LL40 1YD

Tel: 01341 422525
Fax: 01341 423565

12 bedrooms, all with private bathroom; Free House with real ale; Historic interest; Children welcome; Bar food, restaurant evenings only, plus Sun. lunch; Car park (100); Dolgellau 2 miles; ££££.

Beautifully situated at the head of the Mawddach Estuary, this charmingly individual establishment was once two separate buildings, pub and ship chandlers, which were united over a century ago to form the George III Hotel. Overnight guests may choose between accommodation in the hotel itself or in the Lodge a short step away. All rooms have private bathrooms, colour television, tea and coffee tray, hairdryer, direct-dial telephone and trouser press. Bar meals are served every day, and Sunday lunch and excellent evening meals may be taken in the restaurant. Children are very welcome in the newly refurbished Cellar Bar. Free fishing permits for guests; mountain bike hire. ❦❦❦❦ *Highly Commended, AA**RAC, Egon Ronay, Ashley Courtenay, Johansens, Best Loved Hotels of the World.*

THE WEST ARMS,
Llanarmon D.C., Near Llangollen,
North Wales LL20 7LD

Tel: 01691 600665
Fax: 01691 600622

12 bedrooms, all with private bathroom; Free House with real ale; Historic interest; Children welcome; Bar meals, restaurant evenings only; Car park (12); Llangollen 7 miles; £££.

Originally a farmhouse and some 400 years old, the West Arms remains as charming and unpretentious as in the days when it was a simple country inn. It has recently been refurbished to a high standard but, epitomised by its slate floors, vast inglenooks, timberwork and period furnishings, its character remains dominant. Dining here is quite an experience to savour, its superb country cooking complementing the beautiful surrounding countryside. The accommodation vies with the best hotels, all rooms having private facilities and the decor throughout is most appealing. The actively inclined will find the area offers invigorating walks and pony trekking and fishing may be arranged. There are three good golf courses within half-an-hour's drive. ❦❦❦❦ *Highly Commended, Good Pub Guide, Good Food Guide.*

MINFFORDD HOTEL,
Talyllyn, Tywyn,
North Wales LL36 9AJ

Tel: 01654 761665
Fax: 01654 761517

6 bedrooms, all with private bathroom; Historic interest; Restaurant meals; Car park (12); Machynlleth 10 miles; ££.

Homely, informal and with a reputation for good food, this little gem of a hostelry nestles in a landscape of rugged grandeur, the way to the summit of Cader Idris starting from the bottom of the home field. This we found to be a rewarding but breathless experience. We'll try anything once! Flocks of sheep still graze in the fields surrounding this 17th century drovers inn and despite the exigencies of a modern age, tranquillity rules supreme. Discover the lovely Dysynni Valley, Talyllyn Lake, Dolgoch Falls, the famous toy-like Talyllyn Railway and a panoply of mountains and streams in one's meanderings. Always, at this happy retreat there is companionship and comfort, all the tastefully furnished rooms having en suite facilities. *WTB* ♛♛♛♛ *Highly Commended, AA Red Rosette, RAC Three Merit Awards, Taste of Wales, Ashley Courtenay, Good Food Guide, Good Hotel Guide.*

FOR THE MUTUAL GUIDANCE OF GUEST AND HOST

Every year literally thousands of holidays, short breaks and overnight stops are arranged through our guides, the vast majority without any problems at all. In a handful of cases, however, difficulties do arise about bookings, which often could have been prevented from the outset.

It is important to remember that when accommodation has been booked, both parties – guests and hosts – have entered into a form of contract. We hope that the following points will provide helpful guidance.

GUESTS: When enquiring about accommodation, be as precise as possible. Give exact dates, numbers in your party and the ages of any children. State the number and type of rooms wanted and also what catering you require – bed and breakfast, full board etc. Make sure that the position about evening meals is clear – and that about pets, reductions for children or any other special points.

Read our reviews carefully to ensure that the proprietors you are going to contact can supply what you want. Ask for a letter confirming all arrangements, if possible.

If you have to cancel, do so as soon as possible. Proprietors do have the right to retain deposits and under certain circumstances to charge for cancelled holidays if adequate notice is not given and they cannot re-let the accommodation.

HOSTS: Give details about your facilities and about any special conditions. Explain your deposit system clearly and arrangements for cancellations, charges etc. and whether or not your terms include VAT.

If for any reason you are unable to fulfil an agreed booking without adequate notice, you may be under an obligation to arrange suitable alternative accommodation or to make some form of compensation.

While every effort is made to ensure accuracy, we regret that FHG Publications cannot accept responsibility for errors, omissions or misrepresentations in our entries or any consequences thereof. Prices in particular should be checked because we go to press early. We will follow up complaints but cannot act as arbiters or agents for either party.

Dyfed

Cardiganshire, Carmarthenshire and Pembrokeshire.

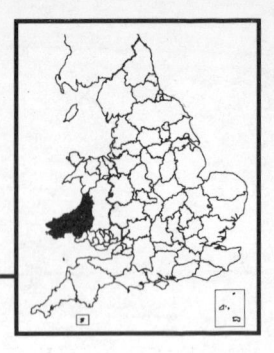

TREWERN ARMS HOTEL,
Nevern, Newport,
Dyfed SA42 0NB

Tel: 01239 820395

9 bedrooms, all with private bathroom; Free House with real ale; Children welcome; Bar meals, restaurant evenings only; Car park (75); Newport 2 miles; ££.

Set deep in a forested and secluded valley on the banks of the River Nevern, this picturesque, 16th century hostelry has a warmth of welcome that is immediately apparent in the interestingly-shaped Brew House Bar with its original flagstone floors, stone walls, old settles and beams decorated with an accumulated collection of bric-a-brac. Bar meals are served here from a popular grill area. By contrast, the Lounge Bar is furnished on cottage lines and the fine restaurant has received many accolades from far and wide for its culinary delights. The tranquil village of Nevern is ideally placed for Pembrokeshire's historic sites and uncrowded, sandy beaches and the accommodation offered at this recommended retreat is in the multi-starred class. ♛♛♛ *Highly Commended.*

Available from most bookshops, the 1997 edition of THE GOLF GUIDE covers details of every UK golf course – well over 2000 entries – for holiday or business golf. Hundreds of hotel entries offer convenient accommodation, accompanying details of the courses – the 'pro', par score, length etc.

Endorsed by The Professional Golfers' Association (PGA) and including Holiday Golf in Ireland, France, Portugal, Spain and the USA.

£8.99 from bookshops or £9.80 including postage (UK only) from FHG Publications, Abbey Mill Business Centre, Paisley PA1 1JT

Powys

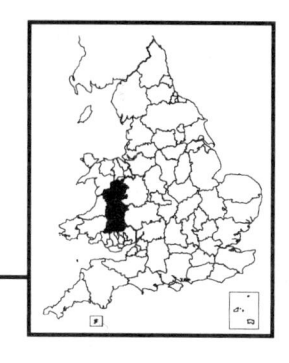

HUNDRED HOUSE INN,
Hundred House, Llandrindod Wells,
Powys LD1 5RY
Tel: 01982 570231

4 bedrooms, 1 with private bathroom; Free House with real ale; Children welcome; Bar and restaurant meals; Car park (40); Newbridge 4 miles; £.

With a character-filled Farmers' Bar serving fine real ale, cosy lounge bar and large beer garden and river terrace, this centuries-old village hostelry was originally a drovers' inn serving weary farmers travelling the Welsh hills to market their sheep. Today, it is a comfortable haven for travellers and villagers alike, a wonderful place in which to unwind and forget about time (other than closing time!) and sample good food and drink and the magnetic charms of the surrounding countryside. Excellent Bed and Breakfast accommodation is available, all rooms having colour television, clock radio and tea and coffee-making facilities. This cosy retreat sports an extensive à la carte restaurant menu. *Member of Guild of Master Caterers.*

SEVERN ARMS HOTEL,
Penybont, Llandrindod Wells,
Powys LD1 5UA
Tel: 01597 851224/851344
Fax: 01597 851693

10 bedrooms, all with private bathroom; Free House with real ale; Historic interest; Children and pets welcome; Bar meals, restaurant evenings only plus Sunday lunch; Car park; Llandrindod Wells 4 miles; ££.

A handsome early Victorian coaching inn, the Severn Arms enjoys an enviable reputation for first-class service and hospitality at reasonable prices — a reputation which the friendly proprietors are determined to maintain. Olde worlde bars provide tasty and wholesome snacks and meals, while the à la carte restaurant is a most pleasant setting for the enjoyment of the fine cuisine offered there. Cosy bedrooms, all with private bathrooms and colour television, provide overnight accommodation, and the inn's position on the A44 makes it a perfect stop for travellers and tourists visiting the many attractions in the Welsh heartland. ♚♚♚ Commended, *Les Routiers, CAMRA, Egon Ronay.*

THE DOLBRODMAETH INN,
Dinas Mawddwy, Machynlleth,
Powys SY20 9LP

Tel: 01650 531333
Fax: 01650 531339

7 bedrooms, 6 with private bathroom; Free House with real ale; Children welcome; Bar and restaurant meals; Car park; Aberystwyth 16 miles; £/££.

The spectacular natural beauty of this unspoilt corner of the Principality attracts visitors from near and far and those in search of a friendly base while exploring this haven for nature lovers, artists, photographers, and all who enjoy outdoor activities will find a warm welcome and traditional hospitality here at this former farmhouse, set on the banks of the River Dovey. Meals, freshly prepared in the hotel kitchens, are served all day, either in the Bar or the Riverside Restaurant, with an extensive selection ranging from freshly cut sandwiches to sirloin steak with all the trimmings. Neatly furnished double and twin en suite rooms, some on the ground floor, provide comfortable accommodation. *WTB* ♛♛♛, *Egon Ronay, Green Award for Tourism.*

DRAGON HOTEL,
Montgomery,
Powys SY15 6PA

Tel and Fax: 01686 668359

15 bedrooms, all with private bathroom; Free House with real ale; Historic interest; Children and pets welcome; Bar and restaurant meals; Welshpool 7 miles; ££.

Parts of this historic black and white timbered inn in the middle of the Welsh Borders date back to the mid-17th century when it was a noted coaching inn. Evidence of those days still exists in company with skilfully introduced modern facilities, the en suite guest rooms now blessed with central heating, colour television, direct-dial telephone and tea-makers. The Dragon draws a great deal of enthusiastic custom by reason of its highly regarded restaurant, dishes prepared to the highest standards and personally supervised by proprietor, Sue Michaels. The well-appointed bar is a popular meeting place and a bonus for guests is a superb heated indoor swimming pool. ♛♛♛♛ *Commended, AA**.*

THE HARP INN,
Old Radnor, Presteigne,
Powys LD8 2RH

Tel and Fax: 01544 350655

4 bedrooms, 2 with private bath; Free House with real ale; Historic interest; Well-behaved children and pets welcome; Bar meals, restaurant evenings only; Car park (20); Hereford 24 miles, Kington 4; £.

Peacefully situated amidst the dramatic splendour of the Welsh Marches with unrivalled views over Radnor Valley, this fine 15th century country inn offers a tranquil and most comfortable base away from the bustle of modern life. After a peaceful night's sleep and a hearty Welsh breakfast, what could be more relaxing than a stroll across the village green to inspect the architectural splendours of St Stephen's Church, with its ancient organ screen and font. Those actively inclined will find plenty to occupy them, and at various times of the year sheepdog trials, Eisteddfods, trotting races and even rodeos attract locals and visitors alike. Slate-flagged floors, exposed beams and stone walls and interesting antiques enhance the period charm of the interior, where good food and ale are dispensed with friendly and professional ease. *Egon Ronay, Good Pub Guide, CAMRA Good Beer Guide.*

South Wales

(formerly Glamorgan and Gwent)

Blaenau Gwent, Bridgend, Caerphilly, Cardiff, Merthyr Tydfil, Monmouthshire, Neath & Port Talbot, Newport, Rhondda Cynon Taff, Swansea, Torfaen, and Vale of Glamorgan.

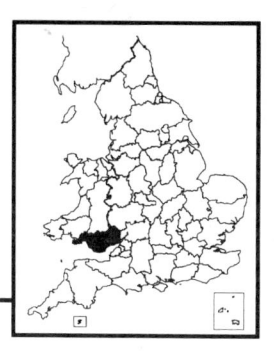

THE ANGEL
Cross Street, Abergavenny,
South Wales NP7 5EW

Tel: 01873 857121
Fax: 01873 858059

29 bedrooms, all with private bathroom; Real ale; Historic interest; Bar and restaurant meals; Car park (30); Pontypool 9 miles; ££.

Nestling on the borders of the Brecon Beacons, The Angel was once one of the great coaching inns on the busy London to Fishguard road. Of considerable architectural interest, the hostelry retains a haunting aura of the past whilst providing a high standard of modern comforts and conveniences. Dine in our inviting restaurant which serves traditional home-cooked fayre, or perhaps relax in the Foxhunter Bar with its enjoyable selection of snacks to complement the real ale. Guest rooms each have a private bathroom, colour television, radio, direct-dial telephone and tea and coffee-making facilities. The Angel is an ideal base for a relaxing holiday and opportunities exist for a wide range of leisure and sporting activities.

CLYTHA ARMS,
Clytha, Near Abergavenny,
South Wales NP7 9BW

Tel: 01873 840206

3 bedrooms, all with private bathroom; Free House with real ale; Historic interest; Children and pets welcome; Bar meals (not Fri/Sat evenings), restaurant meals (not Mon.); Car park; Abergavenny 6 miles; £££.

A converted Dower House set in its own grounds alongside the old Abergavenny to Raglan road (B4598), the Clytha Arms is known primarily for its superb food; furthermore, it is very unpublike in its appearance and its facilities equate more to a distinguished country hotel. Indeed, the accommodation, limited though it may be, is of the highest calibre, the en suite rooms prettily decorated and sumptuously appointed. Nevertheless, this lovely retreat, in the hands of Andrew and Bev Canning, still maintains traditions of a wayside inn with six real ales and snacks available in the public bar. However, it is culinary art and expertise that is the big attraction here — imaginative fare, delightfully presented.

LLANWENARTH ARMS HOTEL,
Brecon Road, Abergavenny,
South Wales NP8 lEP

Tel: 01873 810550
Fax: 01873 811880

18 bedrooms, all with private bathroom; Free House with real ale; Historic interest; Children welcome; Bar and restaurant meals; Car park (60); Pontypool 9 miles; ££££.

With delightful views of the River Usk and Sugarloaf Mountain, this renovated 16th century inn, so well run by D'Arcy and Angela McGregor, makes the most of its beautiful situation by offering good company and sustenance in its bars, including an interesting selection of real ales, whilst the restaurant is a popular venue for imaginative, home-cooked fare. Children are especially welcome and have their own menu. Golf, riding and hang-gliding are among the many sporting opportunities to be found locally and the hotel possesses two excellent stretches of salmon and trout water available to guests. Well-appointed double and twin-bedded rooms add further encouragement to stay in this lovely, peaceful area. ♛♛♛♛ Commended, AA** and Rosette.

KING ARTHUR HOTEL,
Higher Green, Reynoldston, Gower, Swansea,
South Wales SA3 1AD

Tel: 01792 391099

7 bedrooms, all with private bathroom; Children welcome; Bar meals; Swansea 11 miles; £.

Set in the Gower Peninsula, home of Arthurian legend, this is a friendly old traditional inn with a relaxed atmosphere. There are log fires in winter, a cosy restaurant and tasteful en suite bedrooms (some with four-poster beds). The King Arthur is renowned for delicious home cooked meals, with extensive seasonal fish and game menus. It is situated close to all the finest beaches and is an ideal base for a walking holiday.

RECOMMENDED SHORT BREAK HOLIDAYS IN BRITAIN

Introduced by John Carter, TV Holiday Expert and Journalist

Specifically designed to cater for the most rapidly growing sector of the holiday market in the UK. Illustrated details of hotels offering special "Bargain Breaks" throughout the year.
Available from newsagents and bookshops for £4.25 or direct from the publishers for £4.80 including postage (UK only).

FHG PUBLICATIONS LTD
Abbey Mill Business Centre, Seedhill,
Paisley, Renfrewshire PAl ITJ

SCOTLAND

Aberdeenshire

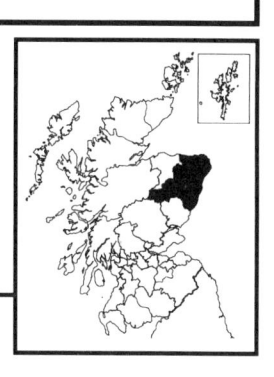

THE GREEN INN,
9 Victoria Road, Ballater,
Aberdeenshire AB35 5QQ
Tel and Fax: 013397 55701

3 bedrooms, all with private bathroom; Children and pets welcome; Restaurant meals; Aberdeen 17 miles, Braemar 14; ££.

Situated in the heart of Royal Deeside, this friendly hotel offers accommodation in three comfortable en suite bedrooms (one double and two twin), all with television and tea/coffee making facilities. Featuring Taste of Scotland dishes, the cosy restaurant serves the best of the fine fresh produce that this area is renowned for. This is an ideal base for exploring the many historic castles, gardens, and other places of interest in the area, as well as enjoying the extensive leisure pursuits such as golf, fishing, walking and ski-ing. ❦❦❦ *Commended.* **See also Colour Advertisement on page 7.**

KILDRUMMY INN,
Kildrummy, Alford,
Aberdeenshire AB33 8QS
Tel: 01975 571227

4 bedrooms; Free House; Historic interest; Children and pets welcome; Bar and restaurant meals; Car park (50); Alford 7 miles; £.

This small family-run inn is situated in the Grampian Highlands, within easy reach of several good golf courses and ideal for touring, fishing, hill walking and pony trekking. Accommodation is available in two family and two double bedrooms, all with washbasins, tea-making facilities and television. There is a residents' dining room, a lounge bar serving bar lunches and suppers, a public bar with several draught beers on tap and a good range of whisky, and a sun lounge where meals, coffees, snacks etc are also served. The inn is situated on the A97 Strathdon to Huntly road, with easy access and good parking facilities, and is a good base for scenic round trips. **See also Colour Advertisement on page 7.**

GORDON ARMS HOTEL,
Kincardine O'Neil,
Aberdeenshire AB34 5AA

Tel: 013398 84236
Fax: 013398 84401

7 bedrooms, 5 with private bathroom; Free House with real ale; Historic interest; Children welcome; Bar and restaurant meals; Car park; Banchory 7 miles; £.

Early Victorian in origin when it was a coaching inn, the Gordon Arms is situated amidst the beautiful scenery of Royal Deeside where castles abound, including Balmoral, only half an hour away. The superb cuisine here is widely acknowledged, chef-inspired home-cooked dishes featuring locally caught salmon as well as succulent steaks and tempting sweets. Vegetarians are also well catered for. An interesting selection of organic wines is kept and also a fine range of real ales. Active outdoor pursuits to be enjoyed in the area include tennis, golf, fishing, pony trekking, water ski-ing and even gliding. For such enthusiasts, comfortable accommodation in period style may be arranged. 👑👑👑 *Approved.*

Angus

FISHERMAN'S TAVERN HOTEL,
Fort Street, Broughty Ferry, Dundee,
Angus DD5 2AD

Tel: 01382 775941
Fax: 01382 477466

8 bedrooms; Free House with real ale; Historic interest; Children and pets welcome; Bar lunches, restaurant summer evenings only; Dundee city centre 4 miles; £.

A "must" for real ale aficionados who find themselves in this traditional little resort just on the edge of Dundee, the Fisherman's Tavern boasts of having been elected "Best in UK" by CAMRA. But whatever your tipple, this comfortably rambling inn is a pleasant spot for relaxation and good conversation, and in addition offers a good bar food menu which ranges from sandwiches and burgers to more substantial dishes such as steak pie and lasagne. The usual menu is supplemented by a choice of daily specials which are well worth looking out for. Centrally heated bedrooms provide cosy accommodation, and the very reasonable room rate includes a full Scottish breakfast. 👑 *Commended.*

PLEASE MENTION THIS GUIDE WHEN YOU WRITE

OR PHONE TO ENQUIRE ABOUT

ACCOMMODATION.

IF YOU ARE WRITING, A STAMPED,

ADDRESSED ENVELOPE IS ALWAYS APPRECIATED.

Argyll

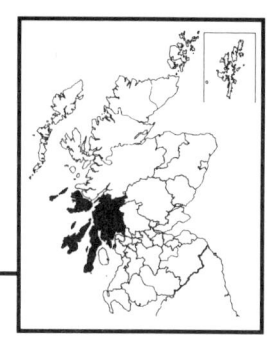

CAIRNDOW STAGECOACH INN,
Cairndow,
Argyll PA26 8BN

Tel: 01499 600286
Fax: 01499 600220

12 bedrooms, all en suite; Free House with real ale; Historic interest; Children welcome; Bar and restaurant meals; Car park (35); Arrochar 12 miles, Inveraray 10; ££.

Amidst the beautiful scenery which characterises the upper reaches of Loch Fyne, this historic stagecoach inn enjoys a spectacular sheltered position. In the delightful restaurant one may dine well by candlelight from the table d'hôte and à la carte menus; bar meals are served all day. There is also a new functions bar and games room. Bedrooms are centrally heated, with radio, television, direct-dial telephone, baby listening, and tea-making facilities. There are two de luxe rooms with two-person spa baths, king-size beds and 20" television! This is an ideal spot for touring Oban, the Western Highlands, Glencoe, the Trossachs, the Cowal Peninsula, Kintyre and Campbeltown. The inn is under the personal supervision of hosts Mr and Mrs Douglas Fraser, and the area offers fine opportunities for many outdoor pursuits and visits. Lochside beer garden, exercise room, sauna and solarium.

The £ symbol when appearing at the end of the italic section of an entry shows the anticipated price, during 1997, for single full Bed and Breakfast.

Under £25	£	Over £36 but under £45	£££
Over £25 but under £36	££	Over £45	££££

This is meant as an indication only and does not show prices for Special Breaks, Weekends, etc. Guests are therefore advised to verify all prices on enquiring or booking.

COYLET INN,
Loch Eck,
Argyll PA23 8SG
Tel: 01369 840426

4 bedrooms; Free House with real ale; Historic interest; Children welcome; Bar and restaurant meals; Car park (30); Dunoon 8 miles; £.

Far away from fuss and fumes and splendidly set amidst the leafy fastness of the Argyll Forest Park, the homely Coylet Inn lies on the eastern shore of Loch Eck in an area that will appeal to all who enjoy outdoor pursuits in natural surroundings. Boating, sea angling, hill walking, pony trekking and golf are all rewarding local diversions and the Younger Botanic Garden is only two miles away. A one-time coaching inn dating back to the 18th century, this happy retreat has open log fires to banish chill weather and four small but comfortable bedrooms. Bar meals are available with an à la carte menu on offer in the dining room. *Egon Ronay.*

Caithness

PORTLAND ARMS,
Lybster,
Caithness KW3 6BS
Tel: 01593 721208/721255

20 bedrooms, all with private bathroom; Free House; Historic interest; Children welcome; Bar lunches, restaurant meals; Car park (40); Wick 12 miles; £££.

As sturdy and enduring as the cliffs of this northern corner, the Portland was built in the early 1800s as a staging post on the new parliamentary road. Enlarged and upgraded to a high standard, accommodation today comprises 20 beautifully furnished guest rooms, all with private bath or shower, electric blanket, telephone, colour television, and tea and coffee facilities; some with four poster or half-tester bed. The traditional Scottish meal of High Tea is served in the restaurant from 5pm to 6.30pm, as an alternative to the fine table d'hôte dinner, and bar snacks ranging from soups, sandwiches and baked potatoes to baked sole, sirloin and gammon steaks. ☻☻☻☻ *Commended, Taste of Scotland.*

Dumfriesshire

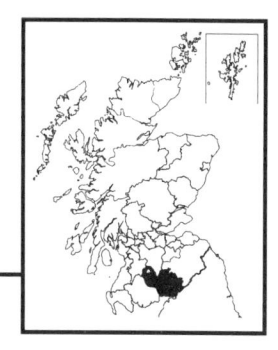

RIVERSIDE INN,
Canonbie,
Dumfriesshire DG14 0UX
Tel: 013873 71512/71295

7 bedrooms, all with private bathroom; Free House with real ale; Historic interest; Children welcome, pets by arrangement; Bar meals, restaurant evenings only; Car park (20); Langholm 6 miles; £££.

Only just over the border, this pretty black-and-white hostelry overlooks the River Esk and is ideally placed for touring that unspoilt area, as well as the Solway Coast and Northern Lakes. En suite guest bedrooms are equipped with colour television, electric blanket, tea tray and fruit basket, and residents who do not wish to use the cheerful lounge bar have their own private sitting room in which to relax in peace and comfort. The dining room boasts a good daily-changing menu, and varied and imaginative lunches and suppers are served either in the bar or, weather permitting, on the sunny terrace. AA Inn of The Year 1983, Pub of the Year 1992.

CRIFFEL INN,
New Abbey, Near Dumfries,
Dumfriesshire DG2 8BX
Tel: 01387 850305

5 bedrooms, 3 with private bathroom; Free House; Historic interest; Children and pets welcome; Bar and restaurant meals; Car park; Dumfries 6 miles; £.

Attractions such as first-class food served in the bar and dining room featuring fresh local produce and home baking, neat bedrooms (including three en suite) with colour television and tea making facilities, and a pretty garden patio for fine weather relaxation make this an ideal spot for rest and refreshment whatever the season. Set in the beautiful Scottish Borders, the village of New Abbey is famed as the site of the 13th century Sweetheart Abbey and is a most convenient base for exploring this unspoiled part of the country. Leisure activities available locally include golf, sea angling, and river and loch fishing.

DINWOODIE LODGE COUNTRY HOUSE HOTEL,
Johnstonebridge, Near Lockerbie,
Dumfriesshire DG11 2SL   Tel and Fax: 01576 470289

7 bedrooms, 3 with private bathroom; Free House; Historic interest;
Children and pets welcome; Bar and restaurant meals; Car park; Dumfries 11 miles; ££.

This Grade B Listed small country house hotel is ideally situated for touring the Borders, Galloway, Edinburgh and Glasgow (approximately 70 miles). Local activities include fishing, golf and shooting. Breakfast, lunch, bar meals and traditional high teas are served, as well as vegetarian meals. There is a licensed bar and separate pool room with dartboard. All bedrooms, including a family room sleeping two adults and three children under 10 years, have colour television and tea/coffee facilities; one room is suitable for disabled visitors. There is a caravan park and holiday cottages adjacent for those who prefer a self-catering holiday. **See also Colour Advertisement on page 7.**

BALMORAL HOTEL,
High Street, Moffat,   Tel: 01683 220288
Dumfriesshire DG10 9DL   Fax: 01683 220451

16 bedrooms, 6 with private bathroom; Free House with real ale; Historic interest;
Children welcome; Bar and restaurant meals; Car park; Dumfries 19 miles; ££.

Once the centre of the Scottish woollen trade and a popular spa, Moffat nestles in the gentle Annandale valley, providing both a good centre for touring the Border country and a rather pleasing holiday venue in itself, with good golfing, fishing, shooting, hill-walking and pony trekking. Accommodation in this substantial old inn run by John and Pip Graham comprises sixteen comfortable and well furnished bedrooms, some en suite and all with tea and coffee facilities and colour television. A character-filled lounge bar, dining room and residents' lounge complete the guest accommodation, and fine Scottish fare is served with charm and quiet courtesy.

BLACK BULL HOTEL,
Churchgate, Moffat,   Tel: 01683 220206
Dumfriesshire DG10 9EG   Fax: 01683 220483

8 bedrooms, 6 with private bathroom; Scottish Brewers House with real ale; Historic interest; Bar
and restaurant meals; Children welcome, no pets in bedrooms; Dumfries 19 miles; ££.

Much care has been taken to preserve the authentic atmosphere of this famous, 16th century inn. Many colourful characters have sat within these hospitable walls taking food and drink amongst convivial company, most notably, one Rabbie Burns, a regular patron, who complemented his mood by writing 'The Famous Epigram to a Scrimpit Nature' here and possibly other whimsies. The warm welcome is still there with good real ale and a selection of bar snacks available, whilst the Mail Coach Restaurant is renowned for its top quality food and friendly service. Excellent fishing and golf may be enjoyed locally, further reasons for taking advantage of the high standard of modern accommodation. ❦❦ *Commended, Welcome Host, Egon Ronay, CAMRA, Good Pub Guide.*

Inverness-shire

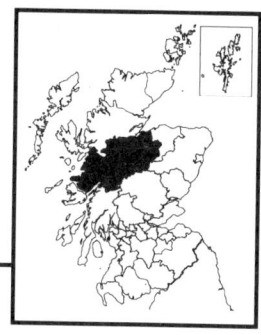

ARISAIG HOTEL,
Arisaig,
Inverness-shire PH39 4NH

Tel: 01687 450210
Fax: 01687 450310

15 bedrooms, all with private bathroom; Free House; Historic interest; Children and pets welcome; Bar and restaurant meals; Car park (30); Fort William 37 miles, Mallaig 7; ££.

This historic Jacobite inn stands on the shores of Loch Nan Ceal with views across the bay to the isles of Rum and Eigg. The proprietors, Malcolm and Jacqueline Ross, welcome you to their warm family atmosphere, where you can relax and enjoy the chance to explore this unspoiled area. All bedrooms have private bathrooms, direct-dial telephones, remote-control colour television and tea/coffee making facilities. Cuisine is based upon traditional and modern presentation of fresh produce from Scotland's natural larder, especially locally caught seafood, and can be enjoyed in the restaurant, or, more informally, in the bar. An extensive wine list is available, as well as a superb range of malt whiskies. 👑👑👑 Commended, AA and RAC **.

NETHER LOCHABER HOTEL,
Onich, Fort William,
Inverness-shire PH33 6SE

Tel: 01855 821235

5 bedrooms; Free House; Historic interest; Bar and restaurant meals; Car park, garages (2); Edinburgh 121 miles, Glasgow 91, Oban 48, Fort William 10; £.

An ideal centre from which to explore Lochaber, the Ardnamurchan Peninsula and Glencoe. This old Highland inn may be small, but it is a homely place which has been run by the MacKintosh family since 1923. Traditional home cooking goes hand in hand with homely service, comfortable accommodation and private facilities. The inn stands on the shores of beautiful Loch Linnhe at Corran Ferry.

Isle of Arran

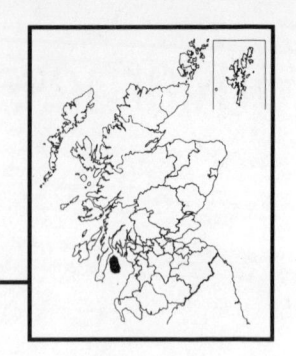

ALDERSYDE HOTEL,
Lamlash,
Isle of Arran KA27 8LU
Tel: 01770 600219/600732

Brodick 3 miles; £.

This small family-run hotel is situated in the delightful village of Lamlash and enjoys outstanding views over the bay to Holy Island. This is an ideal location for golf, walking, fishing and sailing. Guests can enjoy good home cooking, and as an added attraction, there is live music in the lounge bar during the main holiday season. Rates for Bed and Breakfast or Bed, Breakfast and Evening Meal are extremely attractive, with special discounts for party bookings, long stays or out of season breaks. Please contact June for further information.

Isle of Skye

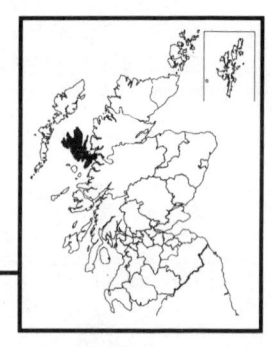

ARDVASAR HOTEL,
Ardvasar, Sleat,
Isle of Skye IV45 8RS
Tel: 01471 844223

10 bedrooms, all with private bathroom; Free House with real ale; Historic interest; Children welcome; Bar meals, restaurant evenings only; Car park (30); Broadford 25 miles; ££.

Since the 1700s this solid white-washed hotel has gazed over the Sound of Sleat to the Knoydart Mountains and the beautiful Sands of Morar, and as well as being one of the oldest coaching inns on the west coast, it is surely one of the most idyllically situated. Not surprisingly, seafood features extensively on the menu here, together with local venison and other fine Scottish produce, and tasty bar lunches and suppers are offered as an alternative to the more formal cuisine served in the restaurant. A private residents' lounge warmed by a gas fire is furnished to the same high standard of comfort as the cosy guest rooms, all of which have private facilities.

Kirkcudbrightshire

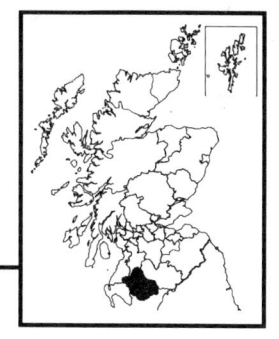

BANK O' FLEET HOTEL,
Gatehouse of Fleet,
Kirkcudbrightshire DG7 2HR
Tel and Fax: 01557 814302

6 bedrooms, 5 with private bathroom; Free House; Historic interest; Children and pets welcome; Bar and restaurant meals; Kirkcudbright 6 miles; £.

Situated in the heart of this historic and picturesque town, the Bank O' Fleet Hotel is an ideal base for touring and enjoying Galloway, with its miles of unspoiled countryside leading from uplands down to the sea. Accommodation includes single, double and family rooms, all en suite with colour television and tea/coffee making facilities. There is a lounge bar, a dining room for evening meals, a residents' lounge and a large function room with regular entertainment. The hotel is the "home" of the Stewartry Pipe Band, and there is always a piper available. This is an ideal base for country activities such as fishing (river, loch and sea), golf, birdwatching and walking, or just simply relaxing away from the hustle and bustle. ✤✤ Approved, RAC. **See also Colour Advertisement on page 8.**

KEN BRIDGE HOTEL (Ref 2),
New Galloway, Castle Douglas,
Kirkcudbrightshire DG7 3PR
Tel and Fax: 01644 420211

10 bedrooms, 6 with private bathroom; Free House; Children and pets welcome; Bar and restaurant meals; Car park; £.

In the heart of the beautiful Galloway countryside, famed for its associations with Robert the Bruce, this friendly Victorian coach house offers a traditional Scottish welcome and good home cooking. It stands on the banks of the river and residents have free fishing rights. Husband and wife team, Andrew and Ann Ramsay, provide comfortable accommodation in single, double/twin and family rooms. Private parking. Open all year. ✤ Approved, AA, RAC Approved. **See also Colour Advertisement on page 8.**

KENMURE ARMS HOTEL,
New Galloway, Castle Douglas,
Kirkcudbrightshire DG7 3RL
Tel and Fax: 01644 420240

12 bedrooms, 8 with private bathroom; Free House; Children and pets welcome; Bar and restaurant meals; Car park (12); Kirkcudbright 17 miles; £.

Situated in the centre of New Galloway, the Kenmure Arms could not be better placed to enjoy the considerable attractions of South West Scotland. Accommodation is available in 12 modern bedrooms, most with en suite facilities, all with washbasins, razor points and central heating, and guests can relax in the lounge bar, residents' lounge with television, and games room. The 50-seater restaurant offers home-cooked fare from a varied menu. This is an ideal base for a golfing holiday, with 22 courses less than an hour's drive away; other activities which can be enjoyed locally include fishing and walking in the Galloway Forest Park.

Peeblesshire

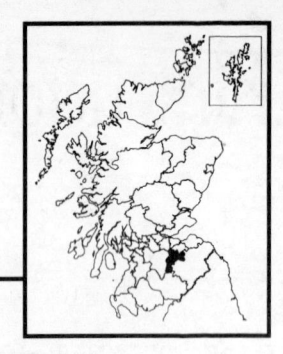

TRAQUAIR ARMS,
Traquair Road, Innerleithen,
Peeblesshire EH44 6PD

Tel: 01896 830229
Fax: 01896 830260

10 bedrooms, all with private bathroom; Free House with real ale; Children and pets welcome; Bar and restaurant meals; Car park (18); Peebles 6 miles; ££.

A solidly constructed traditional 19th century Scottish inn, just 40 minutes from Edinburgh and 10 minutes from Peebles, in a delightful Borders valley. Hugh and Marian Anderson run it as a relaxing, friendly, family-run hotel with genuine concern for the comfort of their guests. Imaginative menus utilise the best local produce, and in appropriate weather can be enjoyed beside a blazing log fire in the dining room or al fresco in the secluded garden. The bar prides itself on its real ales. Egon Ronay's *Good Pub Guide* says "Bed and breakfast is recommended, particularly the handsome Scottish meal complete with superb kippers". *STB* 👑👑👑 Commended, Taste of Scotland, CAMRA, Best Breakfast in Britain 1990, "In Britain" Scottish Finalist 1993.

NOTE

All the information in this book is given in good faith in the belief that it is correct. However, the publishers cannot guarantee the facts given in these pages, neither are they responsible for changes in policy, ownership or terms that may take place after the date of going to press. Readers should always satisfy themselves that the facilities they require are available and that the terms, if quoted, still apply.

Perth & Kinross

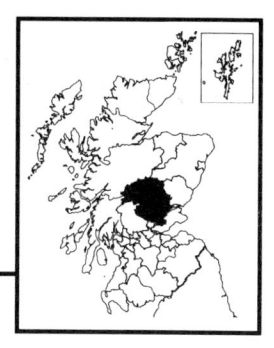

**THE MUIRS INN KINROSS,
49 Muirs, Kinross,
Perth & Kinross KY13 7AU** Tel: 01577 862270

5 bedrooms, all with private bathroom; Free House with real ale; Historic interest; Bar lunches, restaurant meals; Car park (9); Dunfermline 9 miles; £££.

Open all year round and listed as one of Scotland's best pubs, it is a traditional Scottish Country Inn — at its best. With all bedrooms en suite it is full of character and boasts its own Award Nominated Restaurant which serves Home-Cooked fresh Country Cuisine at sensible prices every day. Scottish Real Ales and Malt Whiskies are a speciality at this charming inn where you spend time and not a fortune. Historic Kinross is ideal for business or for pleasure and is a superb holiday centre with 130 golf courses and all major cities within driving distance. This Inn is simply something special. Details of special mid-week and weekend breaks sent on request. ☙☙☙ Commended, AA QQQ, Guinness Pub Food Award nomination, Taste of Scotland Appointed, Featured in CAMRA Pub Guide.

Taking a pet on holiday? Then buy
"PETS WELCOME"
THE ANIMAL LOVERS' HOLIDAY GUIDE
Details of Hotels, Guest Houses, Furnished Accommodation, Caravans, etc, where holiday makers and their pets are made welcome.
Available from most newsagents and bookshops price £4.60
or from Publishers (£5.50 including postage, UK only).

**FHG PUBLICATIONS LTD
Abbey Mill Business Centre, Seedhill,
Paisley, Renfrewshire PA1 1TJ**

Ross-shire

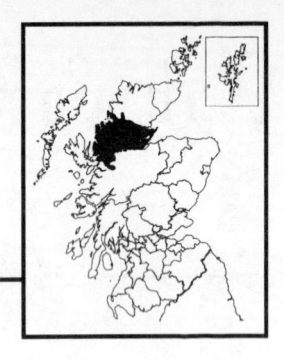

THE OLD INN,
Gairloch,
Ross-shire IV21 2BD

Tel: 01445 712006
Fax: 01445 712445

14 bedrooms, all with private bathroom; Free House with real ale; Historic interest; Bar and restaurant meals; Car park (50); Inverness 71 miles, Ullapool 56; £££.

Recently featured on TV's top holiday programme, "Wish You Were Here!" The famous gardens of Inverewe are just seven miles from this solid and welcoming family-run inn, and guests booking for three nights' bed and breakfast may visit them free of charge. Real ales are a speciality, and good bar food is served here daily. An à la carte menu is offered in the dining room, locally caught seafood, trout and salmon vying for the gourmet's attention with fine Aberdeen Angus beef and skilfully prepared venison. Colour television, beverage makers, direct-dial telephones and child/baby listening facilities are provided in each of the en suite guest rooms, all of which are furnished for comfort as well as being pleasing to the eye. STB ❀❀❀ Commended, AA/RAC**.

GLENELG INN,
Glenelg, By Kyle of Lochalsh,
Ross-shire IV40 8JR

Tel: 01599 522273
Fax: 01599 522373

6 bedrooms, all with private bathroom; Free House; Historic interest; Children and pets welcome; Bar meals, restaurant evenings only; Car park; Shiel Bridge 10 miles; ££££ (DB&B).

Where the strait narrows between the Scottish mainland and the Isle of Skye, this hospitable and delightfully furnished inn welcomes visitors to an area of unspoilt beauty, a land of quiet sea lochs, remote beaches, secret places and an abundance of wildlife. Standing in extensive grounds, the genial Glenelg Inn lies a short distance south of the ferry (and infamous bridge!) to Skye and in the area there are opportunities for pony trekking, golf, fishing, birdwatching and hill walking. Visitors and locals can meet in the cosy and welcoming public bar in the lively atmosphere of the ceilidh, where the traditional music of the pipe and the fiddle are the order of the evening. Fresh seafood specialities are served every night in the dining room.

Wigtownshire

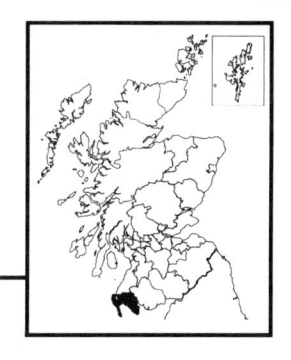

CROWN HOTEL,
North Crescent, Portpatrick,
Wigtownshire DG9 8SX

Tel: 01776 810261
Fax: 01776 810551

12 bedrooms, all with private bathroom; Free House; Children and pets welcome; Bar and restaurant meals; Stranraer 6 miles; £££.

Seafood is a particular speciality of this fine, family-run hotel — hardly surprising as it is only a few steps from the water's edge, facing westwards over the harbour of picturesque Portpatrick village to the Irish Channel beyond. Fresh caught crab, lobster, prawns and scallops are on offer in the bar, together with the usual steaks and sandwiches, and the pleasant thirties-style restaurant caters amply for more formal dining. A gracious conservatory opens on to sheltered well-planned gardens, and guest accommodation is attractively furnished and comfortable in the extreme, all rooms having en suite facilities and television. *Egon Ronay, Which?*

PHEASANT INN,
Sorbie, Newton Stewart,
Wigtownshire DG8 8EL

Tel: 01988 850223

3 bedrooms, all with private bathroom; Free House; Bar and restaurant meals; Newton Stewart 14 miles; ££.

The Pheasant Inn is situated in uncrowded Wigtownshire with its landscape of forest, farmland and coastline. As well as peace and quiet there are opportunities for golf, fishing, cycling, walking and birdwatching. The inn has two comfortable bars and a cosy restaurant for good home-cooked meals at reasonable prices. There is a private lounge for residents and a large garden. Well furnished bedrooms have colour television and tea and coffee making facilities. You are assured of a warm welcome at the Pheasant Inn. **See also Colour Advertisement page 8.**

TORRS WARRREN HOTEL,
Stoneykirk, Stranraer,
Wigtownshire DG9 9DH

Tel and Fax: 01776 830204

8 bedrooms, all with private bathroom; Free House with real ale; Historic interest; Children welcome; Bar and restaurant meals; Car park; Stranraer 5 miles; £.

The hotel is situated in South West Scotland, just six miles from Portpatrick and 15 minutes from the ferry to Ireland. All around is tranquil countryside, with secluded coves, rugged cliffs, enchanted forests and sandy beaches. It is ideally placed for exploring sub-tropical gardens, castles and standing stones. We can arrange most activities for you and we have put together special all-in packages for golf and sea angling. Originally the church manse but now converted into a comfortable family-run hotel, the Torrs Warren is set in its own grounds with ample parking. *STB Listed Approved.* **See also Colour Advertisement on page 8.**

Are you ready to take the place of her mum?

Leaving mum can be scary for a small puppy. But if you feed Beta Puppy at least the food's as good as mum's was. For details on the full Beta range call the Beta Petcare Advice Service on FREEPHONE 0800 738 2273 or write to PO Box 53, Newmarket, Suffolk CB8 8QF.

BETA *petfoods*
Food for Life

The Golden Bowl Supplement for Pet-Friendly Pubs

BETA
Petfoods

When Beta Petfoods launched its search for Britain's warmest pet welcome with their Golden Bowl Award Scheme, the response was staggering. Hundreds of people nominated their favourite pubs for a Golden Bowl Award, where kind hearted publicans ensure a fresh bowl of water is available for their canine customers!

The pick of the pet pubs (and hotels) have gone into this Supplement to enable owners travelling, holidaying or just walking their dogs to find a warm welcome for everyone in the party when they stop for refreshment. We only wish we had room to include more!

Help Your Dog Beat the Heat on the Road

Follow these three tips from John Foster B.VSc., Cert.V.Ophthal., M.R.C.V.S., consultant vet to Beta Petfoods, and you could make your dog's life in the car considerably more comfortable during the summer months.

When travelling with your dog carry plenty of fresh water and a drinking bowl. An average 20kg dog will drink about $1^1/_2$ pints per day. In the heat this can increase by 200-300%.

Always ensure that your dog has plenty of fresh air. Placing a dog in the back of an estate car without an open rear window is undesirable, probably cruel, and may be fatal.

When you leave your car parked in the shade, remember how quickly the sun moves. As the shade disappears, the inside of the car can quickly reach oven-hot temperatures — up to 140 degrees. Heat stroke can happen within minutes.

BETA — THE BETTER WAY TO NUTRITIONAL CARE

Beta Petfoods make caring for your dog easy — at every stage of his life! From puppy to working dog, family pet to older dog, the Beta choice is extensive and the difference between each product clear. Check the Beta complete food packs and you will see each of the seven highly palatable, easily digestible lifestage products has been carefully balanced to meet a dog's different nutritional requirements.

From **Beta Puppy**, high in energy and protein, you can be assured of a smooth nutritional transition in the first six months to **Beta Junior** and then to **Beta Recipe** or **Beta Pet** for the family dog, **Beta Light** for the older or less active dog with a tendency to put on weight, **Beta Field** for the working dog, and **Beta Champion** for breeding and racing dogs.

Beta also produce **Beta Bravo** and **Beta Brutus** — tasty flake foods, plus crunchy wholewheat mixers and delicious treats.

If you want to know more about Beta Petfoods call the Spillers Petcare Service on **Freephone 0800 738 2273.**

The Golden Bowl Supplement for Pet-Friendly Pubs

BERKSHIRE

THE GREYHOUND (known locally as 'The Dog')
The Walk, Eton Wick, Berkshire (01753 863925).
Dogs allowed throughout the pub.

Pet Regulars: Include Lady (GSD), at one o'clock sharp she howls for her hot dog; Trevor (Labrador/Retriever), who does nothing; Skipper (Jack Russell), the local postman's dog and Natasha (GSD) who simply enjoys the ambience.

THE QUEEN
Harts Lane, Burghclere, near Newbury, Berkshire (01635 278350).
Dogs allowed throughout the pub.

Pet Regulars: Sam (Border Terrier), makes solo visits to the pub to play with resident long-haired Dachshund Gypsy.

NOTE
A few abbreviations and 'pet' descriptions have been used in this section which deserve mention and, where necessary, explanation as follows: **GSD:** German Shepherd Dog. ... *-cross:* a cross-breed where one breed appears identifiable. *57:* richly varied origin. You will also encounter *'mongrel', 'Bitsa'* and *'???!'* which are self evident and generally affectionate.

THE SWAN
9 Mill Lane, Clewer, Windsor, Berkshire (01753 862069).
Dogs allowed throughout the pub.
Pet Regulars: Include Luke (Samoyed), enjoys a glass of Tiger beer.

THE TWO BREWERS
Park Street, Windsor, Berkshire (01753 855426).
Dogs allowed, public and saloon bars.
Pet Regulars: Missy and Worthey (Huskies), prefer to remain outside; Sam (Golden Retriever), will retrieve any food and eat it while owner is not looking; Bumble (Highland Terrier), better known as the Highland Hooverer.

BUCKINGHAMSHIRE
WHITE HORSE
Village Lane, Hedgerley, Buckinghamshire SL2 3UY (01753 643225).
Dogs allowed at tables on pub frontage, beer garden (on leads), public bar.
Pet Regulars: Digby (Labrador), the entertainer; Cooper (Boxer), tries hard to better himself - also drinks!

CAMBRIDGESHIRE
YE OLD WHITE HART
Main Street, Ufford, Peterborough, Cambridgeshire (01780 740250).
Dogs allowed in non-food areas.
Pet Regulars: Henry and Robotham (Springer Spaniels), 'pub dog' duties include inspection of all customers and their dogs and, on occasion, seeing them home after last orders.

CHESHIRE
JACKSONS BOAT
Rifle Road, Sale, Cheshire (0161 973 3208).
Dogs allowed throughout with the exception of the dining area.
Pet Regulars: Bix (Labrador), will share pork scratchings with pub cat, chases beer garden squirrels on solo missions; hamburger scrounging a speciality.

CORNWALL

THE WHITE HART
Chilsworthy, near Gunnislake, Cornwall (01822 832307).

Dogs allowed in non-food bar, car park tables, beer garden.

Pet Regulars: Joe (Terrier-cross), sleeps on back under bar stools; Max (Staffordshire-cross), lager drinker; Tatler (Cocker Spaniel), pork cracklings fan; Sheba (GSD), welcoming committee.

WELLINGTON HOTEL,
The Harbour, Boscastle, Cornwall (01840 250202).

Dogs allowed in bedrooms and pub.

Own private 10-acre woodland walk. Dogs welcome free of charge.

CUMBRIA

BRITANNIA INN
Elterwater, Ambleside, Cumbria (015394 37210).

Dogs allowed throughout (except dining area).

Pet Regulars: Bonnie (sheepdog/Retriever), beer-mat catching, scrounging, has own chair.

THE MORTAL MAN HOTEL
Troutbeck, Windermere, Cumbria LA23 lPL (015394 33193).

Dogs allowed throughout and in guest rooms.

Pet Regulars: Include James (Labrador) who will take dogs for walks if they are on a lead and Snip (Border Collie), makes solo visits.

STAG INN
Dufton, Appleby, Cumbria (017683 51608).

Dogs allowed in non-food bar, beer garden, village green plus B&B.

Pet Regulars: Bacchus (Newfoundland), enjoys a good sprawl; Kirk (Dachshund), carries out tour of inspection unaccompanied - but wearing lead; Kim (Weimaraner), best bitter drinker; Buster (Jack Russell), enjoys a quiet evening.

WATERMILL INN

School Lane, Ings, near Staveley, Kendal, Cumbria (01539 821309).

Dogs allowed in beer garden, Wrynose bottom bar.

Pet Regulars: Smudge (sheepdog); Gowan (Westie) and Scruffy (mongrel). All enjoy a range of crisps and snacks. Scruffy regularly drinks Theakstons XB. Pub dogs Misty (Beardie) and Thatcher (Lakeland Terrier).

DERBYSHIRE

DOG AND PARTRIDGE COUNTRY INN & MOTEL

Swinscoe, Ashbourne, Derbyshire (01335 343183).

Dogs allowed throughout, except restaurant.

Pet Regulars: Include Mitsy (57); Rusty (Cairn); Spider (Collie/GSD) and Rex (GSD).

RIFLE VOLUNTEER

Birchwood Lane, Somercotes, Derbyshire DE55 4ND (01773 602584).

Dogs allowed in non-food bar, car park tables, beer garden.

Pet Regulars: Flossy (Border Collie), bar stool inhabitant; Pepper (Border Collie), has made a study of beer mat aerodynamics; Tara (GSD), pub piggyback specialist.

WHITE HART

Station Road, West Hallam, Derbyshire DE7 6GW.

Dogs allowed in all non-food areas.

Pet Regulars: Ben and Oliver (Golden Retrievers) drinking halves of mixed; Sid (Greyhound), plays with cats.

DEVON

BRENDON HOUSE HOTEL

Brendon, Lynton, North Devon EX35 6PS (01598 741206).

Dogs very welcome and allowed in tea gardens, guest bedrooms.

Pet Regulars: Mutley (mongrel), cat chasing; Pie (Border Terrier), unusual 'yellow stripe', was once chased - by a sheep! Farthing (cat), 20 years old, self appointed cream tea receptionist. Years of practice have perfected dirty looks at visiting dogs.

THE BULLERS ARMS
Chagford, Newton Abbot, Devon (01647 432348).

Dogs allowed throughout pub, except dining room/kitchen.

Pet Regulars: Miffin & Sally (Cavalier King Charles Spaniels), celebrated Miffin's 14th birthday with a party at The Bullers.

CROWN AND SCEPTRE
2 Petitor Road, Torquay, Devon TQ1 4QA (01803 328290).

Dogs allowed in non-food bar, family room, lounge.

Pet Regulars: Samantha (Labrador), opens, consumes and returns empties when offered crisp packets; Toby & Rory (Irish Setters), general daftness; Buddy & Jessie (Collies), beer-mat frisbee experts; Cassie (Collie), scrounging.

THE DEVONSHIRE INN
Sticklepath, near Okehampton, Devon EX20 2NW (01837 840626).

Dogs allowed in non-food bar, car park, beer garden, family room, guest rooms.

Pet Regulars: Bess (Labrador), 'minds' owner; Annie (Shihtzu), snoring a speciality; Daisy (Collie), accompanies folk singers; Duke (GSD) and Ben (Collie-cross), general attention seeking.

THE JOURNEY'S END INN
Ringmore, near Kingsbridge, South Devon TQ7 4HL (01548 810205).

Dogs allowed throughout the pub.

Pet Regulars: Lager, Cider, Scrumpy and Whiskey (all Terriers) - a pint of real ale at lunchtime between them.

THE ROYAL OAK INN
Dunsford, near Exeter, Devon EX6 7DA (01647 252256).

Dogs allowed in non-food bars, beer garden, accommodation for guests with dogs.

Pet Regulars: Tom Thumb (Jack Russell), pub bouncer - doesn't throw people out, just bounces.

THE SEA TROUT INN
Staverton, near Totnes, Devon TQ9 6PA (01803 762274).

Dogs allowed in non-food bar, car park tables, beer garden, owners' rooms (but not on beds).

Pet Regulars: Billy (Labrador-cross), partial to drip trays; Curnow (Poodle), brings a blanket.

THE WHITE HART HOTEL
Moretonhampstead, Newton Abbot, Devon TQ13 8NF (01647 440406).

Dogs allowed throughout, except restaurant.

Pet Regulars: Poppie, Rosie (Standard Poodles) and Bobby (Collie).

DURHAM

TAP AND SPILE
27 Front Street, Framwellgate Moor, Durham DH1 5EE (0191 386 5451).

Dogs allowed throughout the pub.

Pet Regulars: These include Smutty (Labrador) who brings her own beer bowl and is definitely not a lager Lab - traditional brews only.

ESSEX

THE OLD SHIP
Heybridge Basin, Heybridge, Maldon, Essex (01621 854150).

Dogs allowed throughout pub.

Pet Regulars: Toby (57), monopolising bar stools; Tag (Spaniel), nipping behind the bar for biscuits; Toto (57), nipping behind the bar to 'beat up' owners' Great Dane; Happy (terrier), drinking beer and looking miserable.

THE WINGED HORSE
Luncies Road, Vange, Basildon, Essex SS14 1SB (01268 552338).

Dogs allowed throughout pub.

Pet Regulars: Gina (Newfoundland), visits solo daily for a pub lunch biscuits and a beer; Roxy (Bull Terrier), fond of making a complete mess with crisps and loves a glass of beer. There are 14 canine regulars in all, not including the pub dog Tinka.

GREATER LONDON

THE PHOENIX
28 Thames Street, Sunbury on Thames, Middlesex (01932 789163).

Dogs allowed in non-food bar, beer garden, family room.

Pet Regulars: Pepe (57), fire hog; Cromwell (King Charles), often accompanied by small, balled-up sock. Drinks Websters, once seen with a hangover. Fred (Labrador), would be a fire hog if Pepe wasn't always there first; Oliver (Standard Poodle), still a pup, pub visits are character-building!

THE TIDE END COTTAGE
Ferry Road, Teddington, Middlesex (0181 977 7762).

Dogs allowed throughout the pub.

Pet Regulars: Angus (Setter), "mine's a half of Guinness"; Dina (GSD), guide dog, beautiful, loyal and clever; Harry (Beagle), partial to sausages, a greeter and meeter; Lady (cross), likes a game of tug o' war with Angus.

HAMPSHIRE

THE CHEQUERS
Ridgeway Lane, Lower Pennington, Lymington, Hants (01590 673415).

Dogs allowed in non-food bar, outdoor barbecue area (away from food).

Pet Regulars: Otto (Hungarian Vizsla), eats beer-mats and paper napkins. Likes beer but not often indulged.

THE VICTORY
High Street, Hamble-le-Rice, Southampton, Hampshire(01703 453105).

Dogs allowed throughout the pub.

Pet Regulars: Sefton (Labrador), his 'usual' chew bars are kept especially.

NOTE

A few abbreviations and 'pet' descriptions have been used in this section which deserve mention and, where necessary, explanation as follows: **GSD:** German Shepherd Dog. ... *-cross:* a cross-breed where one breed appears identifiable. **57:** richly varied origin. You will also encounter **'mongrel', 'Bitsa'** and **'???!'** which are self evident and generally affectionate.

FLYING BULL

London Road Rake, near Petersfield, Hampshire GU33 7JB (01730 892285).

Dogs allowed throughout the pub.

Pet Regulars: Flippy (Labrador/Old English Sheepdog), partial to the biscuits served with coffee. Status as 'pub dog' questionable as will visit The Sun over the road for a packet of cheese snips.

HERTFORDSHIRE

THE BLACK HORSE

Chorly Wood Common, Dog Kennel Lane, Rickmansworth, Hertfordshire (01923 282252).

Dogs very welcome and allowed throughout the pub.

Pet Regulars: Spritzy (mongrel), pub hooligan, former Battersea Dogs' Home resident.

THE FOX

496 Luton Road, Kinsbourne Green, near Harpenden, Hertfordshire (01582 713817).

Dogs allowed in non-food bar, car park tables, beer garden.

Pet Regulars: A tightly knit core of regulars which includes assorted Collies, German Shepherd Dogs and Retrievers. Much competition for dropped bar snacks.

THE ROBIN HOOD AND LITTLE JOHN

Rabley Heath, near Codicote, Hertfordshire (01438 812361).

Dogs allowed in non-food bar, car park tables, beer garden, pitch and putt.

Pet Regulars: Willow (Labrador), beer-mat catcher. The locals of the pub have close to 50 dogs between them, most of which visit from time to time. The team includes a two Labrador search squad dispatched by one regular's wife to indicate time's up. When they arrive he has five minutes' drinking up time before all three leave together.

ISLE OF WIGHT

THE CLARENDON HOTEL AND WIGHT MOUSE INN

Chale, Isle of Wight (01983 730431).

Dogs allowed in pub but not hotel dining room.

Pet Regulars: Guy (mongrel), calls in for daily sausages. Known to escape from house to visit solo. Hotel dog is Gizmo (Spoodle - Toy Poodle-cross King Charles Spaniel), child entertainer.

KENT

KENTISH HORSE

Cow Lane, Mark Beech, Edenbridge, Kent (01342 850493).

Dogs allowed.

Pet Regulars: Include Boozer (Greyhound), who enjoys a beer and Kylin (Shihtzu), socialising. Pub grounds also permanent residence to goats, sheep, lambs, a horse and geese.

THE OLD NEPTUNE

Marine Terrace, Whitstable, Kent CT5 IEJ (01227 272262).

Dogs allowed in non-food bar and beach frontage.

Pet Regulars: Josh (mongrel), solo visits, serves himself from pub water-bowl; Bear (GSD), insists on people throwing stones on beach to chase, will drop stones on feet as quick reminder; Trigger (mongrel), accompanied by toys; Poppy & Fred (mongrel and GSD), soft touch and dedicated vocalist - barks at anything that runs away!

PRINCE ALBERT

38 High Street, Broadstairs, Kent CT10 lLH (01843 861937).

Dogs allowed in non-food bar.

Pet Regulars: Buster (King Charles), a health freak who likes to nibble on raw carrots and any fresh veg; Suki (Jack Russell), Saturday-night roast beef sampler; Sally (Airedale), official rug; Bruno (Boxer), particularly fond of pepperami sausage.

THE SWANN INN

Little Chart, Kent TN27 OQB (01233 840702).

Dogs allowed - everywhere except restaurant.

Pet Regulars: Rambo (Leonbergers), knocks on the door and orders pork scratchings; Duster (Retriever?), places his order - for crisps - with one soft bark for the landlady; Ben (GSD), big licks; Josh (Papillon), hind-legged dancer.

UNCLE TOM'S CABIN

Lavender Hill, Tonbridge, Kent (01628 483339).

Dogs allowed in non-food bar, beer garden.

Pet Regulars: Bob Minor (Lurcher); Tug (mongrel); Bitsy (mongrel); Tilly (Spaniel): 10pm is dog biscuit time!

LANCASHIRE

ABBEYLEE

Abbeyhills Road, Oldham, Lancashire (0161 678 8795).

Dogs allowed throughout.

Pet Regulars: Include Susie (Boxer), so fond of pork scratchings they are now used by her owners as a reward in the show ring.

MALT'N HOPS

50 Friday Street, Chorley, Lancashire PR6 OAH (01257 260967).

Dogs allowed throughout pub.

Pet Regulars: Freya (GSD), greets everyone by rolling over to allow tummy tickle; Abbie (GSD), under-seat sleeper; Brandy (Rhodesian Ridgeback), at the sound of a bag of crisps opening will lean on eater until guest's legs go numb or he is offered a share; Toby (Labrador), valued customer in his own right, due to amount of crisps he eats, also retrieves empty bags.

BETA *petfoods*

BETA PETFOODS
THE BETTER WAY TO
NUTRITIONAL CARE

LEICESTERSHIRE
CHEQUERS INN
1 Gilmorton Road, Ashby Magna, near Lutterworth, Leicestershire (01455 209523).

Dogs allowed throughout the pub.

Pet Regulars: Bracken (Labrador), barmaid; Jessie (Labrador), socialite; Blue (English Setter), 'fuss' seeker.

LINCOLNSHIRE
THE BLUE DOG INN
Main Street, Sewstern, Grantham, Lincs NG33 SQR (01476 860097).

Dogs allowed in non-food bar, beer garden. Dog-hitching rail outside.

Pet Regulars: The Guv'nor (Great Dane), best draught-excluder in history; Jenny (Westie) shares biscuits with pub cats; Jemma (98% Collie), atmosphere lapper-upper; JoJo (Cavalier King Charles), enjoys a drop of Murphys.

MERSEYSIDE
AMBASSADOR PRIVATE HOTEL
13 Bath Street, Southport, Merseyside PR9 ODP (01704 543998).

Dogs allowed in non-food bar, lounge, guest bedrooms.

THE SCOTCH PIPER
Southport Road, Lydiate, Merseyside (0151 526 0503).

Dogs allowed throughout the pub.

Pet Regulars: Pippa (Rescued Russell), one dog welcoming committee, hearth rug, scrounger. Landlord's dogs very much second fiddle.

MIDLANDS
AWENTSBURY HOTEL
21 Serpentine Road, Selly Park, Birmingham B29 7HU (0121 472 1258).

Dogs allowed in non-food bar, car park tables, beer garden.

Pet Regulars: Well-behaved dogs welcome.

TALBOT HOTEL

Colley Gate, Halesowen, West Midlands.

Dogs are allowed throughout the pub.

Pet Regulars: Include Inga, Gil, Jack and Red, all Border Collies. Every Christmas canine customers are treated to gift-wrapped dog chews.

NORFOLK

MARINE HOTEL

10 St Edmunds Terrace, Hunstanton, Norfolk PE36 5EH (01485 533310).

Dogs allowed throughout, except dining room.

Pet Regulars: Many dogs have returned with their owners year after year to stay at The Marine Bar.

THE OLD RAILWAY TAVERN

Eccles Road, Quidenham, Norwich, Norfolk NR16 2JG (01953 888223).

Dogs allowed in non-food bar, beer garden.

Pet Regulars: Maggie (Clumber Spaniel); Indi (GSD), Soshie (GSD) and pub dogs Elsa (GSD) & Vell (Springer). Elsa is so fond of sitting, motionless, on her own window ledge that new customers often think she's stuffed!

THE ROSE AND CROWN

Nethergate Street, Harpley, King's Lynn, Norfolk (01485 520577).

Dogs allowed in non-food bar, car park tables.

Pet Regulars: A merry bunch with shared interests - Duffy (mongrel); Tammy (Airedale); Bertie & Pru (Standard Poodles), all enjoy pub garden romps during surnmer and fireside seats in winter.

OXFORDSHIRE

THE BELL INN

High Street, Adderbury, Oxon (01295 810338).

Dogs allowed throughout the pub.

Pet Regulars: Include Wilf (mongrel), supplies full cabaret including talking to people and singing.

SHROPSHIRE
LONGMYND HOTEL
Cunnery Road, Church Stretton, Shropshire SY6 6AG (01694 722244).

Dogs allowed in owners' hotel bedrooms but not in public areas.

Pet Regulars: Sox (Collie/Labrador), occasional drinker and regular customer greeter; Kurt (GSD), entertainments manager; Sadie (Retriever), self appointed fire-guard.

REDFERN HOTEL
Cleobury Mortimer, Shropshire SY14 8AA (01299 270395).

Dogs allowed throughout and in guests' bedrooms.

SOMERSET
THE BUTCHERS ARMS
Carhampton, Somerset (01643 821333).

Dogs allowed throughout the pub.

Pet Regulars: Lobo and Chera (Samoyeds), eating ice cubes and drinking; Emma (Spaniel), a whisky drinker; Benji (Spaniel-cross), self-appointed rug. Jimmy, a pony, also occasionally drops in for a drink.

HALFWAY HOUSE
Pitney, Langport, Somerset TA10 9AB (01458 252513).

Dogs allowed throughout (except kitchen!).

Pet Regulars: Pip (Lurcher), enjoys bitter, cider and G&T; Bulawayo (Ridgeback-cross), the advance party, sometimes three hours in advance of owner; Potter (57), sits at the bar.

THE SHIP INN
High Street, Porlock, Somerset (01643 862507).

Dogs allowed throughout and in guests' rooms.

Pet Regulars: Include Buster, Hardy and Crackers (Jack Russells), terrorists from London; Bijoux (Peke), while on holiday at The Ship enjoys Chicken Supreme cooked to order every evening.

SURREY
THE CRICKETERS
12 Oxenden Road, Tongham, Farnham, Surrey (01252 331340).

Dogs allowed in non-food bar, beer garden.

Pet Regulars: Include Lucy (a 'Bitsa'), surreptitious beer drinker and Chocolate Labradors Marston - after the beer and Tullamore Dew - after the whisky.

SUSSEX
CHARCOAL BURNER
Weald Drive, Furnace Green, Crawley, West Sussex RH10 6NY (01293 526174).

Dogs allowed in non-food bar areas and front and back patios.

Pet Regulars: Lucy (Irish Setter), dedicated to cheese snips.

THE FORESTERS ARMS
High Street, Fairwarp, near Uckfield, East Sussex TN22 3BP (01825 712808).

Dogs allowed in the beer garden and at car park tables, also inside.

Pet Regulars: Include Scampi (Jack Russell) who enjoys a social interlude with fellow canine guests.

THE INN IN THE PARK (CHEF & BREWER)
Tilgate Park, Tilgate, Crawley, West Sussex RH10 5PQ (01293 545324).

Dogs allowed in non-food bar, beer garden, upstairs lounge and balcony.

Pet Regulars: Tuffy (Staffordshire Bull Terrier) leans, on hind legs, on bar awaiting beer and nibbles; Ted (Weimaraner), a 'watcher'; Jacko (Dalmatian), a crisp howler who, once given a pack, opens them himself; Meg (Border Collie), hoovers fallen bar snacks.

THE PLOUGH
Crowhurst, near Battle, East Sussex TN33 9AY (01424 830310).

Dogs allowed in non-food bar, car park tables, beer garden.

Pet Regulars: Kai (Belgian Shepherd), drinks halves of Websters; Poppy and Cassie (Springer Spaniels), divided between the lure of crisps and fireside.

Pet-Friendly Pubs

THE PRESTONVILLE ARMS

64 Hamilton Road, Brighton, East Sussex (01273 701007).

Dogs allowed in beer garden, throughout the pub (no food served).

Pet Regulars: These include Katie and Susie, a Yorkie and a ???!, who have been known to jump onto the pool table and help out by picking up the balls.

QUEENS HEAD

Village Green, Sedlescombe, East Sussex (01424 870228).

Dogs allowed throughout the pub.

Pet Regulars: Misty (Whippet) partial to Guinness and Bacardi and Coke. Hogs the dog biscuits kept especially for guests' dogs - proceeds to Guide Dogs for the Blind.

THE SLOOP INN

Freshfield Lock, Haywards Heath, West Sussex RH17 7NP (01444 831219).

Dogs allowed in non-food bar, at car park tables, beer garden, family room, public bar.

Pet Regulars: Pub dogs are Staffordshire Bull Terriers Rosie and Chutney. Customers include Solo (Labrador), crisp burglar, beer drinker; Tania (Rottweiller), sleeping giant. All bedraggled gun-dogs are especially welcome to dry out by the fire.

THE SMUGGLERS' ROOST

125 Sea Lane, Rustington, West Sussex BN16 25G (01903 785714).

Dogs allowed in non-food bar, at car park tables, in beer garden, family room.

Pet Regulars: Moffat (Border Terrier), beer makes him sneeze; Leo (Border Terrier), forms instant affections with anyone who notices him; Max (Cocker Spaniel), eats crisps only if they are 'plain'; Tim (King Charles Spaniel), quite prepared to guard his corner when food appears. The landlord owns a Great Dane.

Pet-Friendly Pubs

THE SPORTSMAN'S ARMS
Rackham Road, Amberley, near Arundel, West Sussex BN18 9NR (01798 831787).
Dogs allowed throughout the pub.

Pet Regulars: Ramsden (Labrador), likes pickled onions. Landlord's dogs will not venture into the cellar which is haunted by the ghost of a young girl.

WELLDIGGERS ARMS
Lowheath, Petworth, West Sussex GU28 OHG (01798 342287).
Dogs allowed throughout the pub.

Pet Regulars: Angus (Labrador), crisp snaffler; Benji (Cavalier King Charles), hearth rug.

THE WYNDHAM ARMS
Rogate, West Sussex GU31 5HG (01730 821315).
Dogs allowed in non-food bar and at outside tables.

Pet Regulars: Henry (wire-haired Dachshund), hooked on Bristol Cream Sherry; Blot (Labrador), welcoming-committee and food fancier; Scruffy (Beardie), completely mad; Oscar (Labrador), floor hog.

WILTSHIRE

ARTICHOKE
The Nursery, Devizes, Wiltshire SN10 2AA (01380 723400).
Dogs allowed throughout pub.

Pet Regulars: Heidi (mongrel), pub tart; Monty (Dalmatian), trifle fixated; Rosie (Boxer), customer 'kissing'; Triffle (Airedale) and Shandy (mongrel) pub welcoming-committee.

NOTE
A few abbreviations and 'pet' descriptions have been used in this section which deserve mention and, where necessary, explanation as follows: ***GSD:*** German Shepherd Dog. ... ***-cross:*** a cross-breed where one breed appears identifiable. ***57:*** richly varied origin. You will also encounter *'mongrel'*, *'Bitsa'* and *'???!'* which are self evident and generally affectionate.

Pet-Friendly Pubs

THE PETERBOROUGH ARMS

Dauntsey Lock, near Chippenham, Wiltshire SN15 4HD (01249 890409).

Dogs allowed in non-food bar, at car park tables, in beer garden, family room (when non-food).

Pet Regulars: Include Winston (Jack Russell), will wait for command before eating a biscuit placed on his nose; Waddi (GSD), can grab a bowling ball before it hits the skittle pins; Harry 4 Legs (GSD), always wins the Christmas prize draw.

THE THREE HORSESHOES

High Street, Chapmanslade, near Westbury, Wiltshire (01373 832280).

Dogs allowed in non-food bar and beer garden.

Pet Regulars: Include Clieo (Golden Retriever), possibly the youngest 'regular' in the land - his first trip to the pub was at eight weeks. Westbury and District Canine Society repair to the Three Horseshoes after training nights (Monday/Wednesday). The pub boasts six cats and two dogs in residence.

WAGGON AND HORSES

High Street, Wootton Bassett, Swindon, Wiltshire (01793 852326).

Dogs allowed in non-food bar.

Pet Regulars: Include Gemma, a very irregular Whippet/Border collie cross. She likes to balance beer-mats on her nose, then flip them over and catch them, opens and shuts doors on command, walks on her hind legs and returns empty crisp bags. She is limited to one glass of Guinness a night.

YORKSHIRE

BARNES WALLIS INN

North Howden, Howden, East Yorkshire (01430 430639).

Guide dogs only

Pet Regulars: A healthy cross-section of mongrels, Collies and Labradors. One of the most popular pastimes is giving the pub cat a bit of a run for his money.

Pet-Friendly Pubs

KINGS HEAD INN

Barmby on the Marsh, East Yorkshire DN14 7HL (01757 638357).

Dogs allowed in non-food bar.

Pet Regulars: Many and varied!

THE FORESTERS ARMS

Kilburn, North Yorkshire YO6 4AH (01347 868386).

Dogs allowed throughout, except restaurant.

Pet Regulars: Ebony (Labrador) and Jess (Labrador), eating ice cubes off the bar and protecting customers from getting any heat from the fire.

FOX INN

Roxby Staithes, Whitby, North Yorkshire (01947 840335).

Dogs allowed throughout including guests' bedrooms, but not in bar.

Pet Regulars: B&B guests include Lucy and Mouse (Jack Russell & Dachshund); Mattie & Sally (Spaniels) and Meg and George (Bassetts); Lady (57) and another Lady, also a Heinz 57.

THE GREENE DRAGON INN

Hardraw, Hawes, North Yorkshire DL8 3LZ (01969 667392).

Dogs allowed in bar, at car park tables, in beer garden, family room but not dining room or restaurant.

THE HALL

High Street, Thornton Le Dale, Pickering, North Yorkshire YO18 7RR

Dogs allowed usually throughout the pub.

Pet Regulars: Include Lucy (Jack Russell), she has her own beer glass at the bar, drinks only Newcastle Brown and Floss (mongrel), partial to Carlsberg.

NEW INN HOTEL

Clapham, near Settle, North Yorkshire LA2 8HH (015242 51203).

Dogs allowed in non-food bar, beer garden, family room.

Pet Regulars: Ben (Collie-cross), a model customer.

PREMIER HOTEL

66 Esplanade, South Cliff, Scarborough, North Yorkshire YO11 2UZ (01723 501062).

Dogs allowed throughout in non-food areas of hotel.

Pet Regulars: enjoy sharing their owners' rooms at no extra cost. There is a walking service available for pets with disabled owners.

SIMONSTONE HALL

Hawes, North Yorkshire DL8 3LY (01969 667255).

Dogs allowed throughout hotel except dining area.

Pet Regulars: account for 2,000 nights per annum. More than 50% of guests are accompanied by their dogs, from Pekes to an Anatolian Shepherd (the size of a small Shetland pony!) Two dogs have stayed, with their owners, on 23 separate occasions.

THE SPINNEY

Forest Rise, Balby, Doncaster, South Yorkshire DN4 9HQ (01302 852033).

Dogs allowed throughout the pub.

Pet Regulars: Shamus (Irish Setter), pub thief. Fair game includes pool balls, beer mats, crisps, beer, coats, hats. Recently jumped 15 feet off pub roof with no ill effect. Yan (Labrador), a dedicated guide dog; Sam (Boxer), black pudding devotee.

THE ROCKINGHAM ARMS

8 Main Street, Wentworth, Rotherham, South Yorkshire S62 7LO (01226 742075).

Dogs allowed throughout pub.

Pet Regulars: Tilly (Beardie), does nothing but has adopted the quote of actor Kenneth Williams- "Sometimes I feel so unutterably superior to those around me that I marvel at my ability to live among them"; Sasha & Penny (Terriers), enjoy a social coffee; Kate & Rags (Airedale and cross-breed), prefer lager to coffee; Holly (terrier and pub dog), dubbed 'the flying squirrel', likes everyone, whether they like it or not!

THE SHIP

6 Main Street, Greasbrough, Rotherham, South Yorkshire S61 4PX (01709 551020).

Dogs allowed throughout the pub.

Pet Regulars: Include Hans (Guide Dog), reverts to puppy behaviour when 'off duty' and Ben (Border Terrier), 'frisks' customers for tit-bits.

ROTHERHAM COMPANIONS CLUB

The Fairways, Wickersley, Rotherham, South Yorkshire (01709 548192).

Dogs on leads allowed throughout the pub (some restrictions if wedding party booked).

Pet Regulars: All chocolate fanatics who receive their favourite treat on arrival include Viking (Springer), Duke (Chow), Max (Border Collie) and Willie (Yorkshire Terrier). Viking keeps a box of toys and a ball behind the bar.

THE GOLDEN FLEECE

Lindley Road, Blackley, near Huddersfield, West Yorkshire (01422 372704).

Dogs allowed in non-food bar, at outside tables.

Pet Regulars: Ellie & Meara (Rhodesian Ridgebacks), starving dog impressions, animated hearthrugs.

WALES

ANGLESEY

THE BUCKLEY HOTEL

Castle Street, Beaumaris, Isle of Anglesey LL58 8AW (01248 810415).

Dogs allowed throughout the pub, except in the dining room.

Pet Regulars: Cassie (Springer Spaniel) and Rex (mongrel), dedicated 'companion' dogs.

DYFED

THE ANGEL HOTEL
Rhosmaen Street, Llandeilo, Dyfed (01558 822765).

Dogs allowed throughoue the pub.

Pet Regulars: Skip (Spaniel/Collie), a Baileys devotee; Crumble (GSD), a devotee of anything edible.

SCOTLAND

ARGYLL

THE BALLACHULISH HOTEL
Ballachulish, Argyll PA39 4JY (01855 811606).

Dogs allowed in the lounge, beer garden and guests' bedrooms, but not in bar.

Pet Regulars: Thumper (Border Collie/GSD-cross), devoted to his owner and follows him everywhere.

INVERNESS-SHIRE

ARISAIG HOTEL
Arisaig, Inverness-shire (01687 450210).

Dogs welcome.

Pet Regulars. Regulars in the public bar include Luar (Lurcher), Cindy (Collie), Whisky (Terrier) and Raith (Jack Russell), plus resident dog Noodle, available for walks at any time.

KIRKCUDBRIGHTSHIRE

CULGRUFF HOUSE HOTEL
Crossmichael, Castle Douglas, Kirkcudbrightshire DG7 3BB (01556 670230).

Dogs allowed in family room, guest bedrooms, but must be kept on leads outside.

Pet Regulars: A cross-section of canine visitors.

MORAYSHIRE

THE CLIFTON BAR
Clifton Road, Lossiemouth, Morayshire (01343 812100).

Dogs allowed throughout pub.

Pet Regulars: Include Zoe (Westie), has her own seat and is served coffee with two lumps and Rhona (Labrador) who makes solo visits.

ROYAL OAK
Station Road, Urquhart, Elgin, Moray (01343 842607).

Dogs allowed throughout pub.

Pet Regulars: Murphy (Staffordshire Bull Terrier) - food bin. Biscuits (from the landlady), Maltesers (from the landlord), sausages and burgers (from the barbecue).

PERTHSHIRE

CLACHAN COTTAGE HOTEL
Lochside, Lochearnhead, Perthshire (01567 830247).

Dogs allowed in all non-food areas.

Pet Regulars: Regulars are few but passing trade frequent and welcome. Previous owner's dog was a renowned water-skier.

CHANNEL ISLANDS

JERSEY

LA PULENTE INN
La Pulente, St Brelade, Jersey (01534 41760).

Dogs allowed throughout the pub.

Pet Regulars: Include Bridie (Border Collie), darts, pool, watching TV, beer-mat skiing, stone shoving. Also responsible for fly catching. Drinks Bass and Guinness.

"FAMILY FRIENDLY"
Pubs, Inns and Hotels

These are establishments which make an extra effort to cater for parents and children. The majority provide a separate children's menu or they may be willing to serve small portions of main course dishes on request; there are often separate outdoor or indoor play areas where the junior members of the family can let off steam while Mum and Dad unwind over a drink.

CORNWALL
WRINGFORD DOWN, Cawsand (01752 822287). Children's suppers, indoor and outdoor play areas, indoor heated pool, laundry room, baby listening — and lots more!

CUMBRIA
GLEN ROTHAY HOTEL, Rydal, Ambleside (015394 32524). Children's menu; garden; cots and high chairs; baby listening and early evening meals.

COLEDALE INN, Braithwaite, Near Keswick (017687 78272). Children's menu and family rooms; outdoor play area with climbing net; cots and high chairs.

MANOR HOUSE INN, Oxen Park, Near Ulverston (01229 861345). Family room and children's menu; cots and high chairs.

GLOUCESTERSHIRE
WYNDHAM ARMS, Clearwell, Near Coleford (01594 833666). Children's menu and family room; cots and high chairs; nappy changing facilities; baby listening in bedrooms.

HAMPSHIRE
HIGH CORNER INN, Linwood, Near Ringwood (01425 473973). Children's menu and family rooms; outdoor adventure playground; indoor pool table and Lego; nappy changing room; babysitting.

HEREFORD & WORCESTER
THE GREEN MAN INN, Fownhope (01432 860243). Children's menu and family room; outdoor play area with swing; cots and high chairs; baby listening.

ROYAL OAK HOTEL, South Street, Leominster (01568 612610). Children's menu and family room; cots and high chairs.

ISLE OF WIGHT
CLARENDON HOTEL & WIGHT MOUSE INN, Chale (02983 730431). Children's menu and family room; outdoor play area with swings, climbing frame, pets' corner, bouncy castle, etc; Shetland pony rides; cots and high chairs; nappy changing room; babysitting.

KENT
RINGLESTONE INN, Harrietsham, Near Maidstone (01622 859900). Full Children's Licence; children's portions; 2 acres of gardens with hopscotch (unsupervised); high chairs.

OXFORDSHIRE
SHEHERDS HALL INN, Witney Road, Freeland (01993 881256). Children's menu and family room; indoor and outdoor play areas; cots and high chairs.

SOMERSET
THE HATCH INN, Hatch Beauchamp, Taunton (01823 480245). Children's menu and family rooms; garden; cots.

MALT SHOVEL INN, Blackmoor Lane, Cannington, Bridgwater (01278 653432). Children's menu and family room; garden; cots and high chairs.

WEST SUSSEX
BAT AND BALL, Newpound Lane, Wisborough Green (01403 700713). Children's menu and family room; outdoor play area; high chairs.

NORTH YORKSHIRE
THE TRADDOCK HOTEL, Austwick, Near Settle (015242 51224). Children's menu and family rooms; garden and toy cupboard; cots and high chairs; radio baby listeners.

BUCK INN, Thornton Watlass, Near Bedale, Ripon (01677 422461). Children's menu; garden with slide, climbing frame, swings, bouncy bike; cots and high chairs.

FORESTERS ARMS, Main Street, Grassington, Near Skipton (01756 752349). Family room and children's menu; cots and high chairs.

SCOTLAND

ABERDEENSHIRE
GORDON ARMS HOTEL, Kincardine O'Neil (01339 884236). Children's menu and small portions; family room.

DUMFRIES-SHIRE
BALMORAL HOTEL, High Street, Moffat (01683 220288). Children welcome.

ROSS-SHIRE
THE OLD INN, Gairloch (01445 712006). Children's menu and family room; outdoor play area with rope swing; cots and high chairs; baby listening in bedrooms.

The *Countryman*

Discover the countryside that belongs to us all.

There's always plenty to read in *The Countryman*. This little green book first appeared back in 1927. With nearly 200 pages in every issue, this bi-monthly magazine brings you stories and poems of country ways and insights into country life, as well as keeping a keen eye open for changes that threaten our glorious British countryside.

Our offices in the Cotswolds are a former coaching inn and readers are always welcome to visit the delightful garden with views of the Windrush valley across the stone roofs of the village.

Subscribe now, and for just £13.20 we will deliver the countryside direct to your door six times a year.

SUBSCRIPTIONS HOTLINE
CALL 0181 646 6672

quote ref FHG97

The Countryman makes the perfect gift for anyone who loves the countryside. If you make a gift subscription we send the recipient a greetings card to tell them you have thought of them.

ONE FOR YOUR FRIEND 1997

FHG Publications have a large range of attractive holiday accommodation guides for all kinds of holiday opportunities throughout Britain. They also make useful gifts at any time of year. Our guides are available in most bookshops and larger newsagents but we will be happy to post you a copy direct if you have any difficulty. We will also post abroad but have to charge separately for post or freight. The inclusive cost of posting and packing the guides to you or your friends in the UK is as follows:

Farm Holiday Guide ENGLAND, WALES and IRELAND
Board, Self-catering, Caravans/Camping, Activity Holidays. £5.50

Farm Holiday Guide SCOTLAND
All kinds of holiday accommodation. £4.00

SELF-CATERING HOLIDAYS IN BRITAIN
Over 1000 addresses throughout for Self-catering and caravans in Britain. £5.00

BRITAIN'S BEST HOLIDAYS
A quick-reference general guide for all kinds of holidays. £4.00

The FHG Guide to CARAVAN & CAMPING HOLIDAYS
Caravans for hire, sites and holiday parks and centres. £4.00

BED AND BREAKFAST STOPS
Over 1000 friendly and comfortable overnight stops. Non-smoking, The Disabled and Special Diets Supplements. £5.50

CHILDREN WELCOME! FAMILY HOLIDAY & ATTRACTIONS GUIDE
Family holidays with details of amenities for children and babies. £5.00

SCOTTISH WELCOME
Introduced by Katie Woods. A new guide to holiday accommodation and attractions in Scotland. £4.80

Recommended SHORT BREAKS HOLIDAYS IN BRITAIN
'Approved' accommodation for quality bargain breaks. Introduced by John Carter. £4.80

Recommended COUNTRY HOTELS OF BRITAIN
Including Country Houses, for the discriminating. £4.80

Recommended WAYSIDE AND COUNTRY INNS OF BRITAIN
Pubs, Inns and small hotels. £4.80

PGA GOLF GUIDE Where to play. Where to stay
Over 2000 golf courses in Britain with convenient accommodation. Endorsed by the PGA. Holiday Golf in France, Portugal, Spain and USA. £9.80

PETS WELCOME!
The unique guide for holidays for pet owners and their pets. £5.50

BED AND BREAKFAST IN BRITAIN
Over 1000 choices for touring and holidays throughout Britain.
Airports and Ferries Supplement. £4.00

THE FRENCH FARM AND VILLAGE HOLIDAY GUIDE
The official guide to self-catering holidays in the 'Gîtes de France'. £9.80

Tick your choice and send your order and payment to FHG PUBLICATIONS, ABBEY MILL BUSINESS CENTRE, SEEDHILL, PAISLEY PA1 1TJ (TEL: 0141-887 0428. FAX: 0141-889 7204). **Deduct** 10% for 2/3 titles or copies; 20% for 4 or more.

Send to: NAME ....

ADDRESS ....

....

....POST CODE ....

I enclose Cheque/Postal Order for £...

SIGNATURE ....DATE ....

Please complete the following to help us improve the service we provide. How did you find out about our guides?

☐ Press ☐ Magazines ☐ TVRadio ☐ Family/Friend ☐ Other.

MAP SECTION

The following seven pages of maps indicate the main cities, towns and holiday centres of Britain. Space obviously does not permit every location featured in this book to be included but the approximate position may be ascertained by using the distance indications quoted and the scale bars on the maps.

Map 1

Map 2

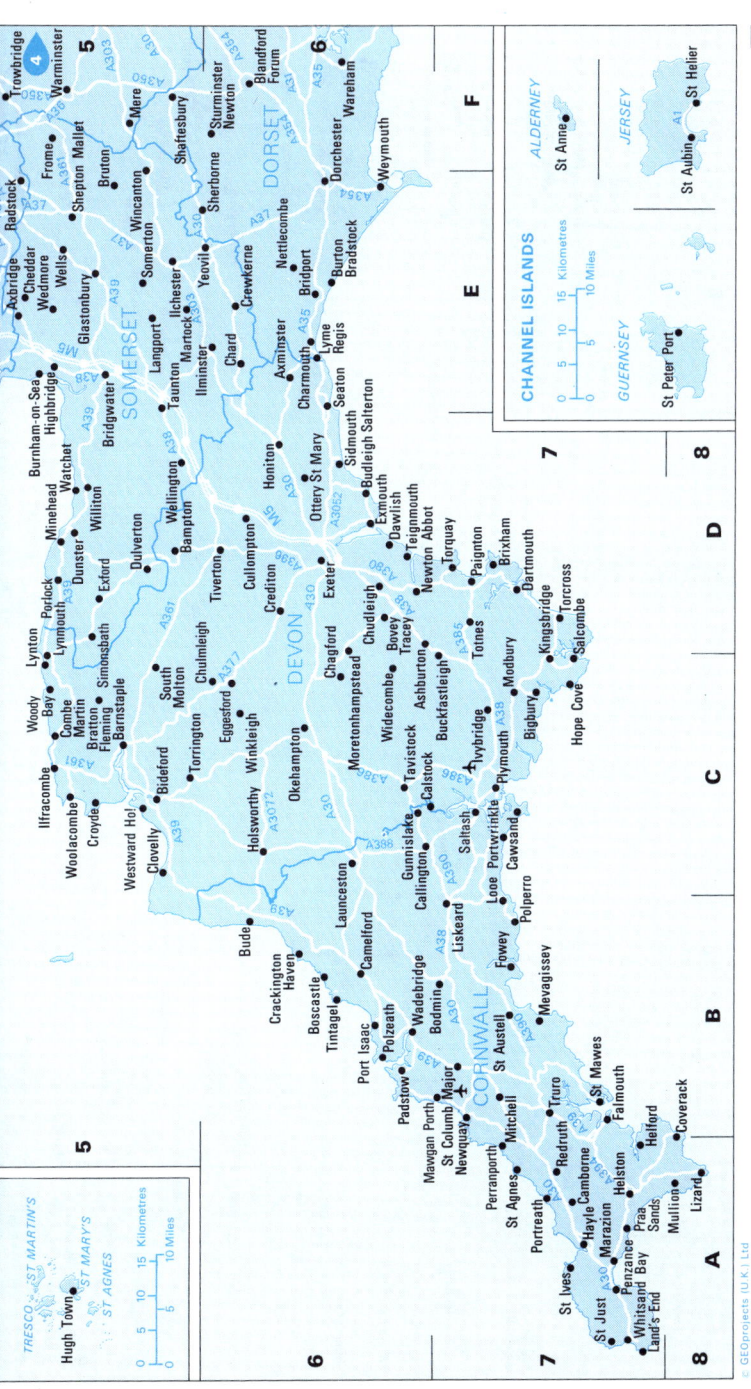

Map 3

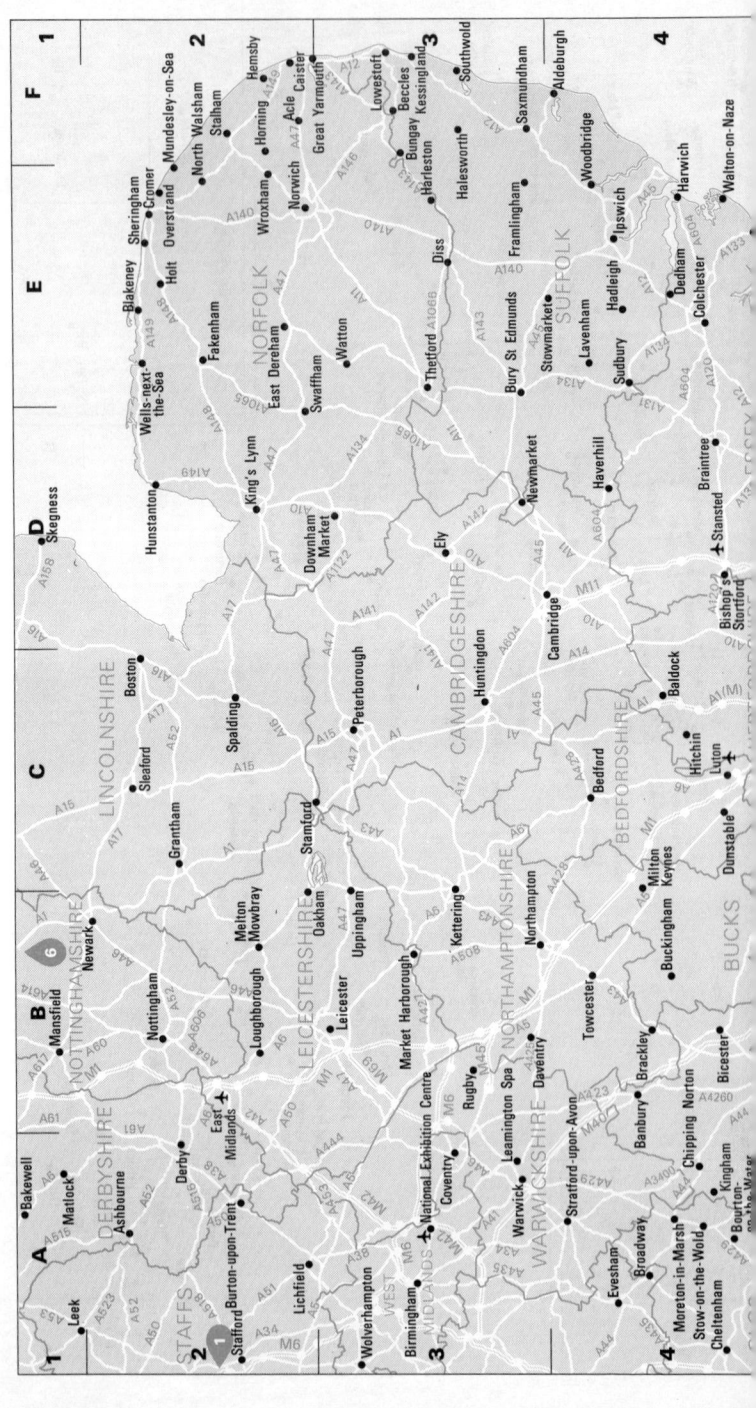

Map 4

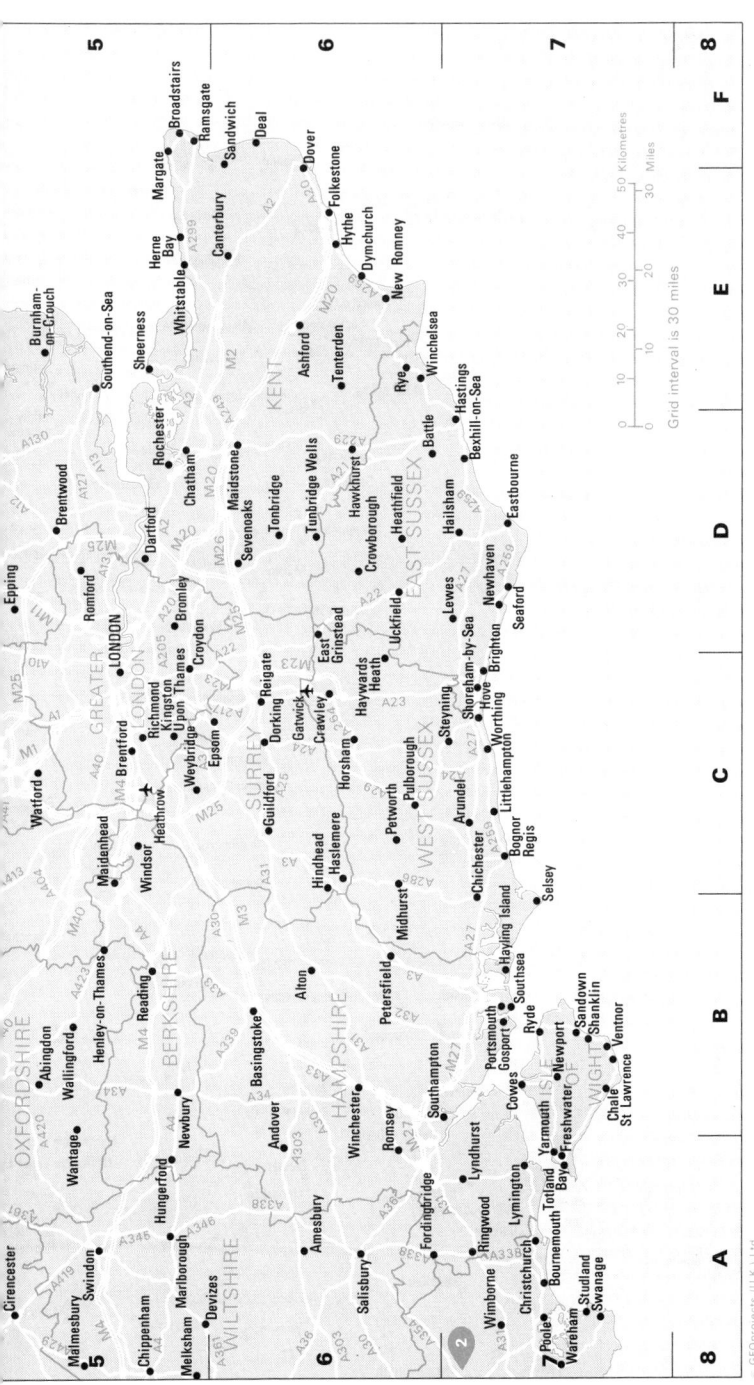

Map 5

Map 6

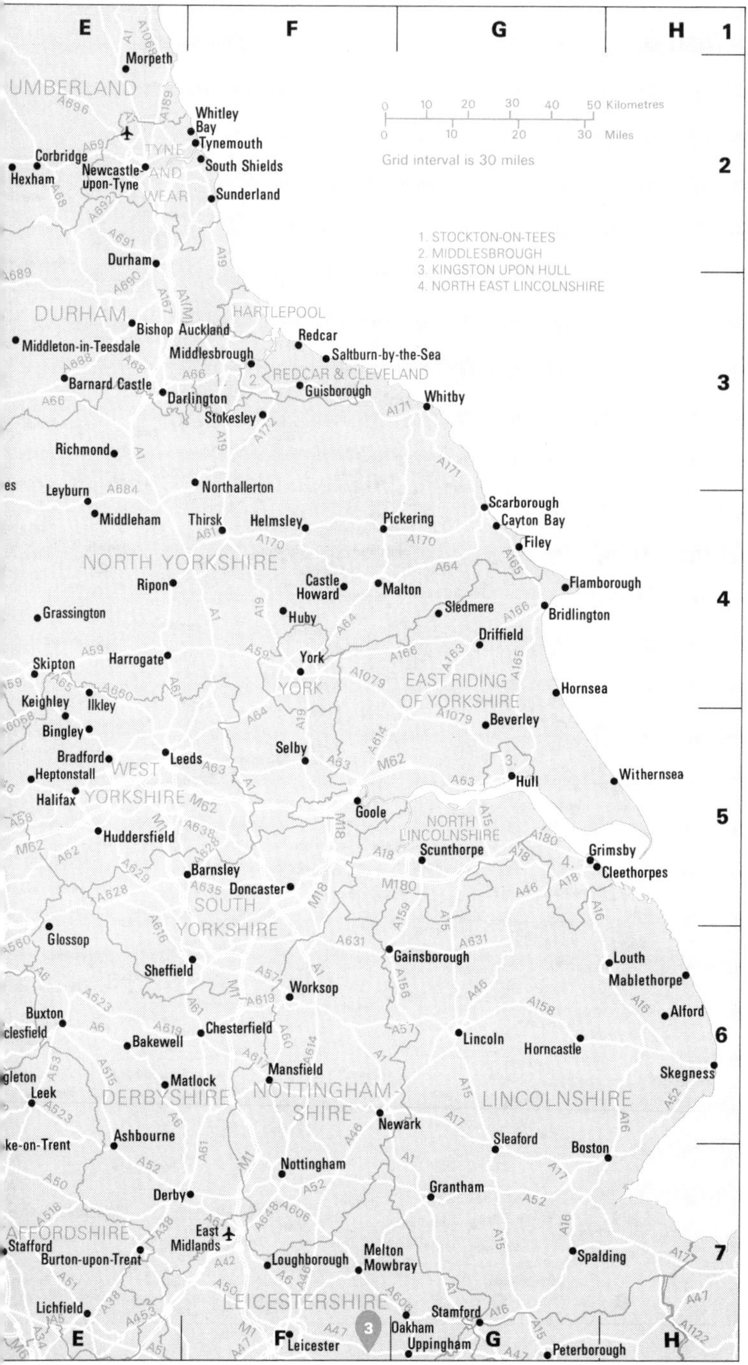
E
F
G
H
1
2
3
4
5
6
7
0 10 20 30 40 50 Kilometres
0 10 20 30 Miles
Grid interval is 30 miles
1. STOCKTON-ON-TEES
2. MIDDLESBROUGH
3. KINGSTON UPON HULL
4. NORTH EAST LINCOLNSHIRE
UMBERLAND
TYNE AND WEAR
DURHAM
HARTLEPOOL
REDCAR & CLEVELAND
NORTH YORKSHIRE
YORK
EAST RIDING OF YORKSHIRE
WEST YORKSHIRE
NORTH LINCOLNSHIRE
SOUTH YORKSHIRE
DERBYSHIRE
NOTTINGHAM-SHIRE
LINCOLNSHIRE
AFFORDSHIRE
LEICESTERSHIRE
Morpeth
Whitley Bay
Tynemouth
South Shields
Corbridge
Hexham
Newcastle-upon-Tyne
Sunderland
Durham
Bishop Auckland
Middleton-in-Teesdale
Middlesbrough
Redcar
Saltburn-by-the-Sea
Guisborough
Barnard Castle
Darlington
Stokesley
Whitby
Richmond
Leyburn
Northallerton
Middleham
Thirsk
Helmsley
Pickering
Scarborough
Cayton Bay
Filey
Ripon
Castle Howard
Malton
Flamborough
Grassington
Huby
Sledmere
Bridlington
Driffield
Skipton
Harrogate
York
Keighley
Ilkley
Hornsea
Bingley
Beverley
Bradford
Leeds
Selby
Heptonstall
Hull
Withernsea
Halifax
Goole
Huddersfield
Scunthorpe
Grimsby
Cleethorpes
Barnsley
Doncaster
Glossop
Gainsborough
Louth
Sheffield
Mablethorpe
Worksop
Buxton
Alford
clesfield
Chesterfield
Lincoln
Bakewell
Horncastle
Mansfield
Skegness
gleton
Matlock
Leek
Newark
Ashbourne
Sleaford
Boston
ke-on-Trent
Nottingham
Grantham
Derby
East Midlands
Stafford
Burton-upon-Trent
Loughborough
Melton Mowbray
Spalding
Lichfield
Stamford
Oakham
Leicester
Uppingham
Peterborough
3

Map 7

0 10 20 30 40 50 Kilometres
0 10 20 30 Miles
Grid interval is 30 miles

SHETLAND ISLANDS

ORKNEY ISLANDS
MAINLAND
Stromness
Kirkwall
HOY

MAINLAND
Lerwick
YELL
Sumburgh

Durness
Bettyhill
Thurso
John o'Groats
Tongue
Scourie
Wick
LEWIS
Lochinver
Helmsdale
WESTERN ISLES
Lairg
Golspie
Ullapool
Bonar Bridge
Dornoch
Gairloch
Poolewe
Tain
Dingwall
Cullen
Fraserburgh
HIGHLAND
Rosemarkie
Elgin
Banff
Fortrose
Forres
Fochabers
Portree
Beauly
Nairn
Keith
Turriff
Peterhead
SKYE
Croy
Kilravock Castle
MORAY
Huntly
Broadford
Kyle of Lochalsh
Inverness
Daviot
Kyleakin
Dornie
Grantown-on-Spey
Inverurie
Carrbridge
Tomintoul
ABERDEENSHIRE
CITY OF ABERDEEN
Aviemore
Fort Augustus
Kingussie
Aberdeen
Mallaig
Braemar
Banchory
Stonehaven

INNER HEBRIDES
Fort William
Kinloch Rannoch
Kinlochleven
Pitlochry
Brechin
Tobermory
Ballachulish
Glencoe
Aberfeldy
Dunkeld
Forfar
Montrose
MULL
Blairgowrie
Arbroath
Oban
Taynuilt
Killin
Lochearnhead
Monifieth
Carnoustie
Dalmally
PERTH & KINROSS
Perth
Dundee
1. CITY OF DUNDEE
Crianlarich
Crieff
St Andrews
2. CLACKMANNANSHIRE
Inveraray
Arrochar
Callander
Auchterarder
3. FALKIRK
Tarbet
Aberfoyle
Cupar
FIFE
4. WEST LOTHIAN
ARGYLL & BUTE
Kinross
5. CITY OF EDINBURGH
Lochgilphead
Luss
STIRLING
6. MIDLOTHIAN
JURA
Ardrishaig
Drymen
Stirling
Kirkcaldy
North Berwick
7. EAST LOTHIAN
Balloch
Dumbarton
Dunfermline
Dunbar
Tarbert
Dunoon
Gourock
EDINBURGH
Eyemouth
ISLAY
Rothesay
Greenock
Paisley
Glasgow
Dalkeith
Haddington
Largs
Hamilton
Chirnside
Beith
NORTH AYRSHIRE
Lanark
Lauder
Duns
Brodick
Ardrossan
Kilmarnock
SOUTH LANARKSHIRE
Peebles
Coldstream
Berwick upon Tweed
KINTYRE
Irvine
Troon
Biggar
Galashiels
Cornhill-on-Tweed
Lamlash
Prestwick
EAST AYRSHIRE
Selkirk
Kelso
Wooler
Campbeltown
Ayr
Abington
SCOTTISH BORDERS
Jedburgh
ARRAN
Maybole
Hawick
Alnwick
New Cumnock
8. INVERCLYDE
Moffat
9. RENFREWSHIRE
SOUTH AYRSHIRE
Beattock
10. WEST DUNBARTONSHIRE
Girvan
11. EAST DUNBARTONSHIRE
Langholm
NORTHUMBERLAND
12. NORTH LANARKSHIRE
DUMFRIES & GALLOWAY
Bellingham
13. CITY OF GLASGOW
14. EAST RENFREWSHIRE
New Galloway
Dumfries
Gretna
Longtown
Newcastle-upon-Tyne
Newton Stewart
Annan
Greenhead
Hexham
Corbridge
Stranraer
Castle Douglas
Carlisle
Portpatrick
Wigtown
Gatehouse of Fleet
CUMBRIA
Alston
Durham
Port William
Kirkcudbright
Silloth
Bassenthwaite
Penrith

© GEOprojects (U.K.) Ltd
Crown Copyright Reserved